Escape

To the student soldiers
who perished in World War II

Author: Professor Uhm Young-Sik (嚴永植)

1996 년 3 월 (Uhm Young-Sik completed the draft manuscript.)

2005 년 1 월 (First edition published by Yasmedia, Seoul, Korea)

2025 년 7 월 (Revised edition, Epsilon Advisors, Inc., NJ, U.S.A.)

Cover: China in Twilight
Oil on Canvas (30" x 24")
Sim Joo Yoon (윤심주)
Ehwa Women's University, College of Art.
Exhibited at the Aegis Gallery in Saratoga, CA 2012.

ISBN: 979-8-9919082-3-8
First Printing, 2005 (야스미디어, Seoul, Korea)
First Revision, 2025 (Epsilon Advisors, Inc., New Jersey, U.S.A.)

Contents

Author Profile: Professor Uhm Young-Sik (嚴永植)

Birth and Education

- January 22, 1920: Born as the second son of Uhm Jin-seung in Iksong-dong, No. 1056, Galsan-myeon, Jeongju-gun, North Korea
- March 1938: Graduated from Osan Middle School
- March 1941: Completed studies at the Second Waseda Preparatory School in Tokyo
- December 1943: Graduated from the Department of Oriental History, Faculty of Literature, Waseda University
- April 1975: Received Doctor of Literature degree from Kyung Hee University Graduate School

Career

- January 1944: Forcibly conscripted as a student soldier while in school (Private, Japanese Army, Xuzhou Unit)
- August 1944: Escaped from the Japanese military barracks
- April 1946: Teacher at Osan Middle School, North Korea
- April 1947: Moved to South Korea; teacher at Seoul High School
- September 1954: Assistant Professor at Kyung Hee University
- September 1958: Associate Professor at Ewha Womans University
- September 1960: Professor at Kyung Hee University
- September 1985: Retired and became Professor Emeritus at Kyung Hee University

In Remembrance of My Father

In the summer of 1995, during a brief visit to Seoul to spend time with my parents before returning to the United States, my father handed me a bundle of manuscripts, saying simply, "Just read it sometime." That fall and winter, with both of my children having gone off to college and the house left empty, I had no time to feel sadness or loneliness. I spent those months reading and organizing my father's manuscripts, and it became a truly busy and joyful time.

Though I had lived completely disconnected from computers and was virtually computer-illiterate, I gradually learned to use the Hangul Korean word processor with the enthusiastic help of my husband. Fueled by a desire to awaken in today's younger generation—who are the true protagonists of our time—a deeper awareness of Korea's modern history, which is fading from memory, I found the process enjoyable.

But more than anything, what brought me the greatest joy was that, through organizing these writings, I came to deeply understand and empathize with my father's sincere and humble attitude to life—marked by a flowing sense of quiet romanticism and a distinctly fatalistic nature.

This book is, from my father's perspective, an unfinished work. He had intended to write further about the Korean War and the events following the recapture of Seoul on September 28, but he refrained from picking up the pen, saying he had no desire to contribute to the flood of autobiographies circulating at the time. He not only avoided editing the manuscript but also insisted that his writings no longer be discussed.

It has now been eight years since I first organized the draft of his manuscript. On August 9 of this year, my father quietly left my side in response to God's calling, longing to be reunited with my mother, who had gone to her eternal home four years earlier.

Now, my siblings and I have come together to compile his writings into a book—something he did not wish for during his lifetime—as a way to ease our sorrow, to hold his memory close in our hearts, and to wait in hope for the day we meet again.

In just a couple of years, my elder brother—born in the year of Korea's liberation following the American victory in the Pacific War—will soon turn sixty. And our children have now reached the age at which our father was forcibly taken as a student soldier into the Japanese army. Yet, our children seem to show little interest or understanding of the turbulent and sorrow-filled lives their grandparents endured during the loss of our nation. On the contrary, some have turned away from the painful lessons of that generation and, alarmingly, embrace communism—claiming that the Korean War was not a North Korean invasion.

This reality is not merely the fault of our children, the second generation, but rather a consequence of our generation—their parents—having failed to cultivate a proper understanding of our parents' arduous lives and a correct view of history. Instead, we pursued only the goal of building a materially prosperous society, and this is the fruit we have reaped.

Now, albeit belatedly, I hope that by introducing the painful struggles of my father's youth—his turbulent twenties, spent in hardship yet lived quietly, without resisting the natural course of life, and with unwavering compassion and integrity toward others—we may reflect together on our shared Korean roots. I also hope that our children will come to understand that the freedom and abundance they enjoy today were built on countless sacrifices, and that they will live with gratitude, planting seeds for the future through honesty and diligence.

Lastly, I would like to express my deep gratitude to Mr. Ahn Gook-ju (安國柱), who read the first draft of this book eight years ago, helped correct parts where my father's memory was unclear, and offered valuable guidance (though we've lost contact since he was last known to be in Washington, D.C. four years ago), and to Mr. Heo Bong-man of Yasmedia, who willingly took on the task of publishing this book.

November 2004, Cherry Hill, New Jersey, USA

Daughter, Uhm Sun-young

Editor's Note

It has already been 20 years since Professor Uhm Young-sik's book *Escape* was published by Yas Media. As the book has gone out of print and is no longer available, we decided to republish it so that today's readers can access it. To make the book more engaging, we included photos of related individuals and relevant Map s found online in this revised edition.

To date, various writings about student soldiers (學兵, hakbyeong) have appeared in books, magazines, and newspapers in Korea. Among them is also a book titled *Escape* by Mr. Shin Sang-cho. However, Professor Uhm's *Escape* uniquely covers a wide range of experiences: the situation in Korea before conscription, the author's own despair at being forced to serve, the anguish of his parents, the complex emotions of a Korean donning a Japanese military uniform and landing deep in China's interior at Xuzhou, the life-risking escape, his journey toward Yan'an, the revolutionary heartland of the Chinese Communist Party, as a member of the Korean Volunteer Army, and the thrill and anticipation he felt upon hearing the news of Korea's liberation on August 15, 1945. It also includes rare accounts of yet another escape, this time from the Korean Volunteer Army, amid fear and discouragement; his imprisonment in a North Korean jail; his arduous journey south across the 38th parallel; and his eventual settlement in South Korea. These are stories not found in any other writing about student soldiers.

After escaping from the Japanese army in the heart of the vast Chinese continent, the author, supported by the Eighth Route and New

Fourth Armies, carried with him the pride of being a member of the Korean Volunteer Army. He endured all hardship and physical suffering in the hope of one day returning to a liberated homeland. Through his story, he candidly expresses the helplessness and despair experienced by the generation of student soldiers, whose country had been taken from them. Furthermore, he shares the small joys and gratitude he found through encounters with poor Chinese farmers and offers insights into how the Chinese Communist Party managed to overcome Chiang Kai-shek's Nationalist forces and gain control of China's vast territory. I believe this is the only book that describes such experiences.

As the editor, the past few months spent preparing this revised edition have been truly fulfilling. I am deeply grateful for the courage and sacrifices of our parents' generation, who, though forced to serve as student soldiers in the prime of their youth under Japanese rule, managed to return alive.

July 2025

Editor, Professor Y.I. Cho, Drexel University, Philadelphia, PA

(Son-in-law)

Chapter 1

The Origins of Japanese Militarism

The Situation in 1943 in the East Asia

The beginning of Japanese militarism can be traced back to June 4, 1930, when Zhang Zuolin (張作霖), who was fleeing from Beijing and returning to Fengtian (奉天, Bongcheon), was assassinated on a train at the intersection of Kyongwon Railway and Namman Railway. The plot was clearly orchestrated by junior Japanese officers of the Kwantung Army (關東軍). Emperor Hirohito ordered a thorough investigation and severe punishment for those involved. However, the military leadership decided to cover up the truth, fearing that it would have negative implications for their control over the army and would be disadvantageous internationally. As a result, Tanaka Giichi (田中義一郎), the Minister of War at the time, resigned, and the masterminds behind the incident were let off lightly. This incident clearly demonstrated that the military was not afraid to act against the Emperor's orders to advance their aggressive plans.

From that time onward, the Japanese government not only failed to restrain the militaristic forces repeatedly engaging in aggression under the pretext of national interest but was rather drawn into their ambitions. Furthermore, in 1932, the military established the so-called "puppet state" of Manchukuo (滿洲國), which allowed them to gain control over China's three northeastern provinces (東三省). Having tasted success in their acts of aggression, the Japanese military gradually penetrated deeper into China's territory, disregarding international opinions. In the same year, 1932, they invaded Shanghai, followed by Inner Mongolia and North China, and eventually escalated to a full-scale war with China in July 1937.

(Editor's Note: Zhang Zuolin (張作霖, 1875–1928) was a powerful Chinese warlord and political figure during the chaotic Warlord Era of early 20th-century China. He was often referred to as the "Old Marshal" and controlled Manchuria (Northeastern China) as the leader of the Fengtian Clique, 奉天軍閥.)

On December 13, 1937, the Japanese army occupied Nanjing (南京). The atrocities, massacres, and looting carried out by General Kawashima (川島) in Nanjing were the most heinous acts the world had ever witnessed. Regarding this, Edgar Snow described the events in his book "The Battle for Asia" as follows:

2

"The Japanese army massacred around 42,000 people in Nanjing alone. During their advance from Shanghai to Nanjing, approximately 300,000 people died at the hands of the Japanese army. Women, ranging from 10 to 70 years old, were all subjected to rape, and refugee mothers often found it inevitable for their young breastfeeding infants to suffer the same fate. Some soldiers heartlessly suffocated young children by covering their heads with grenades before mercilessly committing rape. Certain officers turned their quarters into comfort stations, where they engaged in sexual relations with new captives each day."

"Even in broad daylight, the streets were scenes of terror and pillaging. Japanese soldiers would have intercourse with women they encountered on the streets and then kill them by stabbing them with bayonets. Approximately 5,000 Japanese soldiers plunged into a horrifying abyss of rape, massacre, and looting, unlike anything previously witnessed in history."

At that time, Japan's General Sugiyama boasted, "A force more fearsome than tigers will drive the Japanese army deep into the Chinese mainland, and the war will be over in three months." After the fall of Nanjing, Chiang Kai-shek (蔣介石) relocated the capital to Hankou (漢口), and when Hankou also fell (in December 1938), he moved it again to Chongqing (重慶), seeking support from the United States, Britain, and the Soviet Union to prepare for a protracted war.

By the end of 1938, the Japanese army had occupied all major transportation hubs, including the Beijing-Suiyuan (京綏) Railroad in the north, and the Beijing-Hankou (京漢), Jinpu (津浦), and Yonghai (龍海) Railways in the central region, as well as key areas along the Yangtze River.

Figure 1: The entry of the Japanese Kwantung Army into Fengtian (present-day Shenyang) on September 18, 1931.

As 1940 approached, the nature of the Sino-Japanese War underwent significant changes. The Japanese army mainly occupied critical transportation routes such as railways and roads in China, but the vast rear areas of the Japan-occupied territories became the active

4

theater of operations for the Communist Eighth Route Army (八路軍)(Ba Lu Jun) and the New Fourth Army (新四軍)(Xin Si Jun).

The Eighth Route Army operated in the northern regions, particularly in the areas of Hebei (河北) and Shanxi (山西), while the New Fourth Army operated in the lower reaches of the Yangtze River (長江). They established their bases and engaged in guerrilla warfare with great vigor. As a result, the activities of the Communist forces, represented by both the Eighth Route Army and the New Fourth Army, intensified in these regions.

In "The History of the Chinese Revolution in Recent One Hundred Years," Young Mengyuan (榮孟源) noted that in 1941, 75% of the Japanese invasion forces were directed towards attacking the liberated areas (解放區), which were under the control of the Communist forces. This highlights the significant role played by the Communist forces in countering the Japanese invasion and their efforts to expand the liberated territories.

The Japanese invasion forces employed the so-called "Three Alls Policy" (三光政策) (San Guang Zheng Ce) towards the liberated areas, which involved burning all houses, looting all resources, and killing all inhabitants, a brutal scorched earth strategy. Faced with such ruthless military actions, the local residents realized that the only way to resist the Japanese invasion was to fight back using similar methods, which strengthened their spirit of resistance.

Desperate to achieve their ambitions of invasion, Japan eventually collaborated with the pro-Japanese regime of Wang Jingwei (汪精衛)

and established the Puppet (衛) National Government in Nanjing. However, the Chinese people did not yield to these deceptive tactics and refused to cooperate with the puppet government for Japan's invasion purposes.

As Japan's invasion of China reached a stalemate, Europe was experiencing the expansion of the war into World War II. In June 1940, when France surrendered to Germany, Japan, fascinated by Germany's overwhelming victory, connected the Second Sino-Japanese War to the global conflict. In other words, Japan formed the Axis Powers with Germany and Italy (the Tripartite Pact on September 27, 1940), aiming to resolve the "China issue" and even dreaming of achieving global dominance. However, Japan's reckless ambitions greatly provoked the United States and the Allied forces.

Furthermore, when France surrendered, Japan advanced into French Indochina, blocking the supply route to China through the Burma Road. After the Netherlands surrendered to Germany, Japan gained access to war materials such as oil from the Dutch East Indies. In response to Japan's southern expansion policy, the United States strengthened its support for the Chiang Kai-shek government and implemented a tough policy of cutting off the supply of essential resources like iron and oil to Japan, thereby economically strangling Japan.

While taking a firm stance, the United States also showed a policy of persuasion, indicating that if Japan unconditionally returned the regions, it had invaded and occupied in China in 1937, a compromise could be possible.

At that time, moderate figures in Japan, such as Prime Minister Konoe Fumimaro (近衛) and Navy Minister Yonai Mitsumasa (米內), expressed public opinion that Japan should accept the United States' demand for an unconditional withdrawal from the Chinese mainland. However, the Japanese Army promoted a glorified image of the war, stating that "war is the father of creation and the mother of civilization," and added, "Konoe has determined to firmly eradicate the influence of the Communist Party lurking behind the Chiang Kai-shek government." With such propaganda, the Japanese Army effectively suppressed the public opinion favoring withdrawal, choosing to go against the United States' demands.

On June 22, 1941, Germany launched a surprise attack on the Soviet Union and advanced towards the outskirts of Moscow. At this time, Japan faced a crucial decision: should it collaborate with Germany and move eastward into Eastern Siberia, or should it advance southward to acquire war materials and resolve the China issue? The choice between the two options became unavoidable. On July 2, 1941, Japan made a significant decision. Despite the inevitability of war with the United States and Britain, Japan commenced military actions in French Indochina and Thailand (泰國)(Siam).

In response to Japan's decision to advance into French Indochina, the United States took a firm stance and declared that if Japan engaged in any apparent act of force to acquire foreign territories in the Far East, the U.S. would immediately impose economic and financial sanctions. Despite this warning, on July 24, 1941, Japan proceeded with its occupation of French Indochina. In response, the United States promptly froze Japanese assets. The U.S. further warned that if Japan attempted to forcibly seize oil from the Dutch East Indies (蘭印), the Netherlands and Britain would come to its aid, and the United States would support Britain, leading to a highly critical situation.

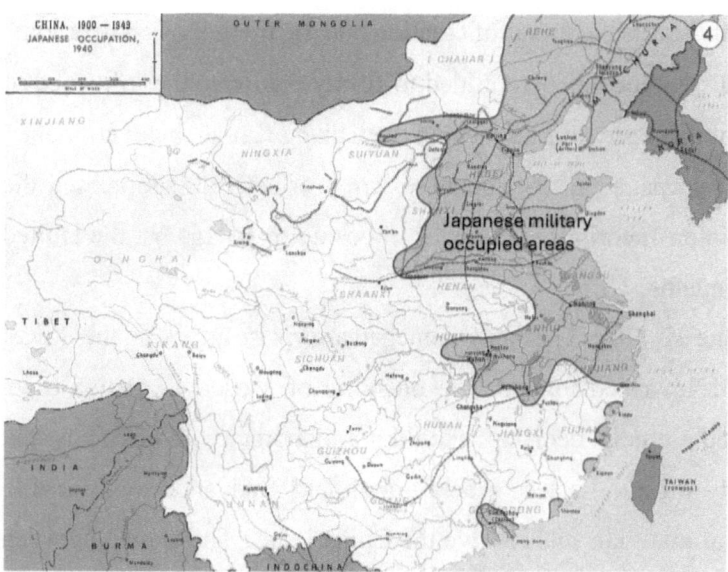

Figure 2: The Expansion of the Japanese Empire in China, 1940.

Indeed, the United States' freezing of Japanese assets effectively meant a ban on exporting oil to Japan. This made it practically impossible for Japan to purchase oil as the only means of payment available to them were the cash reserves they had withdrawn before the freezing order. In 1941, Japan's domestic oil production was only around 3 million barrels, which accounted for a mere 10-20% of its minimum consumption needs. Thus, Japan heavily relied on imports, with around 90% of its oil coming from the United States and Dutch East Indies.

Furthermore, Japan's oil reserves were sufficient for only about a year and a half to two years of consumption, making it evident that the longer Japan delayed the decision to go to war, the more disadvantageous it would be. The situation clearly highlighted the strategic disadvantage Japan faced if it were to engage in warfare.

On September 6, 1941, during the Imperial Conference (御前會議), Japan made the decision to go to war with the United States. Prior to the conference, Admiral Nagano (永野), the Chief of Naval General Staff, argued that Japan should avoid war with the United States. He even suggested that, if necessary to avoid war, Japan should consider withdrawing from the alliance with Germany. However, if war with the United States became inevitable, he believed that Japan had no choice but to take preemptive action. The reason behind this stance was the critical issue of oil supply. Japan's oil reserves would only last for about two years, and the situation was becoming increasingly dire. Considering these factors, Japan ultimately decided to go ahead with the war against the United States.

The Chief of General Staff of the Army, Hajime Sugiyama, responded to the emperor's question, "How long would the Army take to end the war if it were to happen?" by saying, "If we attack in the Southern Direction, we can finish the war in about three months." At this moment, the emperor recalled that four years ago, when Sugiyama was still a Lieutenant General, he had said that the war could be ended in one month from a land-based perspective. The emperor asked, "But even after four years, it still hasn't been concluded, has it?" Sugiyama replied, "China's territory is vast and extensive, which hindered our operations as planned." In response, the emperor expressed his displeasure and said, "If you say China's territory is vast, isn't the Pacific even more extensive? What assurance do you have to claim it will take only three months?"

At that time, the Chief of Naval General Staff responded, "The relationship between Japan and the United States is like that of a patient facing a critical moment. It's a moment of deciding whether to undergo surgery or not. If we don't undergo surgery, we will gradually weaken and die, but if we do, there will be risks, yet it may save our life. The Navy hopes for successful diplomatic negotiations, but if they don't materialize, we have no choice but to proceed with the surgery." From this, it is clear that the emperor did not desire war, and the Navy made efforts to avoid war through diplomacy, while only the Army was keen on pursuing war. This was the true nature of Japan's militarism. The military's unchecked power can be traced back to the failure to properly punish the young officers of the Kwantung Army who were responsible for the assassination of Zhang Zuolin in 1930.

Figure 3: Osami Nagano, Chief of the Naval General Staff.

Figure 4: Hajime Sugiyama, Chief of General Staff of the Army

Figure 5: Emperor Shōwa (Reign: 1926–1989).

The truth of militarism

Prime Minister Konoe Fumimaro (近衛) and General Tojo Hideki (東條英機) often clashed due to their differing opinions. Konoe Fumimaro was a member of the noble class in Japan, having graduated

11

from the Tokyo Imperial University (東京帝国大学) Law School. He became Prime Minister around the time of the 7.7 Incident (the Marco Polo Bridge Incident) and received high expectations from the public. However, he expanded the Sino-Japanese War, which led Japan into a quagmire, and was also responsible for forming the Tripartite Pact with Germany and Italy. While he initially tried to avoid war with the United States, he eventually succumbed to the pressure from the military, as he was a Japanese person unable to escape the national interest they advocated. His decision to take his own life after the war could be seen as acknowledging that he had no other way to survive under those circumstances.

On October 14, 1941, during the Imperial Council meeting, Prime Minister Konoe Fumimaro argued that the war should not be further expanded. In response, General Tojo Hideki criticized him, stating, "Prime Minister Konoe is overly preoccupied with concerns and risks of the future. Ultimately, it's just a difference in our personalities." Tojo demanded the resignation of the entire cabinet, and Prime Minister Konoe, feeling that he could no longer communicate with Tojo, resigned and conveyed his wish to the emperor.

However, the moderate factions agreed to support Tojo as the successor to the Prime Minister, believing that if Tojo became Prime Minister, he would not lead the country into war. Nevertheless, within fifty days of assuming the position of Prime Minister, Tojo ordered the attack on Pearl Harbor, expanding the Second Sino-Japanese War into the wider conflict of World War II.

Figure 6: The surprise attack on Pearl Harbor by the Imperial Japanese
Combined Fleet, December 1941.

I was a first-year undergraduate student at Waseda University at that
time (1941). I wanted to see the expressions of the Japanese people on
the streets of Tokyo, so I wandered around Shinjuku (新宿). The dimly
lit streets felt like a street of death. The faces of people passing by were
stiff and filled with deep emotions. I thought to myself, "Japan has now
fallen into the abyss of destruction!"

The attack on Pearl Harbor by the Japanese Combined Fleet on
December 8, 1941, resulted in the destruction of the United States
Pacific Fleet. Following this success, the Japanese Army occupied the
Philippine capital of Manila in January 1942, followed by the occupation
of Singapore in February and the Burmese capital of Rangoon in March.
Within just five months after the start of the war, Japan had achieved

13

vast territorial gains, stretching from the eastern Rabaul in the South Pacific to Burma in the west.

The early victories of the Japanese in this campaign undoubtedly stirred excitement among the Japanese people. At the beginning of the war, both the Japanese Army and Navy had specific operational plans. However, after securing the occupied territories, their plans became more ambiguous. They focused on annihilating enemies as they encountered them and strengthening their forces by obtaining resources from the southern Asian regions, without having concrete long-term strategies beyond that point.

Figure 7: Prime Minister Fumimaro Konoe.

Japan did not have a firm and concrete operational plan to force the surrender of the United States while engaging in conflict with them. They simply relied on vague assumptions, believing that their ally Germany would achieve victory, and that China and Britain would eventually surrender. Furthermore, Japan speculated that in democratic countries, prolonged warfare would lead to war-weariness among their citizens, causing internal divisions that would eventually lead to the surrender of the United States.

 Figure 8: General Tojo Hideki

However, these calculations were based on uncertain and wishful thinking. Japan lacked a solid strategy to achieve the surrender of the United States and underestimated the determination and resilience of the American forces. As the war progressed, Japan faced formidable resistance from the United States, leading to a prolonged and challenging conflict that ultimately resulted in Japan's defeat.

However, in Europe, the war between Germany and the Soviet Union unfolded differently from Japan's expectations, and the German forces faced a defeat in Leningrad. Meanwhile, Britain managed to withstand the continuous German attacks and prepare for further developments. In the Pacific, on April 18, 1942, sixteen American bombers took off from aircraft carriers and conducted the first bombing raid on Japanese mainland cities such as Tokyo, Yokohama, and Nagoya, with some of the planes flying on to China. I witnessed the destruction of a hospital in front of Waseda University (Tokyo) during that attack. As Japanese citizens directly witnessed the strength of the American air force, they must have felt that the future of the war was far from bright.

The U.S. counterattack in the Central Pacific began with a victory in the Battle of the Coral Sea, which overturned Japan's expectations. However, on June 5th, 1942, Japan decided to gamble on its fortunes and carried out the Battle of Midway in the Central Pacific. In this battle, the Japanese Navy suffered a devastating blow as four of their main aircraft carriers were sunk, leading to a crippling loss for the Japanese Combined Fleet and the loss of air superiority. In August, the U.S. Marines landed on Guadalcanal in the Solomon Islands. Once again, Japan experienced a bitter defeat, losing both elite forces from two divisions and 38 warships, along with all frontline aircraft deployed in the battle. Despite repeated defeats, Japan continued to deceive its people with the illusion of advancement.

As Japan and Germany experienced victories through surprise attacks and blitzkrieg in the early stages, they began to face the path of defeat in 1943. The U.S. forces launched counteroffensives, expanding their control over the Pacific and gaining air superiority. While the U.S. successfully executed the "Island Hopping" strategy, attacking and bypassing islands to secure strategic locations in the South Pacific, the Japanese forces stubbornly clung to their offensive in the direction of New Guinea. In April 18, 1943, the flagship aircraft carrying Admiral

Yamamoto Isoroku (山本五十六) was shot down, leading to his death and the eventual loss of his fleet. In May 1943, U.S. forces landed on Attu Island in the northern Aleutian Islands (Alaska). Within six months, the entire Japanese garrison of 2,500 soldiers was annihilated (玉砕), known as the "Operation Landcrab."

During this period, the tide of the war began to turn against Japan and Germany, and the Allies gained momentum in their efforts to push back and defeat the Axis powers. On the European front, the Soviet forces launched a full-scale offensive, and in July 1943, U.S. and British forces landed on the island of Sicily. In September 1943, Italy surrendered to the Allied forces. With this surrender, Italy stepped away from the Axis powers, leaving the Tripartite Pact. As a result, the Axis powers were dealt a significant blow as one of the members of the Tripartite Pact had now defected.

Figure 9: A scene from the movie *Midway*.

Figure 10: U.S. Marines at the shores of Guadalcanal, 1942.

Figure 11: Admiral Yamamoto Isoroku (山本五十六).

Despite Japan's repeated claims that the advancing U.S. forces would face logistical challenges and disadvantages in their operations, the American counterattacks were swift and on a large scale, catching Japan off guard. In November 1943, the U.S. forces occupied Makin and Tarawa Atolls, and in February 1944, they landed on the Marshall Islands, followed by Truk Atoll. In March, they took control of the Palau Islands, bringing Japan's home islands within bombing range. A massive operation was launched to capture Saipan, which served as Japan's last outer defense line.

I, as a conscripted student soldier (學兵) of the Japanese Army , was sent to the Chinese front in January 1944. At that time, nobody believed that Japan would win the war against the United States. Many people had abandoned the notion that Japan's population of 100 million would fight until the bitter end. There were no more believers that the emperor would be moved to Manchuria to continue the fight if the U.S. forces landed on Japan's home islands.

In 1281, when the Mongols invaded Korea and advanced towards Japan through the Korean Peninsula, Hojo Tokimune (北条時宗) appeared and used a northern wind to repel them. However, now, when the eastern wind is blowing as if to push them into Japan, Tojo Hideki claims that he will stop the invasion, but no one believes him. When the Mongols invaded, the divine wind known as "Kamikaze" struck, leading to the destruction of the Mongol forces. But now, can another miracle really happen? The people's resentment against Japan's militarism has only grown stronger.

Japanese militarism toward the Korean Peninsula

During its colonial rule of the Korean Peninsula, Japan appointed high-ranking military figures as Governors-General to exercise autocratic control. Except for Hasegawa (長谷川) during the March 1st Movement (1919), all the other Governors-General returned to Japan and took on positions as Prime Ministers, leading Japan's militaristic politics.

Japan's policy towards Korea after provoking the war with China was a thorough extermination policy against Korean national identity and culture. In April 1938, Japan unified Korea's education system under its own system. Here, elementary schools were renamed as *shōgakkō* (小學校), middle schools as *chūgakkō* (中學校), and girls' high schools as *kōtō jogakkō* (高等女學校). It was stated that this change was made to align with the school system of mainland Japan and to use the same educational structure, supposedly in order to avoid distinguishing between Japanese and Koreans. However, its true nature was clearly revealed in the elimination of Korean language and Korean history courses from the regular curriculum.

Figure 12: Government-General Building in Seoul, Korea.

20

Next, they created what was known as the "National Oath of Allegiance" (皇國臣民誓詞) and forced people to memorize it, chanting every day that they were loyal Japanese citizens. Furthermore, they erected shrines dedicated to Japan's mythical deity, Amaterasu Omikami (天照大神), and imposed mandatory worship of these shrines throughout the country. In addition to this, Minami (南次郎), the Korean Governor-General, in February 1940, went as far as to enforce a name change policy, demanding that Koreans change their family names to Japanese ones. Anyone who refused to change their ancestral name was labeled as a nationalist and subjected to various forms of pressure and oppression.

As the war approached, the policy of assimilation intensified as part of the overall policy of exterminating Korean identity. They promoted slogans like "Internal Harmony and Unity" (內鮮一體) and emphasized the concept of "Same Roots and Same Ancestors" to suppress any resistance. Consequently, the onset of the war brought about even more aggressive measures in the campaign to exterminate Korean culture. Policies like "Internal Harmony and Unity" and "Same Roots and Same Ancestors" were used to forcefully assimilate the Korean population into Japanese culture. As a result, the entrance of Korean students into prestigious universities was significantly restricted, as providing them with higher education was seen as contradictory to their cultural extermination policy.

Figure 13: General Jirō Minami.

The content of the National Oath of Allegiance (皇國臣民誓詞) is as follows:

- We are subjects of the Empire of Great Japan.
- We unite our hearts and devote our loyalty to His Majesty the Emperor.
- We endure hardship and train ourselves to become fine and strong citizens.

Eventually, the Japanese military government played its last card to strengthen its forces. In October 1942, they started by shortening the university academic term from three years to two years and six months. This allowed the government to conscript university students six months earlier and send them to the battlefield. In October 1943, they promulgated the "Special Measures for Education Law," which abolished the postponement of military service for law and literature students in high schools, technical schools, university preparatory

22

courses, and undergraduate programs. This measure forced Japanese students into the war frontlines.

Amid sending their own country's students to the battlefield, would the Japanese government let colonial Korean students continue their education undisturbed? Colonial rule, by its very nature, implies that the colonized people, having no sovereignty, must not only be fed and sustained but also educated. And yet, didn't Japan not only take 7 to 8 million *seok* of rice from our land every year, but also thoroughly turn it into a military supply base? How could the brutal and ruthless Japanese military allow Korean students in the colony to live in peace and continue their studies, while forcing their own students onto the battlefield? No one with any sense or learning could help but question this.

(Editor's Note: 1 *seok* of rice ≈ 144 kg or about 317 pounds of rice)

Chapter 2

Student Soldier

Wartime Emergency Measures Act

In October 1943, when the "Wartime Emergency Measures Act" was implemented in Japan, I was just one month away from graduating from Waseda University (早稲田大学), Tokyo. At that time, Italy had surrendered in the Axis Powers, and in the Pacific, the Allied forces had started a powerful counterattack with overwhelming naval fleets and aircraft. The Japanese forces were being cornered in the northern Pacific, and the U.S. military was launching a landing operation in the Marshall Islands in the southern Pacific.

There was not a single Japanese citizen who believed that Japan would achieve victory and establish its so-called "Greater East Asia Co-Prosperity Sphere." As the Japanese students set out to the frontlines, they lamented their fate, wondering if they would vanish like flower petals in the southern skies. They cursed the military leaders who were pushing forward with the war.

Watching these Japanese students, I thought, "Isn't it only natural for you to go to the battlefield? Isn't it for the sake of your country? You should bear the responsibility for the aggression committed by your nation." At that time, I couldn't even imagine that the Wartime Emergency Measures Act would soon come knocking at my doorstep as well.

At that time, I had to endure the lamentations of my Japanese classmates who questioned why they had to go to war and die, while looking at me, a Korean student, with envy, saying "you wouldn't have to go to war." My kind Japanese friend named Gushida one day approached me with a request. He said that he had become a sacrificial victim of the militaristic regime and was forced to go to the front lines, but he couldn't help worrying about his family back home. He had his mother and younger sister living in the house, and he said,

"Since you, as a Korean, wouldn't be going to the military, could you consider marrying my sister and take care of things at my home?"

It was a difficult and unexpected proposal for me to receive. I understood the circumstances he was facing, but I also had my own responsibilities and life to live. The burden of such a decision weighed heavily on me, and I had to carefully consider the consequences of my actions.

After that, he took me to his home and introduced me to his sister. At that time, I had never even considered marriage, let alone imagined marrying a Japanese woman. I listened with a smile but didn't take it seriously. It was as if I let the words go in one ear and out the other. However, he seemed to have discussed it deeply with his mother, and the young woman herself seemed interested in the idea of marrying a man who wouldn't have to go to the military, regardless of his nationality. I could only sympathize with him, as he lamented and cursed his fate of having to go to the military. There was nothing more I could do at that moment.

A farewell party was held in appreciation of the teachers at graduation. All nine graduates (two of them were Koreans) from the Department of Oriental History gathered at the Ohoguma Hall located on the university campus. The atmosphere was extremely somber. The head professor, Shimizu Taishi (清水泰次), couldn't find the words to speak and had a gloomy expression on his face. Professor Kemuriyama Sentaro (煙山專太郎) was even shedding tears. Sending off their beloved students into society and blessing their future should have been the occasion, but instead, they were sending them to the battlefield to face death. How could their hearts have felt in such a situation? The atmosphere was filled with curses towards the military authorities. Generally, intellectuals would condemn war itself, but with the war led by the military authorities reaching a dead end and surrounded by dark clouds, how could the professors offer blessings to the graduates? Under the dim lights of a flickering electric lamp, we had a simple meal and parted ways.

As I walked along the familiar street I had always taken to school for the past 3.5 years, I was filled with remorse, saying:

"Now, it has become as clear as day that Japan is facing defeat. Will these arrogant Japanese people, who have oppressed Korea for 36 years, truly hand our beloved country back to the Koreans? Didn't they claim that they would fight to the last man, even if they had to move the Emperor to Manchuria, once the Allied forces land on the mainland?"

I yearned to leave this melancholic longing behind as soon as possible. Now that I had clearly become a full-fledged member of society, I thought I should quickly get a job.

Earlier, a professor informed me that Gyeongseong Middle School (鏡城中學校) in North Hamgyong Province was looking to hire a history teacher, and recommended that I submit my résumé. At that time, Korean students looking for employment needed a certification from Taehwasuk (太和熟) to assess their ideological tendencies, so I had no choice but to visit them for the request. However, Taehwasuk refused to provide the certification, citing the reason that I had not received training from Yeonseonghui (錬成會). Feeling disheartened, I turned back, thinking that unless I adopt the same mindset as the Japanese, it would be difficult for me to find a job in their world.

Having already experienced how difficult it was to find a job, I nevertheless left Tokyo with a vague hope that once I returned to my homeland, Korea, some path would open up for me. Upon arriving in

Kyungsung (京城, Seoul), I stayed for a night and saw an advertisement in Kyungsung Daily News recruiting journalists. Kyungsung Daily News was under the control of the Governor-General's office, and one of the owners was Choi Lin (崔麟), while Seo Chun (徐椿), a graduate of Osan (五山) School, was an executive.

It was, of course, a publication aimed at assimilating Koreans into the Japanese way of life. Feeling that I had nothing to hide, I applied that day and took the exam, which had the topic "Discussing the Greater East Asia Co-Prosperity Sphere." About 170 candidates sat for the exam at the Bumin Hall (府民館). The next morning, when the results were announced, my name was among the eight successful candidates listed.

(**Editor's Note:** *Yeonseong* (研磨育成) referred to the process of "training and fostering" aimed at transforming the Korean people into complete and loyal subjects of the Japanese Emperor. During this period, schools functioned as subordinate institutions to the military, serving as sites for Japanese language instruction and military drills. Even after graduation, students were subjected to pre-military training through the establishment and operation of institutions such as *Yeonseong Training Centers* and *Special Youth Training Centers*.)

I went straight to consult with Kim Do-tae (金道泰), a first graduate of Osan School and the principal of Seoul Girls' Commercial High School. He had a close relationship with my father. I immediately sought a meeting with Seo Chun as Kim Do-tae suggested, and we went to a Chinese restaurant called Daeleukwan located in Susong-dong (Seoul) at that time. Kim Do-tae pointed at me and said, "This child is the second son of Uhm Jin-seung (嚴珍昇). He graduated from Waseda University's Faculty of Literature and passed the first round of the Kyungsung Daily News journalist recruitment exam. Please help him get the job." He made a sincere request to Seo Chun.

Upon hearing this, Seo Chun's face turned pale, and he responded with a deeply regretful expression, "I just finalized the list of three successful candidates and came here. I'm sorry, but there was no one with the surname Uhm on the list."

I sensed an impending mismatch of fate, but still, I calmly showed respect to the senior alumni from my hometown before leaving. The impact on Seo Chun was evident and needless to say, he was shocked. He had been a classmate of my father at Osan School, and since both of them came from poor families and worked at the school to support themselves through their studies, they had developed a deep bond of understanding.

Figure 14: Uhm Jin-seung (right), my father, with a friend.

Student Soldiers

I spent three days in Seoul and returned to my hometown, Jeongju. When I saw my parents, their faces were filled with sorrow. I asked them why, and they explained that the day before, they were forcibly taken to the local authorities and had no choice but to put their signatures on the documents supporting my enlistment in the Japanese army. This was due to the issuance of the Imperial Japanese Army Directive No. 48, titled "Temporary Rules for the Special Army Support Soldier Recruitment," which announced that all Korean students were required to apply to the Japanese army by November 20, 1943. However, although I had graduated, it was six months early, so strictly speaking, I was still considered a student and therefore not exempt from conscription.

If I had already secured a job after graduation, there would have been a valid reason allowing me to postpone the enlistment. However, I was in a situation where I had not found employment yet, so I had no choice but to apply for the enlistment. They called it a voluntary application, but in reality, it was forced upon us. The war was intensifying, and many Japanese were dying on the battlefield. They wanted to silence the educated Koreans, so they devised a cunning scheme to force us into the war under the pretext of conscription as "student soldiers (學兵)." It was a despicable plot to push us to the frontlines of the war.

I had already received the conscription notice in Seoul, and there was nothing I could do but accept that I fell under the category of "student soldier". However, my feelings at that time were like the sky falling on me. It felt like fate was playing a cruel joke on me. Just the

30

thought of becoming a Japanese soldier was enough to make me shudder with fear. Who could I blame? I could only lament the fact that I was born as a Korean, belonging to a country-less people. The reality was so overwhelming that I lost my composure and spent days in despair.

In the dusk of evening, I climbed the hill behind my house. As dusk turned to darkness and then to dawn, I kept thinking — unless some cosmic anomaly occurred where the sun would no longer rise, I could not bring myself to believe that I, of all people, would ever go as a student soldier in the Japanese army. There were ways to avoid being a student soldier. Escaping to Manchuria or China was an option or even being conscripted as a laborer by the Japanese and working in remote and harsh conditions. Some people did manage to escape to Manchuria and similar places to avoid becoming student soldiers, but given my circumstances, it was unimaginable for me. Additionally, refusing to enlist and being conscripted as a laborer were no guarantees of survival, as it was said to be extremely challenging to return alive. I could only hope that some significant event would occur to prevent me from becoming a student soldier.

Though my father was completely worn out, he wished to go to Kyungsung (Seoul) with me, even if only for a short visit. At the conscription office near the train station, they treated sending me off to the military as if it were some great offerings of loyalty to Japan, and so they came day and night to keep watch on me. Because of that, my father and I had to report to the conscription office before we could go down to Kyungsung. In Seoul, we stayed at the Asia Inn in Dadong (茶洞), and my father arranged a gathering with Kim Dotae and Seo Chun there.

In that gathering, my father, with no strength left, must have pleaded with Seo Chun, asking if there was any way to spare his son's life. At that moment, Seo Chun coldly responded, "Joining the military as a student soldier is the ultimate loyalty to the emperor, and under the current circumstances, there's absolutely no way to avoid it." Then he continued, "You have been doing well in your business and even sent your son to study in Japan. As for me, I've been living my whole life on a fixed salary, always calculating every penny. No matter how money comes in unexpectedly, it always ends up being spent on things I never expected. Such is life." Upon hearing Seo Chun's words, my father seemed to resign himself to the fact that sending his son into the enemy's army was now unavoidable.

Enlistment

The day of my enlistment in the Japanese military has already been set for January 20th (1944). While waiting for that day to come, I couldn't truly grasp the fact that I, a Korean, would become a Japanese soldier. How on earth could a Korean person become a Japanese soldier? Still, I couldn't shake the thought that on January 20th, I would indeed become a Japanese soldier, and my future seemed dark and uncertain. On the other hand, I couldn't help but feel resentful that if I had found a job, I could have avoided going into the military. Failing the exam to become a reporter for the Kyungsung Daily News made me even more bitter about the situation.

In truth, that reporter exam was my first path into society, and if I had become a journalist, my life would have taken a completely different direction than it is now. However, looking back now, I can say that going into the military as a student soldier had a more meaningful impact on my life. It allowed me to witness Japan's downfall firsthand and unexpectedly immerse myself in the communist world, witnessing the Chinese Communist Party's victory in China. When I lectured at the university later, I often told my students, "Do not avoid the fate that approaches. Endure it and push through. The goddess of fate is not entirely merciless."

Figure 15: The image of a Korean youth who was forcibly conscripted into the Japanese military in 1944.

There were several friends who managed to avoid becoming a student soldier. One of them was Kim Young-cheol, a senior from Osan School and a fellow graduate from Waseda University's English department. He lived in a remote countryside area near Hadan (下端)

Station. As soon as the student soldier conscription was announced, he climbed up into the ceiling of his house to hide. He spent his days looking down from the ceiling while eating his meals. From up there, he could see Japanese military police and soldiers visiting his parents' home daily and causing them trouble. Remarkably, he managed to endure in the ceiling until the day of liberation, but the fear and anxiety he experienced there left him with mental disturbances. Because of that, during his time as an English teacher after escaping to the South, he was not welcomed wherever he went.

He was originally an athlete and had a romantic and cheerful personality, studying English poetry and reciting works by Shelley and Keats. However, ever since coming down from the ceiling after liberation, he appeared constantly gloomy and as if he was being chased. The experience of hiding in the ceiling had transformed him into a completely different person.

Therefore, I believe that trying to forcibly avoid the fate that has come upon us is not the right thing. Since fate is orchestrated by God, to defy it is to go against God's providence. On January 20, 1944, I became a Private Second Class in the Japanese Army.

Osan School

In my hometown Jeongju (定州) county, there were around 90 young men who were conscripted as student soldiers. It was said that Jeongju county produced the highest number of successful candidates in the civil service examinations during the late Joseon Dynasty. Although not all who passed the exams were appointed to government positions, many people took the exams to bring honor to their families. Even during the Japanese colonial period, many notable figures came from Jeongju county. This was largely because the region had an excellent educational institution—Osan (五山) School.

Osan School was a renowned nationalistic educational institution established by the pioneer Namgang Lee Seung-hoon (李承薫) in 1907. He was inspired by the overflowing patriotism of Dosan Ahn Chang-ho (安昌浩) after attending his lecture in Pyongyang. With the belief that "patriotism is education," Lee Seung-hoon founded the school, devoting himself to its establishment.

The Osan School had notable figures such as Godang Cho Man-sik (曺晚植), Daseok Yu Young-mo (柳永模), Chunwon Lee Kwang-soo (李光洙), Shin Chae-ho (申采浩), and Joo Gi-yong (朱基溶) serving as principals or teachers. They wholeheartedly devoted themselves to education, nurturing students like the poets So-wol (素月), An Seo (岸曙), Ham Seok-heon (咸錫憲), Kim Ki-seok (金基錫), and the Western-style painter Lee Jung-seob (李仲燮), among others, who later became distinguished figures in various fields.

In fact, the presence of Osan School in this region allowed many young people to have early access to education, and even those from less privileged households had opportunities to study abroad in Japan. As a result, it is natural to understand that around 90 young men were conscripted as student soldiers from this area. The availability of Osan School provided ample educational opportunities, which contributed to a significant number of young individuals pursuing higher studies both locally and overseas. Therefore, it is not surprising that 90 or so student soldiers were recruited from this region.

Figure 16: Teacher Ham Seok-heon with the First-Year Class A students of the 1936 school year at Osan School, Jeongju.

Figure 17: Cho Man-sik (曺晚植).

Figure 18: Shin Chae-ho (申采浩).

Figure 19: Lee Kwang-soo (李光洙).

Yeonseong military training

The Japanese colonial authorities arranged a so-called "Yeonseong Training (鍊成會)" for the conscripts to acquire basic military knowledge and to showcase their authority before the conscripts' enlistment on December 10, 1943. The training lasted for a week and took place in the classrooms of the law department at Kyungsung Imperial University (京城帝国大学) and Dongsung Commercial

School (東星商業) in Seoul. All conscripts were required to participate in this training, and failure to do so resulted in severe punishments, as it was seen as avoiding military service.

The one-week preparatory training was rigorous and demanding. Officers and non-commissioned officers oversaw the training, making it no different from regular military training in the barracks. It covered the basics of military movements and even regulated the daily life of the conscripts like the discipline in the regular army. I felt nauseous at how demanding the two superior Korean privates, who were our trainers, were in training us. During the training, when they gave the command "Turn left," all the recruits turned left in unison, but I was the only one who couldn't distinguish left from right and turned right on occasions. Every time that happened, I received harsh criticism and was scolded as if I was a fool.

I detested military training altogether. I couldn't concentrate on the training and often worried about whether I would be able to perform well as a soldier and complete the training properly. I lamented how I ended up in this situation even during the training, and it was natural for the trainers to berate me, saying that I had no sense of the Japanese spirit at all.

As time passed, the one-week training came to an end. On the last night of the training, we gathered at the arrangement of the trainers, feeling regretful about parting ways. The trainers said,

"We are soldiers of the Special Support Unit. It's a painful experience for all of you to join the Japanese army. We may have been overly strict and demanding during the training and harsh in enforcing discipline within the barracks, but it was not out of ill will. We ask for your forgiveness. We heard that Rhee Seungman (李承晩) is involved in the independence movement in the United States, and figures like Kim Gu (金九) have established the Provisional Government of the Republic of Korea and organized the Korean Liberation Army in China. A bright future awaits our nation; the day of independence is not far off. Our decision to join the Japanese army as Special Support soldiers was not to become Japanese but to be of use to our nation. The day will come when our people achieve independence. Please forgive us for being strict with you all this time."

I couldn't help but be astonished by their words. Indeed, the blood of Joseon (Korea) flowed through their veins, and it made me realize that no matter how much the Japanese tried to suppress and exploit our people, they could never change the essence of our identity. Guns and swords may force young men like us to the battlefield, but I became certain that Japan's oppression and exploitation would soon come to an end, and they would ultimately fail.

Figure 20: A Shinto shrine enshrining Amaterasu Ōmikami, the sun goddess in Japanese mythology

On the evening when the training period came to an end, the authorities called all the student soldiers to a public hall (Bumin Hall) and announced that there would be a farewell ceremony. When I was taken to Bumin Hall, it was packed with dispirited student soldiers being dragged in, leaving no room to stand. At the entrance of the hall, a military band played a welcoming performance. In the front rows, there were those wretched pro-Japanese collaborators, Japanese soldiers, and government officials, including Chunwon Lee Kwang-soo, sitting in line. It made me sick to my stomach, talking to myself:

"Pro-Japanese collaborators, do you think you can lead a prosperous life by sacrificing the young people of this nation and dragging them into the valley of death?
You will surely face retribution before our people,"

As I murmured to myself, feeling utter disgust, Governor Koiso, with an air of arrogance, stepped up to the podium and began his prepared speech.

"....As one of the loyal subjects of the Imperial Army (皇軍), I congratulate you all on this opportunity to serve the nation, having completed your training. ....With the determination to fight against the cruel and barbaric United States on the Pacific front, you will dedicate your youth to the country without hesitation. I have no doubt that you will carry out this duty faithfully. Such a death was considered the highest honor for an Imperial subject, and a way to repay the benevolence of the emperor. I wish you good fortune...." his speech went on.

Figure 21: Governor-General Kuniaki Koiso.

As I listened to those words, my anger was about to explode. I had no connection to the emperor, and he was our greatest enemy. Why should I sacrifice my life for him? I thought to myself. In that moment, from the second floor of the auditorium, a brave student soldier's voice echoed, "Governor-General, I have a question." The Hall fell silent as if someone had poured water on it. He asked,

"Can the Governor-General take responsibility for the future of our people after we go off to war?"

The Governor-General smiled calmly and returned to the podium, "Such a question indicates that your training as loyal subjects of the Imperial Army is not yet complete. Of course, I will take responsibility," he responded.

I had long wanted to know who this brave student soldier was, and only recently did I learn that it was none other than the famous Han Un-sa. I was deeply impressed, thinking it was indeed fitting of him.

Figure 22: Han Un-sa (韓雲史)

After the war, the arrogant Governor-General Koiso was brought to trial in the Far East military tribunal and sentenced to 20 years in prison. He disappeared in Sugamo Prison. It is said that when the proud Koiso received his 20-year sentence, he thanked the presiding judge and bowed his head. This act might have been his way of expressing gratitude for avoiding the death penalty.

Becoming a Japanese soldier

As a person born into this world, who could stop the clock's hands! No matter how great a philosopher or scientist one may be, they cannot stop the moving clock hands. The appointed time will inevitably come, and without fail, it was January 19, 1944.

On this day, I left home to become a student soldier in the Japanese army. I could feel that everyone in the village looked at me with eyes full of pity. At that moment, I once again felt that I was truly an unfortunate person. While it may be unavoidable to cause worries to parents or family, I couldn't hide the guilt I felt towards my wife, whom I married just three months ago.

My wife had come to her new home with the hope of living a good life, bringing all kinds of household goods and many gifts, but now she faced a separation with no end in sight. Even if I take responsibility for my own misfortune, who will bear the sorrow and emptiness she feels? In the morning, our family gathered for a meal, and before the meal, my father earnestly prayed,

"May God guide this child with pillars of fire and clouds, just as He showed to Moses..."

I couldn't stop the tears flowing uncontrollably. My mother placed a small family photo in the Bible and gave it to me, saying, "This book is truth and life; cherish it dearly."

At noon on the 19th, I was scheduled to take the train to Pyongyang accompanied by military police. The villagers expressed their regret at our parting and gave me heartfelt gifts. Among them, Grandma Noh (盧氏), who always showered me with special love, gave me a seninbari (千人針, thousand-stitch belt), a charm believed to protect against enemy attacks, to put around my shoulder. Later, while waiting for the train at Goeup (古邑) Station, I noticed several friends who were also going as student soldiers. They must have been feeling the same emotions as I did.

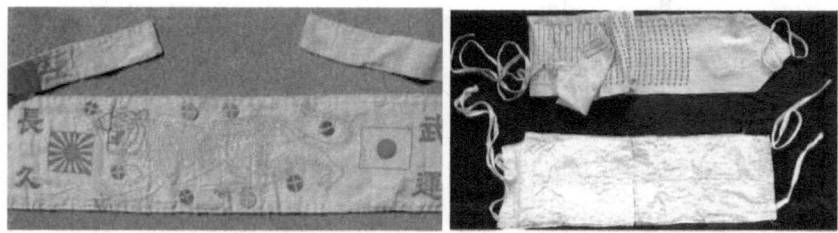

Figure 23: Thousand-stitch belt (千人針: Seninbari)

Seeing my friends who were walking the same path of fate, I couldn't help but feel a sense of resignation. Soon after, we heard the cheer of "Wishing for enduring luck in battle (武運長久)," led by the Japanese principal of Osan High School, where I used to attend.

As the clock struck at noon, the train departed, and we arrived at Pyeongyang Train Station. There, the student soldiers, including myself, stayed together at the inn arranged by the military police. The next day at 10 o'clock a.m., I was to become a Japanese soldier. The induction location was identified as Pyeongyang 42nd Regiment situated in *Sadong* (寺洞), Pyeongyang.

The student soldiers staying at the inn looked at each other's faces and cursed the goddess of fate. They despised anything conventional about their situation on the edge of a cliff. They felt an urge to destroy whatever came their way. Among them was Bang Yong-won (方庸源), a fellow alumnus and classmate from Osan High School. He was tall and well-built, having practiced wrestling as a student and even becoming a sumo wrestler. Despite his imposing physique, he had a strong sense of justice and a gentle heart, always caring for others like a young child. He was a good friend who was always looking out for others.

That day, he drank heavily—even though he normally didn't drink—and when he ran into a Japanese policeman on the street, a fiery burst of hatred erupted in that moment, and he knocked him down with a shoulder tackle. Then, he rushed back to the inn and pounded the wall with his bare fists until it crumbled, all the while crying out, "I have to become a Japanese soldier... I have to kill those bastards!" I consoled him, saying,

"Isn't it because we were born on Korean soil that we find ourselves in this situation? We are enduring the humiliation that a people without a nation must suffer, on behalf of our ancestors."

On that day, even the Japanese military police just watched, no matter what kind of commotion we caused. At the same time, they seemed to mock us, saying, 'Just wait until you enlist—you'll learn exactly what the Japanese army is really like.'

On the early morning of January 20, 1944, the dawn broke clearly. The road to *Sadong* was filled with student soldiers. Parents, lovers, and friends all walked with them, their footsteps marking the path. Everyone urged them to walk faster, afraid they might be late for enlistment. It seemed like they were hurrying to greet someone they were genuinely happy to see. At this point, they had resigned themselves to the situation, feeling as if they had already become Japanese soldiers. As they touched their heads, they realized they had been freshly shaved just two days ago. How melancholy it was!

I passed through the gate of Pyongyang 42nd Division exactly at the designated time. I had crossed the boundary between life and death. A snowstorm passed by. On the other side, it felt warm, but on this side, I felt a cold and desolate sensation. It was only then that I truly realized I had parted with my parents and my wife. A little over an hour later, I put on a shabby Japanese military uniform and wrapped the suit I had worn in a cloth bundle and handed it over to my wife. Seeing me dressed in a military uniform and cap, my parents and my wife must have wept bitterly in their hearts. I did not take the photo that everyone else was taking, because I did not want to leave behind an image of myself in the disgraceful appearance of a Japanese military uniform.

After saying goodbye to my parents and wife at the gate of Pyongyang 42nd Division, I couldn't return home for a full two years. And during those two years, I spent one year and six months in a society under the rule of communism, something I had never even dreamed of.

Chapter 3

Henan Operation

Kagawa Unit

After 20 days of joining the Pyongyang 42nd Division, the enlisted student soldiers were moved to China. Under strict supervision of the military police, they boarded a military train heading north. When the train rolled past my hometown, Osan, lying just beyond the tracks, cloaked in snow and silence, I looked away. As I had already bid farewell to my hometown, I did not want to dwell on the sentimental thoughts of my peaceful home. However, knowing this might be my last glimpse of my beloved hometown, my heart was torn with sorrow, and I couldn't help feeling overwhelmed by sadness.

As the train continued northward, it crossed the Yalu River (鴨綠江) in the middle of the night. Passing through the endless plains of Manchuria and crossing Tianjin (天津), the surroundings remained shrouded in darkness. Among the enlisted soldiers, there were murmurs about making a collective escape once the train reached Tianjin, but nothing significant happened, and the vigilance of the military police only intensified.

After the train reached the Jinpu Line (津浦線), the group of student soldiers disembarked in a city called Xuzhou (徐州). There were around 300 of them who arrived in Xuzhou. At Xuzhou train station square, the soldiers were divided into their respective platoons, and the handover process took place. Even though they found solace in each other's company while gathered as a group, now that they were being separated and assigned to different units, there was no way to suppress the feelings of sadness and loneliness.

I belonged to the Kagawa unit, which was situated about 5 kilometers east of Xuzhou. The commanding officer of the Kagawa unit gathered us in the training field and hung up a sign that read, "We welcome you for joining this honorable unit. Show your loyalty and repay the emperor's grace." It was the first and last time I saw the face of the commanding officer in our unit. In the Japanese military, there was an enormous difference between a second-class soldier like me and the commanding officer. Moreover, within the unit, his position was as distant as the sky from the ground, nearly equal to that of the emperor.

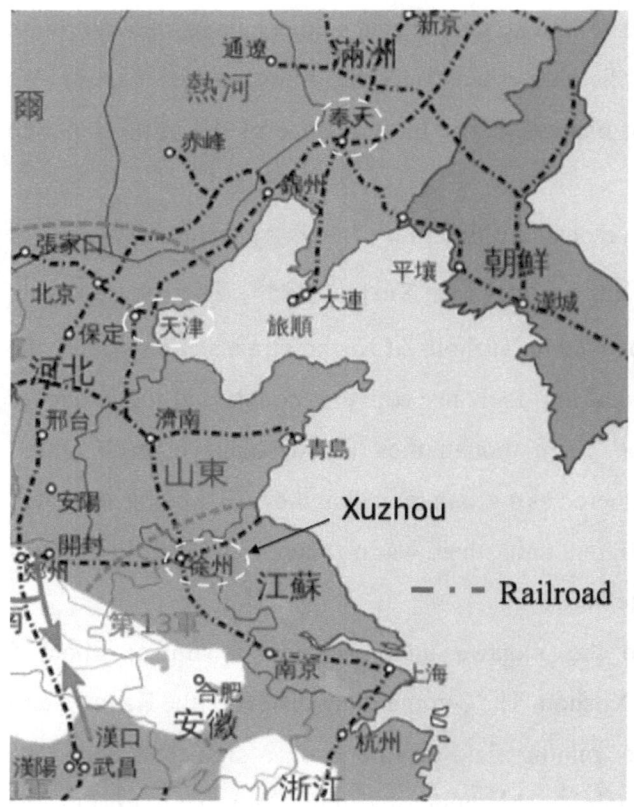

Figure 24: Railroad route through the Japanese-occupied territories,
connecting Fengtian (present-day Shenyang, 奉天), Tianjin
(天津), and Xuzhou (徐州).

My immediate superior in the squad, who was in charge of our
training, was a sergeant named Imagawa. He had a rustic appearance and
thick lips that gave off a cruel impression. He was a seasoned non-
commissioned officer with nearly seven years of experience in the Sino-
Japanese War. From that point on, I underwent training as a new recruit
under his merciless whip.

50

In the Japanese military, the training in the non-commissioned officer class was even more rigorous than regular military training. Here, I was being molded into what they called a "model soldier" for the emperor. In the military, there was no room for freedom or individual rights; absolute obedience to superiors was the only rule. This obedience extended not only to our immediate officers but also to the emperor himself, as a symbol of loyalty. I took part in training with a Type 38 rifle engraved with the Imperial crest said to have been bestowed by the emperor.

I often faced harsh criticism and received disciplinary actions during training. However, since the punishments were physical and not severe, I could endure them without much trouble. Deep down, I knew I wasn't meant to be a soldier in the Japanese military, and that belief shaped my actions, making me appear indifferent to the squad leader's watchful eyes. The squad leader emphasized that surviving the training was crucial for staying alive in combat and, more importantly, for showing loyalty to the emperor. There were 20 new recruits receiving training in the barracks, but only two of us were student soldiers. In comparison to the other trainees who displayed quick movements, wit, and knowledge of military regulations, I felt inadequate. According to the squad leader, I was the odd one out, mentally unfit for the role of a soldier.

The next challenge was enduring hunger, which was quite difficult. Even though the training was physically demanding, I also had to satisfy my hunger with the provided meals, which were often insufficient. I was always hungry. Since we were in the middle of training, we couldn't buy other food to eat. As a result, some of the more experienced soldiers resorted to stealing leftover food, known as "*jjanbong* (殘飯)" or scraps of food, that had been discarded by others. It was a common practice, but if anyone got caught, they would be severely punished, often with a strike from the rice paddle while being scolded, with the justification that "Japanese soldiers don't eat leftovers." Witnessing such incidents made me feel disheartened. I thought, "Even if I were to die, how could I ever stoop so low as to steal the leftovers of those Japanese soldiers?"

One day, while I was out in the field for training, someone gave me a sweet potato. Hiding behind the latrine, I split the sweet potato with another student soldier, but my throat tightened, and I couldn't swallow it. There were also times during the training when we had the chance to roam around the city of Xuzhou. Seeing steaming white dumplings stacked and being sold by the roadside, I found myself wishing I could eat my fill of those dumplings just once before I died. Even now, when I see dumplings being sold on the side of the road, I remember that moment and savor every bite I take. Among all the hardships one can experience in the world, the torment of a hungry stomach was the most profound feeling I endured during my time in the Japanese military.

How could one even think about human rights in the Japanese military? They would point at me and mock, saying, "You're worth only two *sen* (二錢). If you die, we'll just stamp a two-*sen* postage and be done with it." What more can you expect from people with such a mindset? Their cruelty probably stems from the code of the samurai (武士道, bushido) that they held in the past. Moreover, in the Japanese military, there was no such thing as retreat. It was either advance or death. Their disregard for life was a product of the mindset that considered life as light as a feather, which probably originated from the practices of the samurai during the feudal (武家) era.

Four months later, I was promoted to Superior Private, and I treated the new recruit who offered to assist me with warmth and respect. I must say, the most heart-wrenching aspect of the Japanese military was the racial discrimination. Even though I had joined the Japanese army prepared to die alongside them, the attitude of my superiors towards Koreans was disdainful. If I didn't act according to their expectations, they would say, "Aren't you just a Korean?" Being kicked and beaten seemed like a fate we had to endure, but whenever I faced racial humiliation on the battlefield, my blood boiled with anger. Each time, I made a solemn vow to seek revenge someday.

One day, they closely examined a family photo my mother had tucked inside my Bible and said, 'You fool, if we don't defeat the American forces, your family will be torn to pieces.' I thought to myself what pathetic fools they were, silently replying in my heart: Only when the Americans land and you scoundrels are finally destroyed will my family truly find peace.

Henan (Hanam) Operation

During my training as a new recruit, I participated in the "Henan Operation," also known as the "Gyeonghan Line Offensive (京漢線打動作戰)." This operation began on April 18, 1944, shortly after I had arrived in Xuzhou, so it was not even two months since my arrival. Prior to this, the Sino-Japanese War had reached a stalemate since 1938 when Japan occupied Wuhan (武漢三鎭) and the Nationalist

53

Government moved to Chongqing (重慶). Major combat engagements were relatively scarce, and Japan's main warfront was in the Pacific.

Indeed, one of the biggest concerns for Japan was the possibility of U.S. air raids on the Japanese mainland. In April 1942, Japan experienced large-scale air raids on cities like Tokyo, Yokohama, and Nagoya for the first time. Sixteen U.S. bombers took off from aircraft carriers in the Pacific, and some of these bombers, after bombing the Japanese mainland, flew on to Kwangsi (桂林) Province in China. Following this, the U.S. military established airbases in southern Chekiang (浙江省, Zhejiang) and Fukien (福建省, Fujian) provinces, seriously considering the possibility of conducting air raids on the Japanese mainland from these airbases.

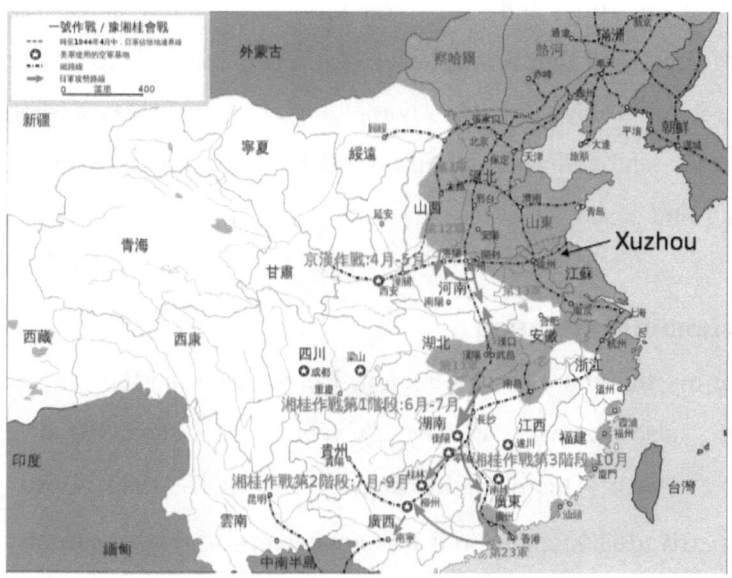

Map 25: Henan Operation, 1944.

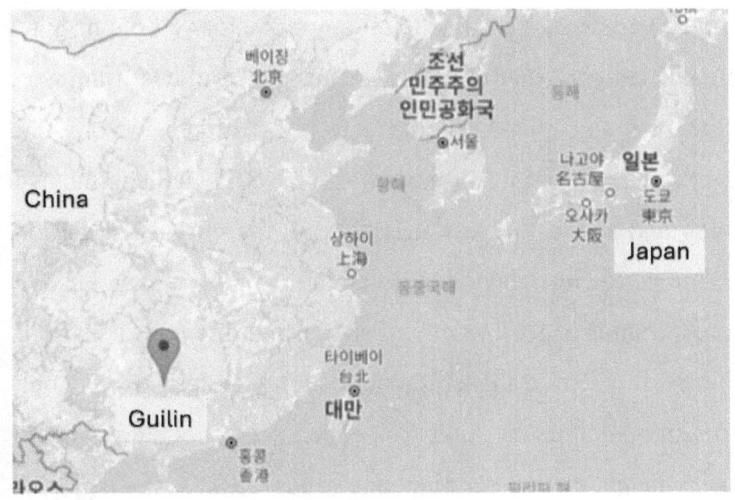

Map 26: Guilin in Kwangsi (Guangxi, 桂林) Province, China.

In November 1943, the U.S. air force gained air superiority in China and had, in fact, planned to build a large-scale airbase in Kwangsi Province (桂林, Guilin). The strategic location of Kwangsi would allow bombers to take off from there, bomb targets in the Japanese mainland, and safely return. In response, the Japanese military launched a desperate operation to occupy this area and prevent the establishment of the airbase. This operation was called the Henan Operation (Gyeonghan Line Offensive). The objective was to seize the area before the U.S. could build the airbase and disrupt their plans to carry out air raids on Japan from this location.

During this operation, not only all Japanese troops stationed in China but also some units from Kwantung Army (關東軍) were mobilized. As a result, the student soldiers who were sent to China automatically participated in the operation. Although they were told they would engage in combat, they didn't feel any particular emotion. Since they had already resigned themselves to the possibility of death and were brought all the way to China, they simply followed orders.

However, the reality of the combat was harsh and challenging, as it involved long and exhausting marches. During the military operation, we were equipped with heavy loads, including 500 rounds of rifle ammunition, 8 rounds of 80-mm mortar shells, and three days' worth of rations. The total weight of this equipment amounted to approximately 16 kan (a traditional Japanese unit of weight). Carrying such a heavy burden during the march was certainly not an easy task, as it weighed as much as our entire body weight.

(Editor's note: 1 kan = approximately 3.8 kilograms or about 8.3 pounds)

Our Kagawa unit arrived at Banbu (蚌埠) by train from Xuzhou (徐州) and set up camp there. It was early spring (194), and the weather was chilly. At night, we lit a bonfire to warm ourselves, but as a new recruit, I felt hesitant to even tend to the fire. Wearing summer military uniform on a cold night must have been really freezing! A senior soldier looked at me and asked if I had ever taken a leave from the unit. When I replied that I hadn't, he said that it would be hard to survive this operation, and it was pitiful that I hadn't even had a single chance to go out. It was then that I realized just how serious this operation was.

According to what I heard, our unit's target for the attack was Fuyang (阜陽) in Anhui Province (安徽省), and the opposing forces were Tang Enbo's (湯恩伯) elite troops, known for their exceptional skills. We continued marching towards Fuyang, facing the arduous journey. At the end of a tiring march, we would camp at forts, where we had to dig trenches outside the fort walls to prepare for potential enemy attacks during the night. We also had to arrange for evening meals and stand guard duty at night. The days were filled with exhausting marches, and the nights were equally challenging, with me, a new recruit, having various difficult tasks to handle.

Even in the midst of all that, there was a certain joy—since most of the student soldiers dispatched to China were taking part in this operation, we would see familiar faces as we marched, sometimes ahead, sometimes behind one another. We could even call each other by name. Realizing, "I'm suffering, but you're alive and suffering too," the joy of meeting one another through just a glance was beyond words.

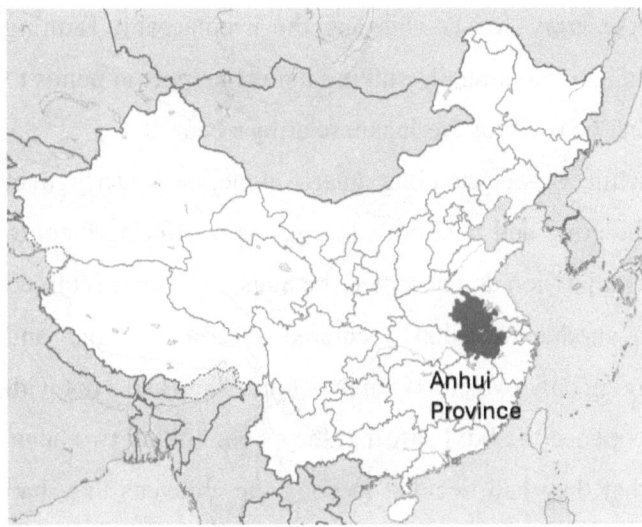

Map 27: Anhui Province (安徽省), China.

The cruelty of the Japanese army

During the operation, the Japanese army revealed its true nature as an invading force. When they arrived at a village or stronghold, it was turned into ruins in no time. They would burn all the farming tools and capture and slaughter livestock such as chickens and pigs. Pigs were killed and their lard extracted, while only the white meat of the chickens was picked to make a dish called "*denpura* (tempura)" and consumed. They sang songs claiming that such operations were enjoyable because they could feast on the abundance of food.

However, when they ordered me to discard the remaining meat, they never allowed me to eat any of it. If they found any alcohol, instead of drinking it themselves, they would pour it out to wash their feet or just simply spill it. It was said that after the Japanese army passed through a village for just one night, the place would become more desolate than if it had suffered from three years of famine. The local residents had fled before the Japanese army arrived, burying the irreplaceable farming tools in the ground and intentionally sinking items like pots in ponds to ensure they couldn't be used for the Japanese army's benefit.

One night, while I was standing guard alone, an elderly man approached me shivering and held out two eggs as if offering them to me. I sensed his compassion and accepted the eggs, but then I returned them to him. On another occasion, I entered a certain village, and everyone fled, leaving only two elderly men behind. They had a pot with them, and when I opened the lid, I saw that they were boiling two hens. They explained that they had decided to cook the chickens they had always wanted to eat before the Japanese soldiers arrived, as they believed the soldiers would surely take the chickens for themselves. Because I understood their state of mind, I pretended not to notice and simply walked past them.

As I marched, I witnessed the miserable lives of Chinese farmers. They simply tilled a handful of land passed down from their ancestors using the same old farming tools, managing at best two meals a day of corn porridge mixed with sweet potatoes. As they grew up, they married, had children, raised them, and then died—realizing this, I was struck once again by the fleeting and futile nature of life.

The forces of the pro-Japanese puppet Chinese National government led by Wang Jingwei (汪靖衛) were more like pitiful bandits than an actual army. They also participated in the Henan (Hanam) Operation, where they would catch chickens whenever they could and stuff several of them into their backpacks to carry while marching. I had heard that in China, those considered useless were sent to the military, and indeed, they were an army of rascals. I had previously held Wang Jingwei in high regard for his fiery revolutionary passion during his youth but seeing him betray the nation and lead a band of thieves was truly disappointing. I thought that, as a *hanjian* (漢奸, traitor to the Han people), the day would soon come when he would face the judgment of the people. In reality, a significant portion of the puppet Nationalist Army (僞軍) sold their weapons to the Communist forces.

There were battles that took place deep within enemy territory. The outskirts of Jungyangkwan (正陽關) saw intense resistance from the enemy. The Japanese forces initiated artillery shelling, followed by airstrikes from Japanese warplanes, which silenced the enemy's resistance. As we advanced into the area, debris was scattered everywhere, and we could see Chinese soldiers fleeing through the barley fields, leaving behind the corpses. This was my first combat experience, where I aimed and fired at the enemy on the Chinese front.

That night, anticipating an enemy counterattack, we spent a tense and grim night in the field. Two enemy prisoners were captured by the Japanese troops. Without any trial or questioning, they were simply labeled as spies and executed in a brutal manner, being stabbed with bayonets and shot. I stood there in shock, witnessing how humans were being slaughtered like animals. It made me realize that war was nothing more than killing and dying, and I trembled at the cruelty of it all.

Figure 28: Jungyangkwan Pass (正陽關) in Anhui Province.

It was that very night. I was assigned to dig a foxhole and stand guard duty, but surprisingly, I was told to go back to the camp and rest. I found it puzzling, but I simply followed orders. However, the next morning, we heard that two days ago, a Korean student soldier had deserted his post and fled to the Chinese lines during combat. The deserter was Lee Mun-hwa (李文華), my junior from Osan High School, whom I knew well. I silently admired his courage and envied his bold decision. Lee Mun-hwa had resolved the inner conflict he faced in the Japanese army with a decisive act of escape, risking his life. I sincerely respected his brave act, and he became the first Korean student soldier to desert, to my knowledge.

After that, for several days, I was not assigned to guard duty during the night, probably because I was a Korean student soldier and they might have suspected I would try to escape as well. Thanks to this, I could enjoy peaceful nights of sleep without worry.

Nationalist Party (Kuomintang)

They said the Henan operation was a success. The unit I belonged to succeeded in occupying Jungyangkwan but withdrew without advancing as far as Fuyang. However, other units were able to occupy Changsha (長沙) in June 1944 and Hengyang (衡陽) in August 1944, thereby gaining control of the land east of the Wulan railway. They also reported occupying Gyerim (Kwangsi) and Yuju (柳州) in November 1944. However, such successful operations by the Japanese army did not contribute to turning the tide of the war. This was because the United States had already taken control of Saipan in the Pacific in June 1944 as an air base needed for bombing the Japanese mainland, making the need for the areas of Gyerim and Yuju in the south of China unnecessary.

In this battle, the Nationalist Army (国民党, Kuomintang) suffered a loss of 500,000 to 600,000 troops, lost 146 large and small cities, and had around 60 million residents pushed into the Japanese-occupied areas. The Nationalist Army's defeat was due to their lack of fighting spirit and their retreat, which was attributed to the extreme corruption within the Nationalist leadership. After the armistice, General Tang Enbai (唐恩伯) betrayed Chiang Kai-shek and switched allegiance to the Communist Party, which also indicates his opportunistic nature. Chiang Kai-shek believed that as long as the United States participated in the war against Japan, the U.S. would emerge victorious, leading to China's victory as well. Therefore, he did not fully exert his forces, with the intention of conserving strength and preparing for a potential conflict with the Communist Party after the armistice.

As expected, the United States also foresaw the possibility of a large-scale civil war between the Nationalists and the Communists in China at the end of the pacific war. This can be inferred from the statement made by O. Lattimore, the political adviser to Chiang Kai-shek, who said,

"China will be victorious, just like the United States. The Soviet Union will also be a winner, and so will the Chinese Communist Party. When the war is over, there will undoubtedly be one more civil war. Therefore, the Nationalist government should keep well-trained troops and new equipment in reserve."

Chiang Kai-shek's repeated retreats during the war against Japan, despite the basic principle that armies become stronger through repeated battles, were foolish and ignored this principle. He did not actively engage in the war with Japan, and this retreat strategy disregarded the fact that an army becomes stronger through continuous combat.

62

Typhoid fever

At the end of a month-long Henan operation, our Kawagawa unit returned to Xuzhou (徐州). However, right after our return, I began to suffer from a high fever that fluctuated between 40 degrees Celsius. I lost consciousness for several days and when I finally regained it, I found myself in the Xuzhou Army Hospital. The diagnosis was "Typhoid fever," which immediately led to my isolation in an infectious disease quarantine ward even within the hospital.

One day, when I opened my eyes, I noticed that my military uniform had three stars on it! However, those stars did not signify a promotion to a Lieutenant General as they were only Private First-Class insignia. In the army, once the required time had passed, even as a Private Second Class, one would naturally be promoted to — that was simply how the system worked.

During my more than a month of isolation in the quarantine ward, I eventually recovered from my illness. However, it wasn't due to medication but rather an inevitable recovery that came with time.

At the Army Hospital, it was customary for patients to be granted a day's outing in the city of Xuzhou before returning to their units. As a new recruit, I had never been allowed to go out to the city during my time in the unit. Thanks to my illness as " Typhoid fever," I finally got the chance to go out to Xuzhou city for the first time since my enlistment. However, it was only an eight-hour free outing. Everything looked fascinating to me as it was my first time experiencing the bustling Chinese street. As my father-in-law had once operated a grain store in

Xuzhou, I grabbed the opportunity to approach fellow countrymen passing by and inquire about the current situation of the grain business.

However, the person I approached saw that I was wearing a Japanese military uniform and asked if I was a student soldier. He had heard that there were many student soldiers around Xuzhou and suggested that we go to his home. It was such a joy to meet a fellow countryman and have a conversation in our language on foreign soil that I eagerly followed him to his house without hesitation.

As soon as we arrived at his home, he said how hungry I must be and welcomed me with a meal of Chinese dishes. Additionally, he mentioned that this year's first batch of grapes had appeared in the market and urged me to try some Chinese grapes. I eagerly devoured the food he served. Proper treatment for Typhoid fever requires carefully regulating one's diet and eating only small portions, but I had foolishly overeaten without thinking.

That night, when I returned to the ward, my stomach began to ache. I tried desperately to vomit the food that was rising up to my throat, but it was in vain, and my vision began to go dark. I thought I was going to die. The patient who had only eaten porridge before ended up overeating greasy Chinese food, and that excessive intake led to unbearable suffering and almost brought death upon me. That night was a torment, but it passed by with great difficulty. It made me realize once again that "life and death are in the hands of God."

The next day, when I finally managed to return to the unit, the platoon leader was taken aback to see me. My pale and exhausted appearance still evident, he asked why I had been discharged from the hospital. Of course, I couldn't say anything in response. However, it seemed that during the few months we had spent together in the unit, we had formed a bond, as he instructed everyone not to assign me any tasks and to take special care of me in the medical unit. The platoon leader's concern and special treatment made me feel touched and grateful. Despite my inability to explain the situation, his understanding and care helped me during my recovery.

Private First Class

My situation in the barracks gradually began to change. I became a Private First Class, and with the influx of new recruits undergoing training, I had some leisure time. The new recruits were old people in their 50s who had been drafted into the reserve forces. Some of them were even former business owners in civilian life. As a result, they all cursed the reckless war conduct of the military, firmly believing that Japan was bound to fail.

The new recruits would often argue over who would take care of my bedding, shine my shoes, and do my laundry during the night. However, I never asked them to do anything for me. I believed that using others for personal gain was a wrong behavior. Instead, seeing these elderly individuals struggle with intense training and not knowing what to do, I felt a sense of pity towards them. War, in my view, was merely the cruel actions of a few individuals who placed themselves above the emperor and certainly not an act for the benefit of the entire nation.

One evening, there was an order for the entire unit to gather. It turned out that we were going to conduct a night training exercise on the back mountain. We all armed ourselves and headed up the mountain. As we reached the top, the company commander informed us that an enemy bomber was appearing in the west and ordered us to shoot at it with our rifles at a 45-degree angle into the air. It was a night practice of shooting down airplanes with our Type 38 rifles, and I understood that this was preparation for the possibility of enemy aerial bombings. At this time, the U.S. forces had already occupied the Saipan Island in the Pacific (known as "Operation Forager") and used it as a base to launch continuous air raids on Japan's mainland. It was then that I began to see the end of the war slowly approaching.

That night, when I returned to the unit, the senior soldiers were visibly furious. They had been fighting and suffering on Chinese soil for seven years, while people on the mainland Japan seemed to be doing nothing. They felt betrayed by the fact that Japan was experiencing nothing but defeat in the Pacific. They were agitated, saying, "Now that the mainland is starting to come under American air raids, doesn't that mean the war is becoming unpredictable?

Afterwards, I was assigned the duty of guarding the military supply and ammunition warehouses in the city of Xuzhou. At night, I would stand guard and look at the nearby Xuzhou Train Station, where trains would come and go. As I observed the trains passing by, I would think, "That train is heading north! Someday, I too will ride this train and return to my beloved hometown." I felt a sense of nostalgia and loneliness. What made it worse was that next to the ammunition depot was a brewery, and when the wind carried the smell of alcohol to my nose, I couldn't help but crave a drink. But when I thought about how I had neither the freedom to board a train and leave nor the means to enjoy a drink, all I could do was sigh.

For student soldiers, there was a path to become officers if they excelled in barracks life and passed the officer candidate exam. By the end of the war, about half of all student soldiers had been commissioned as probationary officers, and their training and life in the barracks were truly impressive. At times, I would look at them and marvel at how they could perform so well even in the enemy's army. I thought they were in no way inferior to Japanese officers.

Indeed, student soldiers who were commissioned as probationary officers played a significant role in the establishment of the Republic of Korea Army after the war. Even during the administration of Prime Minister Chang Myon (張勉) of the Democratic Party, the Chief of Army Staff, Jang Do-yeong (張道暎), was a former student soldier from the Xuzhou unit. As for myself, I was well aware that I was not meant to become an officer in the Japanese military. Therefore, I never attempted to take the officer exam, nor did I seek any recommendations from the unit. My passive attitude stemmed from my idealistic and naive nature, believing that

> "As long as one understands the reality well and adapts accordingly, giving their best effort without compromising principles, the outcome will inevitably be favorable. "

While I couldn't help but feel a twinge of envy when seeing those who became officers, I knew that it was not something I could pursue. I was content with my reality as a Private First Class.

Figure 29: Jang Do-yeong (張道暎)

In the unit, it was said that all senior soldiers were being mobilized for an operation to suppress the Communist forces. But I was left out. The reason given was that I was still suffering from the aftereffects of Typhoid fever. In truth, I wanted to join. I no longer cared about life or death. I simply wanted to escape the stifling barracks, filled with drills and shouting, and to march across the vast Chinese land, feeling the cool wind and firing my rifle. Even if the Japanese military had occupied Xuzhou in 1938, it was only the city center and the railways and roads extending in all directions like the Longhai Line (龍海線) and the Jinpu Line (津浦線). Beyond these points (点) and lines (線), within just 10 *li*

(5 km) there were what they called enemy territories, where the Communist forces or the Nationalist Party had their strongholds.

I had heard such stories from the residents of Xuzhou when I first went out for a break from the army hospital. That's why I had a strong desire to participate in the anti-communist suppression unit, to witness the true nature of the Communist forces and to see the nature of the combat itself. Moreover, I knew that if I managed to escape from the Japanese military barracks, I would likely become a prisoner of either the Nationalist Party or the Communist forces and end up fighting against the Japanese military, which made me even more curious to see the Communist forces' army. However, since I was excluded from the operation, I could do nothing but continue my duty of guarding the military depot in Xuzhou city, waiting for whatever might happen.

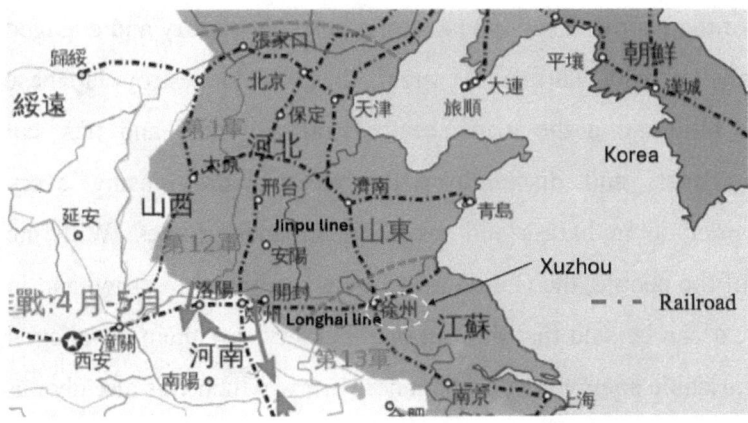

Map 30: Longhai Line and Jinpu Line at Xuzhou.

A week passed, and the members of the anti-communist suppression unit returned to the barracks. They were shaking their heads while sharing stories about how, during their operation against the Communist forces, unexpectedly, the Nationalist Party troops appeared. Instead of attacking the enemy forces, which were their common enemy, they engaged in combat with the Communist forces, who were supposed to be on the same side. They laughed as they recounted the situation. I listened to their words with bewilderment and felt a pang in my heart. How could such a thing happen? How could fellow countrymen, facing a common enemy Japan, turn their guns against each other, giving the invaders the upper hand? I couldn't believe what I was hearing.

However, that was the actual situation in China at that time. Starting from 1944, the Communist forces in the Japanese-occupied rear areas fought against the Japanese in order to protect the civilians and gain the support of the people. They held a strong belief in victory and engaged in brilliant guerrilla warfare. At night, they would destroy Japanese pillboxes built along the roads, remove railroad rails and ties, cut telephone lines, and dismantle defensive structures—using every possible method to harass and resist the Japanese forces. With the support of the people, the Communist forces continued to grow, and in this way, it can be said that the Nationalist Party saw them as an even more formidable enemy than the Japanese army, which was already on the path to defeat.

Decision to Escape

Once again, I couldn't suppress the surge of Korean blood in my veins. It felt utterly unjustifiable for a Korean to become part of the Japanese army that was swallowing Korea, engaging in harsh exploitation and abuse, and guarding ammunition depots with rifles engraved with the Japanese national emblem issued by the emperor. Weren't many independence fighters captured and killed by the treacherous Japanese in Manchuria and China? Even in Chongqing, not far from here Xuzhou, aren't patriots still establishing the Provisional Government of the Republic of Korea and organizing the Korean Liberation Army to fight for our country's independence?

Being a sacrificial pawn for the Japanese invasion, supporting their aggression in any way, no matter the circumstances, felt completely unnatural. The only way out of this unnatural state was to escape. I firmly believed that escaping and joining the Provisional Government to become part of the Korean Independence forces would be the only path for a Korean intellectual like me. Either to fight courageously alongside the Korean Liberation Army against the Japanese, or to assist the Chinese forces resisting the Japanese invasion, it was the only choice that felt right as a Korean intellectual.

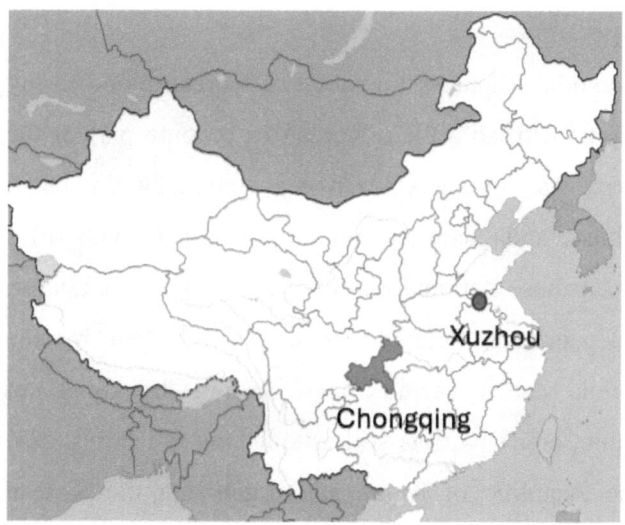

Map 31: Locations of Xuzhou and Chongqing

As I reached this point in my thoughts, the idea of joining the Korean Independence forces didn't seem entirely impossible. I could escape the Japanese army's barracks and make my way to Chongqing. If Chongqing was too far to reach, wasn't it said that just 10 *li* (about 5 kilometers) outside of Xuzhou, there were Chinese forces fighting against the Japanese? Whether they were forces aligned with the Kuomintang, the Communist Party, or Wang Jingwei's (汪兆銘) collaborationist regime, what did it matter? As long as I could aim my rifle at the Japanese and stab their hearts with a knife, that would be enough to achieve my purpose, I thought.

My determination to escape and fight against the Japanese grew stronger as I contemplated the possibility of joining the Chinese forces resisting the invasion. The oppressive weight of serving the Japanese army and abetting their aggression felt unbearable, and I yearned for a path that would align with the spirit of a Korean patriot, even if it meant aligning with foreign forces resisting the Japanese.

Looking back at myself, I was already a soldier of the Japanese army, standing with a rifle on Chinese soil—my life felt like something lived beyond death, a life granted as a bonus. If I could return alive and set foot on my homeland again, I would ask for nothing more. But it seemed unlikely that the ruthless Japanese would let us go freely as their empire was collapsing.

Even so, I firmly believed that God would not abandon me. A verse from the Psalms came to mind: "The Lord is my shepherd; I shall not want. He makes me lie down in green pastures; He leads me beside still waters."

When I thought of that remote area 10 *li* from Xuzhou, far from the railroad and roads, where Chinese soldiers might be hiding, it truly felt like green pastures and still waters. From then on, I acted as if I had already escaped and become part of the Korean Independence army— conducting myself cautiously and waiting for the right opportunity.

As I lay in my bunk after completing my duties in the military camp, distant scenes of my hometown landscape would appear in my mind. The faces of my parents and my wife would come into view. My father, in his youth, was poor and had to work odd jobs at Osan High School to have his tuition waived and graduate. During the March 1st Movement (1919), he bravely sang the independence anthem but soon had to flee to Manchuria to escape the pursuit of the Japanese military police. He stayed in Tonghua (通化), Manchuria, participating in the Korean

Independence movement, but eventually had to hide and return to Osan to avoid capture by the military police.

However, he was still closely monitored, so along with my mother, he sought refuge in the Jinyoung (進永) region of Gyeongsang Province in southern Korea. There, he secured a teaching position at a local school. During their stay, I was born as their second son, and my childhood name was Yeongdeok (永得), which meant "gained in Jinyoung land."

Having spent several years there, my father returned to Osan in northern Korea, where our ancestors' graves were located, and started a business to support our family. He had devoted his youth to the independence movement, so I could only imagine how delighted he would be to hear that I had escaped from the Japanese military in China and was now actively serving in the independence army under the Korean provisional government.

Knowing that my father had signed my papers to join the Japanese military, I was convinced that the best way to show filial piety to him, who was leading a solitary life, was to escape from the Japanese army.

The image of my father unable to conceal his disappointment about Chunwon (春園) came to my mind. Chunwon Lee Kwang-soo was from the same hometown Osan and had returned from studying abroad in Tokyo to work as a teacher at Osan School. At that time, my father was a student. Years later, when Chunwon—by then a complete collaborator with the Japanese—returned to his hometown, the village elders invited him to a restaurant to treat him to dinner. But before beginning his meal, Chunwon reportedly went first to the Kamidana, bowed deeply with utmost formality, and only then began to eat. Witnessing this, my father, who had seen him become a completely different person, couldn't express his disapproval openly but vented his frustrations at home, saying, "How could Lee Kwang-soo become such a treacherous person? To think you had to act like one of those damned Japanese."

My father, who eagerly read the newspapers each day, yearned for the day when Japan would fall. The news of my involvement in the Korean Independence army would undoubtedly be the greatest gift for him.

EOS/Kokugakuin University

Figure 32: Kamidana used for enshrining kami (spirits or deities).

I also missed my kind and gentle mother. On the day I left home to join the Japanese army, she had draped a *senninbari* (thousand-stitch belt) over my shoulder and tucked a family photo into the Bible she had been reading. I remembered how she shut the door, saying she couldn't bear to watch me leave. My mother was a graduate of Boseong Girls' School (寶城女子學校) in Seoncheon (宣川), the only Christian school in the northwestern region of Korea. She was a traditional Korean mother who entrusted both her body and spirit to God and devoted herself entirely to managing the household. Her hope was that I would finish my studies in Tokyo and return home to become a teacher at Osan Middle School. After placing her seal on the document that consigned me to the Japanese army, she went to the village church every single dawn without fail to pray. I thought that, for her prayers to be fulfilled, I must escape from the Japanese army as soon as possible.

My wife's face also came to mind. She had been a student at Ewha Women's College (梨花女子大学), but after marrying me, she came to live in my rural home—and just three months later, she had to send her husband off to the Chinese front! I wondered how she was doing now, living with my parents and trying to get by. She had brought many wedding gifts and household items with her in hopes of a good life—but "who would sleep under those fine silk quilts now? The one who should be there with her was dragged off to war instead." The more I thought about it, the more lonely and desolate I felt. Caught up in these thoughts, I couldn't sleep. But that night, I made the most important decision of my life:

"I will escape from the Japanese army.
Even if I am caught and brought before a court-martial,
I will certainly carry out my plan—no matter what."

The next morning, I went again to the ammunition depot for my sentry duty. But this morning was different from the last—because it was the first day of preparation for my new purpose.

Figure 33: Boseong Girls' School in Seoncheon, Korea.

Comrades

I realized that it would be difficult to escape from the Japanese army on my own. It seemed best to find two or three comrades who shared the same intention. And finding fellow student soldiers to escape with wouldn't be too difficult—most of us had a similar level of awareness, shared the same resentment toward the Japanese military, the same spirit of national identity, and a mutual understanding of our situation. Before long, I was able to find two comrades willing to escape with me, and the three of us quickly reached a consensus.

One comrade was Jung Geun-seok (鄭根碩), who was from Shinuiju (新義州), his hometown. He had graduated from Meiji University (明治大学) and was a devout Christian. He also had thought about escaping and had a plan to flee even if he had to do it alone.

Another comrade was Shim Ha-geun (沈河根), from Sakju, his hometown. He was a student soldier from Dae Pan Foreign Language School (大潘外国语学校) and specialized in studying Chinese. We were pleased to have him with us, as his knowledge of Chinese would greatly help us when dealing with Chinese people after our escape. The three of us met frequently, often gathering at secluded spots or street corners to discuss our plans away from prying eyes.

Around that time, various rumors were circulating within the unit. It was said that two student soldiers had escaped from the barracks and, while wandering through the mountains, encountered Wang Jingwei's puppet army. They allegedly resisted, and one was shot dead by the puppet troops while the other was captured and handed over to the military police. Both of these student soldiers were from North Pyongan Province and had been close to me. However, after the war ended, I learned that the story had been completely false. In fact, the two who had escaped had successfully made their getaway and later played an active role in the independence movement around Fuyang (阜陽).

Another story was heard as well. In the vicinity of Xuzhou, a large number of student soldiers reportedly escaped from a supply unit known as "chijung" (輜重). This was said to be due to the infiltration of Korean provisional government agents who had conducted espionage within the unit. The student soldiers formed groups and confidently passed through the main gate, heading to the provisional government. Among them was Seung Yeong-ho (承永祜), a fellow student from my Osan School days, who was also part of this supply unit. He too managed to escape and traveled all the way to Chongqing, where he joined the provisional government and became significantly involved in its activities.

The three of us who had decided to escape began our preparations in secret. Since we were still living inside a Japanese military camp, it was hardly an environment where proper planning was possible. Ultimately, we had to leave our success or failure to fate. All we could do was quietly gather a few packs of *Asahi* (旭光) brand cigarettes issued by the army and some hardtack from our rations.

Naturally, we had no access to essentials like Map s or a compass—things that would be necessary for an escape. We thought it would be ideal to change into civilian clothes, but since we were not allowed to leave the camp, that too was impossible.

The three of us simply held on to one firm belief: that if we could make it just 10 *li* into the remote countryside, away from the railroad or roads, we would encounter Chinese forces fighting against the Japanese—and that they would welcome us.

Figure 34: Seung Yeong-ho.

It was said that another anti-communist operation was about to begin within the unit. When these operations were underway, the unit would become less active and quieter. We decided to take advantage of this situation to carry out our escape. The day was August 19, 1944. On that day, we each stole a hand grenade. These were intended for use in case escape became impossible, as a means of ending our lives.

I had a word of farewell with Bang Yong-won (方庸源), a fellow student from Osan School who had received officer candidate training. He was being mobilized for the anti-communist operation. I whispered to him, "If you return from the operation and don't see me around, consider me gone." With a final look exchanged between us, we parted ways.

Chapter 4

Escape

Endless Escape

As the fateful hour of midnight on August 19th (1944) approached, I couldn't calm my trembling heart. I urged myself, "Don't look back." I also told my comrades not to think about what might happen behind us. In a situation where we didn't know what hardships lay ahead, hesitating and looking back would only invite misfortune.

Time passed, and after having dinner, it was already night. The three of us planned our shift for sentry duty within the unit. I would take the first watch, then I would switch with Jung Geun-seok (鄭根碩), and after his shift, he would switch with Shim Ha-geun (沈河根). When it was midnight, I would go to a designated spot and wait. Once Shim Ha-geun finished his sentry duty, the three of us would gather at the designated spot without waking the next Japanese soldier on duty and then proceed to jump over the barbed wire fence of the unit.

While receiving training in the daily training field, I had noticed a dilapidated barbed wire fence with holes, as if chewed through by rusted chains. The three of us successfully approached and escaped through the fence using swift movements. Even the military dogs trained by the unit didn't bark, as if aided by a higher power. Now, the three of us had escaped from the Japanese army barracks. We ran with all our might, driven by the single-minded goal of distancing ourselves from the army unit as much as possible. We avoided the railway tracks and stayed away from major roads. Since the Jinpo Line (津浦線) ran to the north and south from Xuzhou, and the Yonghae Line (龍海線) ran to the east and west, we chose a direction in the northeast to evade both railroads.

Map 35: The arrow indicates our intended direction after escape.

But since it was the middle of the night and the temperature had dropped, a thick fog began to roll in. Avoiding the road was absolutely essential, so we ran straight across the fields. We kicked aside sweet potato vines, pushed through tall stalks of sorghum and corn, running and running without exchanging a word. We had to cover 20 *li* (10 km) and disappear into the remote countryside before dawn.

As we ran, a thought struck me—was the direction we were running truly northeast? With the darkness and dense fog, we had no clear landmarks to guide us. Though it felt like we had run at least 10 *li*, the electric lights twinkling in the far east still shone just as brightly as before. We had no idea where we were.

As there was a hill, we decided to rest there for a moment. Lighting up a cigarette helped us to ease our nerves somewhat. I thought to myself, "So this is what freedom feels like." However, this sense of freedom was short-lived, and as I considered our situation, a sense of darkness loomed ahead. It felt like any moment an enemy sentry might appear, or a puppet army or a Chinese resident might suddenly emerge and lead us back to the unit. Running through the foggy night, sweat covered our bodies, and fatigue started to set in. However, compared to the prospect of death, fatigue was not a significant concern.

However, there were a few ominous signs that unsettled our minds. We had been running for a good three hours since starting at midnight, yet the electric light that had been flashing in the east, visible when we crossed the barbed wire fence, hadn't disappeared; it still glowed and continued to shine. The railroad tracks we absolutely needed to avoid suddenly appeared, and we even ended up crossing a larger road unexpectedly. Nevertheless, we couldn't afford to stay in one place, so we just kept running. The dense fog that covered the ground seemed to be thickening, and our clothes were becoming damp from sweat.

Dawn was breaking. The thick fog had turned into a light drizzle. As the sun began to rise, we, dressed in Japanese army uniforms, needed to find a way to conceal ourselves by any means necessary. It was evident that if the local residents spotted us, they would surely report us to the Japanese forces or the puppet army, which is why we had no choice but to venture into a deep, uninhabited mountain to hide ourselves. It wasn't so much a distant mountain as a slightly elevated hill that seemed to loom faintly in the darkness. We considered that place as a hideout and summoned the last of our strength to run toward it.

As we approached, we realized that the mountain was barren, covered in rocks with no trees. As daylight increased, we gathered and stacked large stones, deciding to spend the day there. It seemed like a foolish idea, but we had no other choice.

As we strained to carry the stones, a strange sound reached our ears. Could it be? We looked around and saw military units forming up, soldiers assembling, not for morning roll call, but to gather at the training field! I blinked and looked down again, certain that the training field we were seeing was indeed the very one where we had practiced exercises. And this mountain was unmistakably the same one we had climbed during training. As the three of us exchanged glances, we couldn't see our own faces, but the pale, frightened expressions on each other's faces gave us an idea of how we appeared. Looking down at the neighboring hill, we saw farmers working in their fields.

By then, the day had fully broken, and the misty drizzle that had been falling off and on turned into a steady light rain. One of us said that we no longer had anywhere to go, and that if we stayed here, we would surely be caught by the Japanese. He suggested we return to the unit and turn ourselves in, thinking that surrendering voluntarily might result in a lighter punishment than being captured.

I understood that returning on our own might be one way to save our lives, but to me, the idea of standing trial in a Japanese military court—subjected to a humiliating and degrading process—was a pain worse than death. I firmly said that surrender was out of the question. Turning oneself in was a voluntary act; being captured was by force. I insisted we must run—leave this place and continue our escape.

With that, I dashed off, sprinting over the ridge on the opposite side of the mountain from the unit.

Of course, the other two comrades followed me. The farmers who had been working in the fields paused briefly, casting casual glances as though it was an ordinary sight. Perhaps they assumed that we were Japanese soldiers engaged in training exercises as they saw us running. Being accustomed to seeing Japanese soldiers running and training near the unit, they might have simply thought of it as the sight of three men running by.

There was an underground pillbox, which appeared to be built by the Nationalist Army in the early stages of the war to fight against the Japanese. As soon as we entered the pillbox, the light drizzle that had been falling turned into a heavy downpour, as if it had been waiting for that very moment. The rain poured down relentlessly, and soon it began to flow into the underground pillbox, causing water to pool on the floor. As the water collected, we gradually moved to higher ground inside to avoid it. The rain continued to pour all day long, and since the village houses were spaced far apart, there was no sign of anyone coming or going.

Fortunately, we were able to spend a whole day safely in the underground pillbox. We didn't even smoke cigarettes, as we were concerned that the smoke might waft outside the pillbox and arouse the curiosity of the locals. We ate a few pieces of hardtack, but we couldn't drink any water. After running and sweating through the previous night, we were very thirsty. It was unbearable to go without water all day, but we had to endure it. We encouraged each other, reminding ourselves that if we couldn't bear it, the only outcome would be getting caught by the Japanese soldiers. So, we gritted our teeth and persevered.

Lonely journey

As the rain subsided and darkness fell, we emerged from the underground pillbox. Glancing at my watch, it was 9 o'clock p.m. The pouring rain had suddenly cleared, and a full moon was rising in the eastern sky. The moon, emerging after the rain, was clear and reddish. In the northern sky, the Big Dipper (北斗七星) shone clearly. The harmony of nature was truly mysterious. To think that we had safely spent a day amidst such rain felt like a miracle. What would have become of us if we had been caught in that relentless rain out in the mountains all day?

Our biggest mistake last night was blindly running through the fields to avoid the road, which led to us losing our proper direction. That's why we couldn't get far from the Japanese unit and ended up circling around the unit all night. It's clear that the distant light we saw in the east when we first left was continuously following us. The fact that we had crossed the railway and the major road probably meant we had actually crossed the ones right in front of the unit. Just thinking about it sent shivers down my spine. This time, no matter what happens, I made a vow to determine our direction clearly and proceed straight towards it.

Since it is said that "the moon rises in the east", the direction where the moon appears must be east. And since the Big Dipper constellation is in the north, I reasoned that if we set our course between the two, we would be heading in a northeast direction. The more I thought about it, the more I realized how fortunate that the underground pillbox was prepared for us. We had avoided the rain, concealed ourselves, and now, under a clear sky, we could determine our direction and set off at night. I believed that all of this was God's guidance alongside us.

Soon, we headed towards the northeast. Since we didn't have the strength to run, we walked along the road. Even if there were forts along the way, we couldn't avoid the road; we had to follow it. Even if it meant risking being captured by the Japanese army, we chose to stay on the road. We felt that if we walked about 10 *li* (5 km), we would reach our desired destination.

Walking along the road, we inevitably had to pass by villages. Every time we entered a village, we grew tense. We were apprehensive that someone might suddenly appear and ask a sentinel password, making our bodies shiver at the thought. We were afraid that dogs might bark and give us away. We cautiously passed through, barely even taking a deep breath. Despite the late hour, we reassured ourselves that village people wouldn't likely be wandering around at this time, and we continued to be cautious. We safely passed one village without incident, but we knew we had quite a distance to walk before reaching the next one.

As we continued, a sense of relief gradually settled in. With the tension easing, hunger gnawed at our stomachs and thirst parched our throats. Unlike in Huabei (華北, North China), where rice was cultivated, there were no paddy fields or lakes to provide agricultural water. Fortunately, the heavy rainfall from the previous day had left water pooled in ditches. Despite knowing it wasn't safe to drink, we would sometimes scoop up the water with our hands and sip it. Due to our hunger, we even dug up sweet potatoes from a nearby field, brushing off the dirt and eating them. Walking silently, we were wordless. It wasn't just that we lacked the energy to speak, but the looming uncertainty ahead cast a shadow over us, rendering any conversation difficult.

Exhausted, we sometimes collapsed on the roadside, trying to catch our breath. Looking up at the twinkling stars in the sky while lying down only deepened our sense of melancholy. In the vast expanse of this continent, not knowing where we were and where we were heading, thoughts of whether we were destined to die here crossed our minds. In this eerily tranquil night, akin to the valley of death, where were we truly headed? The words of David's song echoed in my mind:

"Yea, though I walk through the valley of the shadow of death,

I will fear no evil:

for thou art with me;

thy rod and thy staff they comfort me."

I found renewed strength in the belief that the same God who oversees life and death would not abandon us to perish in this place. We pressed on, determined to face whatever lay ahead, fueled by the unwavering conviction that God's presence would guide and protect us through the darkness.

As we journeyed on the road, we encountered a fork in the path. One road held the promise of hope, while the other led to ruin. Which path should we choose? After much hesitation, we ultimately decided to follow the path pointing toward the northeast. We reached the entrance of another village. In the darkness a shabby farmhouse came into view. Checking the time, it was 4 a.m., and we estimated that we had covered about 20 *li* (10 km). We had no more time to spare. Dawn was approaching, and on the vast, endless expanse of land, how could we possibly conceal ourselves?

The only hiding place was within a patch of millet stalks piled up in the middle of a field near the village, left there after harvest. But it wasn't a viable option. As soon as daylight broke, the villagers would surely report the sight of us wearing Japanese military uniforms to nearby Japanese troops or local authorities. We had no choice but to expedite matters before daybreak to make a decision and take action.

The three of us entered the modest farmhouse at the entrance of the village. It couldn't quite be called a house, as it did not have surrounding walls or even a proper gate. It consisted of just one room with a small kitchen attached. As if sensing our presence, the door opened, and an elderly woman emerged. She mumbled something, but we couldn't understand what she was saying. She must have thought we were Japanese soldiers, without a doubt. She must have seen many brutal Japanese soldiers in the past, but now, perhaps because she had nothing left to lose and felt that there was nothing, we could do to an old woman like herself, she showed no sign of fear or intimidation. The old woman fetched water from a jar in the yard, brought it into the kitchen, poured it into a pot, and began to make a fire to boil it.

We approached the old woman and spoke to her in Chinese. Isn't Shim Ha-geun, who studied Chinese at the Osaka School of Foreign Languages, one of us? "We are Koreans," he said. "We are from Korea." "We escaped from the Japanese army and want to join the Chinese forces fighting against them." We asked various questions, such as, "Where are we?" "Is there a place far from here where the Japanese army is not present?"

However, the old woman kept responding that she didn't know. In truth, how could a rural elderly woman possibly know about Koreans or the whereabouts of Chinese forces fighting the Japanese army? Moreover, how could the unsophisticated countrywoman understand what Shim Ha-geun was saying in his Chinese? Hadn't it been said that China is so vast that people from the northern and southern regions cannot understand each other's language?

Failing in our conversation with the old woman, we found ourselves sitting in the courtyard, and before we knew it, we had fallen into a deep sleep. How long had we been asleep? I was jolted awake, and as I opened my eyes, I realized the sun was already shining brightly overhead. Oh no! We've made a huge mistake! I thought to myself as I looked around. The villagers had surrounded us, staring down at us intently. There must have been over 30 of them. Children were there, as well as young adults and even elderly folks puffing on their pipes. They pointed at us, exchanging curious glances and making gestures of astonishment, clearly intrigued by our presence.

As the day grew brighter, it was evident that the bizarre Japanese soldiers had appeared and that the villagers had gathered to witness us, who were deeply asleep in the middle of the courtyard. We, too, were at a loss for what to do, unable to utter a word, and could only stare blankly at them, resigning ourselves to entrust our fate to them. Hunger and thirst were forgotten, replaced by an overwhelming sense of unease, as they held their scabbards, hinting at potential ominous events. The silence between us and them stretched on. They refrained from approaching us and seemed to engage in hushed discussions amongst themselves.

Clad in Japanese military uniforms and each carrying a hand grenade on our belts, it was likely that they perceived us as Japanese informants who had gotten lost and exhausted while gathering information nearby before stumbling upon their village to rest. Finally, a man among them abruptly stood up. He was well over six feet tall, with a gaunt face that exuded a malicious aura. Gesturing towards us, he spoke loudly in Chinese, "If you travel 10 *li* (5 km) to the east, you'll find the Eighth Route Army (八路軍, Ba Lu Jun), and if you go 20 *li* to the west, you'll reach the Japanese garrison. Hurry and go to the Japanese forces!" Although his words were in Chinese, his gestures and expressions conveyed his intent, and given the tense situation, we could sense the urgency. His words suggested that they had assumed we were Japanese stragglers and were concerned about us falling into the hands of the Eighth Route Army, hence offering us guidance.

But this information was truly invaluable to us. Not only did we now know our exact location, but we also gained the conviction that if we traveled just 10 *li* eastward, we would reach our intended destination— the place we had aimed for when we fled the Japanese camp.

In that moment, a flash of realization struck me: "If we go just 10 *li* east, we'll reach the Eighth Route Army. If someone in this village intends to inform the Japanese army about us, they would have to go 20 *li* west, and then it would take another 20 *li* for the Japanese to come here to capture us—that's a round trip of 40 *li*. Meanwhile, we only need to run 10 *li* to reach the Eighth Route Army."

Now, we believed that our escape was as good as successful. With this judgment, our energy was renewed, tiredness dissipated, and our bodies felt lighter. We stood up from where we were and started running towards the east, gazing at the sun. We followed the path if there was one, dashed through the middle of fields, and headed straight towards the east. Perhaps the villagers assumed that we were information agents sympathetic to the Eighth Route Army, running with a mission of conveying their situation.

Eighth Route Army

We ran sweat-soaked for 10 *li*. However, what appeared before us was not the Eighth Route Army, but a large river. The width of the river seemed to be at least 100 meters, yet the water didn't seem to be flowing rapidly. There was no bridge, and not even a raft could be seen. We initially hid ourselves in the dense reed field by the riverbank. From within the reeds, as we looked at the river, our dire situation once again felt stark. When I threw a stone into the river, it seemed deep, and the three of us didn't know how to swim. Fortunately, the reed thicket growing on the riverbank was deep and well-separated from the footpath that ran alongside the river. This allowed us to hide without being noticed by those passing on the path.

Sitting crouched in the reed thicket and looking at the river, we suddenly heard the loud sound of gunfire. Upon hearing the gunshots, it seemed that a battle had erupted not far from our location. The gunshots continued for about 30 minutes, intermittently accompanied by the rapid firing of a machine gun. Eventually, the gunfire ceased, and the surroundings fell quiet. Then, we heard the sound of footsteps approaching along the riverbank footpath. We tensed up, even holding our breaths, and strained our ears. Three women walked by above us, carrying baskets on their heads. One of them said, "Yesterday, three Japanese soldiers fled to this area, prompting the Japanese army to launch a search. However, they were repelled by the Eighth Route Army." While they spoke in Chinese, we were so intensely focused that we could roughly grasp the meaning of their words.

According to a fellow student soldier who had been in the same unit and later told me after the war, the unit waited for a day after our escape, expecting we might return. On the second day, they mobilized a platoon to launch a search operation. It became clear that the intense gunfire we had heard earlier had indeed been, just as the three women had said, a clash between the Japanese troops pursuing us and the Eighth Route Army stationed on the opposite side of the river.

The gunfire ceased, and suddenly from across the river, a loud and rhythmic singing voice could be heard. It was a song sung by the Eighth Route Army to boost morale. With this song, it became clear that the other side of the river was under the control of the Eighth Route Army, while our side was occupied by the Japanese. We even began to consider the possibility that the area we were hiding in might be a buffer zone. As night fell, our plan was to take action – if there was a bridge, we would cross it, and if not, we were confident that there would be a ferry, which would lead us into the territory of the Eighth Route Army. With such hope in mind, our hunger and thirst seemed to fade away, and we eagerly awaited the setting of the sun and the cover of darkness.

Figure 36: Eighth Route Army's Anti-Japanese Campaign.

Just as the evening dew was starting to descend, suddenly a wild boar burst into the thicket of reeds where we were hiding. We couldn't make any noise to shoo it away, but we tried our best to break off reeds and drive it out. Unexpectedly, a farmer appeared and chased the boar into the thicket. Witnessing us, he was taken aback, and with a shout, he quickly retreated. It was beyond his wildest dreams to imagine people hiding in the forest, let alone crossing his path. Moreover, he must have been utterly surprised, mistaking us for Japanese agents conducting some sort of covert operation against the Eighth Route Army across the river. We felt a great sense of unease. We were worried that the villagers might gather in a crowd or that they might alert the Japanese. At that time, it was quite common for people in the Huabei (華北) region to let wild boars graze freely.

Soon, the dew settled, and the bright moon rose. We emerged from the thicket of reeds. Now, driven by the hope of finding a bridge or a ferry, or even if the river narrowed, we could cross the water and reach the Eighth Route Army area. Our steps felt lighter with this hope swelling within us. The moonlight shimmered on the clear river, creating a beautiful scene. We walked along the riverbank for a while, searching for a bridge or a ferry, but found none. We even tried leaning against any large planks we could find to test if they could be used as a makeshift bridge, but it was all in vain. The width of the river neither widened nor narrowed—only the moonlight reflected on the water shone brilliantly. All around was silent, enveloped in stillness, with no sign of human presence whatsoever.

As we continued walking along the riverbank, unable to find any solution, a sudden surge of hunger and thirst, which we had pushed aside amidst our tension and hope, overwhelmed us. We were on the verge of despair and exhaustion, unable to take another step. However, human desires are resilient. We couldn't abandon our hope. We retraced our steps along the familiar path we had taken to dig and eat sweet potatoes from the fields, searching for a ferry, looking for it again and again, hoping to find a bridge or any means of crossing. We must have covered a distance of at least 10 *li*. Looking at the clock, I realized that midnight had passed. We stood there, gazing helplessly at the destination of our hope, the Eighth Route Army area, right in front of us.

River crossing

In China, as mentioned earlier, it was said that a village would always have a forest beneath it. Looking from a distance at the forest, we could see six men sitting and conversing underneath the trees. Despite being quite far away, the moonlight was so bright that we could make out their figures. They seemed to be cooling off from the late summer heat and engaged in a casual conversation by the riverside. We sat on the road and discussed our options.

"Now we're hungry and exhausted, and we can't continue like this. Plus, finding a boat tethered to the riverbank is impossible. Let's leave everything to fate and approach them to explain our situation. They're probably decent villagers and won't harm us without reason, right?"

Gathering our courage, we slowly walked towards the forest. As they sat there peacefully, they suddenly noticed our presence and were taken aback, jumping up in surprise. Naturally, even though we weren't armed, the sight of three men dressed in Japanese military uniforms approaching might have been quite shocking. We confidently sat down next to where they stood in astonishment. Then we began to speak, saying things like, "We are Koreans," "We escaped from the Japanese army," "We are from Korea," and pointing across the river while pleading, "Please help us get to the Eighth Route Army."

Their expressions showed that they didn't fully understand our words. However, it seemed they realized that we weren't arrogant Japanese soldiers but rather desperate refugees, earnestly pleading for something. They didn't show any hostility. Then one of them disappeared, saying he would bring the village head along with a brush and ink.

The night had already grown deep, and the intense heat of the daytime sun had subsided, allowing us to feel the cool river breeze beneath the trees. As we waited for the village head to arrive, it felt like time was passing slowly, as our fate seemed to hang in the balance. Eventually, from a distance, we saw a man wearing traditional Chinese clothing, despite it being summer, with the moonlight casting a glow upon him as he approached us. His face bore a bright smile, radiating a sense of accomplishment and happiness, as if he had achieved something significant. I could now sense that we were safe. The village head handed us a piece of paper and a brush. We quickly wrote down our message:

"我们 朝鲜人 脱出日本军队 希望行 八路军地区"

(We are Korean, escaped from the Japanese army, and wish to go to the Eighth Route Army area).

Upon reading it, the village head repeatedly exclaimed "好的" (Okay) in a delighted manner, seemingly unsure of how to contain his happiness. He then gestured for us to follow him, taking the lead. The other Chinese people nearby also appeared to have grasped our sincere intentions and were visibly pleased.

In this way, we were led by the village head to a nearby house. However, suddenly, the village head who had been guiding us was nowhere to be seen. For a moment, we suspected whether he had deceived us, allowing us to relax before leading us into a trap set by the Japanese soldiers. Doubts began to creep in about his intentions. But then we heard the sound of water boiling in the kitchen and the noise of a chicken being caught. Now, we were hoping to have some water to drink and chicken to eat, swallowing our saliva in anticipation. Just then, a sergeant dressed in worn-out clothes entered the room with a rifle lacking a buttstock, and he excitedly poured cheap Chinese sweets onto a plate before hastily leaving the room. We were left bewildered.

Eventually, the village head reappeared. He informed us that before daybreak, he needed to leave for the Eighth Route Army area, urging us to hurry along. We simply followed him, but it was truly regrettable that we couldn't even take a sip of water or enjoy the chicken we had been longing for.

We arrived once again at the riverbank. Looking along the edge of the river, there it was—the ferryboat we had searched for so desperately! The village head had let us stay at his home and, in the meantime, had prepared the ferry to help us cross. Together with the village head, we boarded the boat rowed by a ferryman and crossed the river. At last, on August 21st—exactly two days after our escape from the Japanese army camp—we reached the land of hope: the Communist-controlled region. The night was still deep, and the full moon was leaning westward in the sky. We breathed in the air of the Communist region with all our might and took our first hopeful steps forward.

Hospitality of the Eighth Route Army

The guide who led us was clearly a local resident associated with the Communist Party. Having survived the clashes between the Eighth Route Army and the Japanese forces in the border region, it was evident that he held strong resentment towards the Japanese forces. He must have held great admiration and support for the Eighth Route Army, which stood against the Japanese forces, and his cooperation with them was likely wholehearted. Judging from his evident joy, it was certain that he would receive substantial rewards from the Eighth Route Army in the days to come.

After crossing the river, the guide led us to a farmhouse. After a brief pause, a young man who seemed to be the owner of the house emerged and the guide handed us over to him. The guide then turned back and left, giving us a reassuring smile and lightly patting our shoulders, as if to indicate that we should follow the young man. It appeared that the young man was the host of this village. When he saw us, he couldn't hide his unexpected joy, like catching an unexpected prize. Following behind the guide, we arrived at another village, where we were handed over once again and continued our journey.

Before we knew it, the sun was rising in the east, glowing red on the horizon. When we arrived at a new village, our guide told us that we had now reached a safe zone. He led us to the largest house in the area and said we could rest easy, as it was far from any Japanese forces. The house had belonged to an absentee landlord—someone who had fled to Nationalist-controlled territory—and was now being used by the Communists as a public facility. At that moment, we could truly feel in our bones that we had successfully escaped. With that realization, our tension melted away, and we fell asleep right where we sat.

As I opened my eyes, the sun had already risen high in the sky, and the courtyard was bustling with activity, resembling a festive gathering at a banquet hall. It seemed that curious residents had gathered, perhaps to witness how the Japanese forces were different from them. Peering through the cracks of the door, we observed the scene, delighted like onlookers watching a newlywed bride enter her new home. With excitement, we swung the door wide open. We, too, wanted to see these genuine folks, who were as curious about us as we were about them. Among them, I spotted a person wearing the uniform of the Eighth Route Army, and it seemed like everyone was celebrating and chatting joyfully, as if welcoming a day of victory.

After our escape, we finally had a chance to wash up and have some tea. It was well past 10 o'clock a.m. when breakfast was served. We

100

couldn't help but be astonished – the table was laid out with an abundance of dishes as if a feast had been prepared! There was even a bottle of huangjiu (黃酒, a high-quality Chinese liquor) placed on the table. Taking a sip of huangjiu was a euphoric experience. When had our situation transformed like this? Just yesterday, we were fleeing and struggling with hunger, and now we were faced with such a spread of food and fine liquor. It felt like we had escaped from hell and arrived in paradise. I resolved that I would fight, even if it meant facing the Japanese forces, for the sake of these people. So there, in the liberated zone of the Communist Party, we enjoyed a hearty meal of Chinese dumplings and dishes that we had been longing for, as if indulging in a long-awaited dream.

Figure 37: Huangjiu, one of the two traditional Chinese liquors.

Chapter 5

Entering the Guerrilla Zone

Propaganda of the Eighth Route Army

Having successfully escaped to the Communist-controlled area (referred to as the liberated zone in China), we finished our first morning meal and once again fell into a deep sleep. When we awoke to the bustling sounds of people gathering outside, the phrase "*chow pah*" (set off) reached our ears. Stepping outside, we were warmly welcomed by everyone, their joyful expressions and cheerful demeanor evident. It seemed like the entire village had gathered to see us. They observed us closely, as if trying to imagine how those Japanese soldiers, dressed in military uniforms and boots, who used to oppress them, might have looked.

Some people playfully said, "*Meshi meshi di ho*" (Eat, eat), while others pointed at us, calling us "*Ilbon kotsu*" (Japanese devil, 鬼子), though it seemed to be done in a good-natured manner. Among them, a soldier wearing the uniform of the Eighth Route Army was so overjoyed that he repeatedly bowed to us and expressed his gratitude.

In that uneasy atmosphere, we continued forward and found three donkeys tied up. A young man in military uniform saw us and motioned for us to ride them. When we hesitated, he gently patted the donkey's back and urged us to get on. He even supported our feet to help us mount, so we gladly climbed onto the donkeys. We were grateful, thinking that since we had come through such a difficult journey and still had a long way ahead, they were being kind by letting us ride—knowing we must be exhausted and our feet in pain. In fact, allowing someone to ride a donkey was considered a great favor in that region, as everyone normally traveled on foot and donkeys were the only means of transportation.

Riding on the donkeys and looking ahead, we saw armed guards leading the way, and there were also several armed soldiers following behind. The young escorts in front and behind wore satisfied expressions as they guided us. For them, having us ride the donkeys in our Japanese military uniforms was a significant display of their strength. In other words, by presenting us – the three Japanese defectors – riding on the donkeys, they aimed to convey the message that if these three Japanese soldiers had willingly defected, anyone could see that they were destined to win against Japan in battle and that Japan would soon surrender.

As I gazed upon the vast expanse of land from the back of the donkey, I couldn't suppress the overwhelming emotion of encountering a new promised land that I had never felt before. Although the fields of barley and corn looked just the same as before, this place had transformed into a battlefield against Japanese imperialism. Even the air

I breathed felt pure and untainted, as if it belonged to a new world untouched by the pollution of the past.

Braving the summer heat, we rode on donkey-back along narrow paths that stretched endlessly between fields on the vast plain. But since the donkeys had no saddles, we soon began to feel an unexpected pain— our buttocks started to chafe and the skin peeled from the constant friction against the donkey's back, causing increasing discomfort. We pleaded with the guards to let us get down and walk, but they pretended not to hear and insisted that we stay on the donkeys. From their perspective, it was likely too good a propaganda image to pass up— Japanese soldiers being led away on donkeys by Communist guards. Eventually, unable to endure it any longer, we even showed them our raw, wounded buttocks and forcefully insisted on getting down. Only then did they reluctantly allow us to walk. It was at that moment that I truly realized how comfortable and liberating it felt simply to walk on my own two feet.

No matter how far we went, it was nothing but open fields—no mountains in sight, and naturally, no sign of a river either. I couldn't help but wonder where that river we had encountered earlier in the buffer zone had come from. With that question lingering in my mind, I quickened my pace. As we walked together, sometimes ahead, sometimes behind one another, it struck me that we had now become bound by a shared fate of life and death. Though they wore shabby clothes and carried rifles without stocks slung over their shoulders, they were soldiers fighting against the Japanese—comrades, in a sense, who shared the same purpose as we did. That thought gave rise to a sense of closeness. Though words didn't flow easily between us, they showed concern with their eyes and gestures, asking whether our feet hurt or if we were feeling unwell. Their kindness was deeply felt, touching something within me.

While walking through the guerrilla zone, something that surprised me was their strong sense of resistance and their expression of it through large posters (大字報). As I entered the entrance of each village, the first thing I encountered was houses with entire walls covered in red paint, displaying slogans like

"Down with Japanese Imperialism 打倒日本帝國主義"

"Long Live the Chinese Communist Party 中國共産黨萬歲" and

"Long Live Mao Zedong 毛澤東萬歲"

These slogans were so provocative! Each time, I truly felt that I was in a completely different society from the past. Seeing these large posters, I gradually realized that I had transformed from a Japanese soldier just a few days ago to now being a member of the Chinese Communist Party, ready to fight and die alongside them. The reality was sinking in, and I could feel it in my skin.

Fraternal Interrogation

As the glowing sun sank in the western sky and the earth was covered with a twilight hue, our group reached a large village. We entered a relatively substantial house (previously owned by an absentee landlord) that appeared to be the largest in the village, constructed with stone pillars and tiled roof. The spacious courtyard indicated that it belonged to a prominent landowner. Many soldiers were milling about within the courtyard, suggesting a significant military presence. In this house, we had our evening meal and spent our first night. The lengthy dining table was laden with ample food, indicating their earnest hospitality towards us. It became evident that even soldiers in the communist-controlled area, not just civilians, had only two meals a day. Given the scarcity of provisions relative to the population, having three meals a day was simply unfeasible due to the prolonged effects of war.

For that reason, in this society, it was rare to see people who were well-fed or overweight. Instead, emaciated faces with protruding bones were commonly seen. It was easy to tell that everyone, without exception, was suffering from malnutrition.

These days, in our society, beautiful women are commonly seen. While beauty may be partly innate, I believe that many become beautiful through good nutrition and a comfortable lifestyle.

After dinner, as the stifling air began to clear, we were led to a certain office. There, the three of us underwent our first interrogation. Two individuals conducted the questioning – they were dressed in military uniforms, with holsters strapped around their waists, and their refined demeanor suggested they held high positions, perhaps even commanding officers or staff officers. At that time, within the Communist army, there was no practice of wearing rank insignia, so this judgment was made based on intuition. Their office was quite modest, with only a worn-out Map hanging on the wall, and a tablecloth and long chairs placed around. It seemed that the interrogators were more

106

focused on putting us at ease through conversation rather than simply investigating our identities. This was evident from their demeanor and the cheerful expressions on their faces.

They first served tea and then asked for our names, the name of the Japanese military unit we belonged to, and the name of our unit commander. We replied that our unit was the 65th Brigade of the North China Front (北支專部隊), and our affiliation was the Kagawa (賀川) Unit. The interrogating officer expressed that they had also infiltrated agents as intelligence sources into that unit, and if we had been in contact with their agents, it would have been easier for us to escape. I personally believed that the brigade commander's words were likely an exaggeration of their intelligence activities rather than being entirely true.

They praised our brave actions enthusiastically and told us that we would now be escorted to the rear to join the Korean Independence Alliance. In this warm and friendly atmosphere, the interrogation was brief and concluded smoothly.

That night, as I lay on the bed, my joy seemed boundless. Truly, I felt that my escape from the Japanese military was in accordance with the will of God, and I realized that He had guided me thus far. With tears in my eyes, I offered a prayer of heartfelt gratitude. Learning that there was a Korean Independence group near this area striving for our homeland's independence, I fervently wished to join them as soon as possible, even if it were just for a single day.

As I drifted off to sleep, a young soldier entered the room carrying a bag with a Red Cross emblem. He sat down next to my bed, looking apologetic, and asked if I had any pain or discomfort. His demeanor was so humble and gentle that it seemed like any pain I might have had would instantly heal. I couldn't help but admire their sincere and modest behavior, and I thought that these were indeed comrades fighting for the liberation of people oppressed and forced to leave their homeland. The medicine they had might have been nothing more than a simple herbal remedy, but their heartfelt kindness surpassed any potent elixir.

Japanese blockade line

The next day, our group was told to take off our Japanese military uniforms and change into communist army uniforms, which they provided. They said the Japanese uniforms we turned in would be used for intelligence operations.

As I put on the communist army uniform, I couldn't help but feel a pang of regret, wondering when I might ever wear the proud uniform of the Korean Independence Army. Still, compared to having worn the detested Japanese uniform and being forced to play the part of a Japanese soldier against my will, wearing the uniform of the Chinese communist forces—though foreign—felt lighter, because I was now among comrades who shared the same cause.

Even changing out of the Japanese military boots into cloth-made Chinese shoes made me feel as if I could fly. Once again, under the escort of guards, we set off toward the vast, endless plain embarking on a new journey.

Originally, northern China, commonly referred to as the Huabei (華北) region, is a vast plain area where the sun rises in the east and sets in the west. In this wide expanse, when it rains, there is nowhere for the water to flow, causing the entire plain to become flooded. With even a small amount of water, crops are at a loss and wither away. If locusts were to swarm in, the fields would turn into desolate wastelands. According to the statistics of that time, in an average year, a successful harvest could only be expected once every three years. The other two years were likely to be plagued either by floods or by crop failures caused by various factors.

During times of crop failure, the peasants would endure by consuming wild roots and plants, but when even those resources were exhausted, they would abandon their homes and migrate to regions where there was plenty of food. Due to the large number of migrating peasants forming groups, they were compared to flowing water and called "Yumin (流民, Flowing People)."

Opportunistic rulers would sometimes take in these Yumin, providing them with food and using them for various purposes, including instigating rebellions or establishing new dynasties if circumstances favored them. This phenomenon is considered by some scholars as one of the frequent causes for the frequent changes of dynasties in Chinese history.

Finally, we arrived at a certain village. The guide informed us that we would need to rest here for a few days. This was because our intended route was blocked by the Japanese military's blockade line, and overcoming this blockade required careful preparation. The blockade line was established along the main road connecting Sukhyeon (宿縣) and Gojin (固鎮). In the cities, powerful Japanese troops were stationed, and along the road, sturdy checkpoints were set up in a line, connected by military vehicles.

For a while, I was consumed by worry and disappointment, but suddenly a young soldier who seemed like a commander appeared. He informed us that the plan was to cross the blockade line before dawn. The period between 1 a.m. and 2 a.m. was the darkest since the moon wouldn't be up, making it an ideal time for the Communist guerrillas to operate. Additionally, he mentioned that the Japanese soldiers generally slept during this time.

The commander emphasized that during the march, there should be absolutely no talking, smoking, or striking matches. Each person should stay close to the one in front and never lose sight of them. He also warned against coughing, and even if a dog barked, he advised us to pet it gently and not to make any noise.

We waited until it was time to move. When the hour came, we began marching in step with the commander's signal, walking along the narrow path between furrows in the fields. Fortunately, the shoes we wore were made from plain cotton fabric, so they made no sound as we marched. We walked and sometimes ran, pushing forward through the darkness for more than an hour. Then suddenly, a deep ravine appeared before us, forcing us to halt. Looking around, we saw electric lights shining brightly not far away—but thankfully, the light did not reach the spot where we stood. It was clear that the place ahead was a Japanese pillbox where enemy troops were stationed.

The trench appeared to be roughly twice the height of an adult's stature. Suddenly, the guides' movements became agile. They leaped down into the trench using a prepared ladder, then quickly hoisted up a rope for us to descend as well. After that, they used another ladder to climb up to the other side and lowered a rope for us. We too descended using the rope. Then, it was time to continue running. Finally, we were informed that we had safely crossed the blockade line that had been blocking our path. A sigh of relief was followed by swift footsteps, as we had to continue walking through the night toward the next hamlet. Considering that Japanese military vehicles were positioned on both sides of the road, it could be inferred that even civilian movement was completely restricted. Indeed, during the daytime, only residents who could present proper identification were allowed to pass through a small pathway beside the military vehicles.

Misery of Chinese Peasants

Having safely crossed the blocked main road, we took a short rest and were served a meal at the village we arrived in. Afterward, we once again set off toward the rear. During the day, we could see farmers harvesting barley in the middle of the fields. As we passed through small hamlets, one thing stood out: there wasn't a single well-built house in sight. The homes were humble thatched cottages, made of mud bricks with barley straw roofs that looked as though they might collapse at any moment. Since there were no chimneys, the area beneath the roofs was blackened with soot. In the sheds, a donkey or two was often tied up, or a few chickens pecked around for food. Yet despite their poverty, on the walls of every house, without exception, were bold words painted in large letters: "Down with Japan".

The livelihood of these peasants in the Huabei (華北) region was literally torn apart by poverty. They eked out a living in simple, crumbling thatched-roof huts passed down from their ancestors, cultivating the tiny patches of land inherited from their forebears using worn-out farming tools that had been in the family for generations. They would marry when the time came, have children, raise them, and eventually pass on their homes, land, and tools to their descendants before passing away. This kind of life didn't just start recently; it has been carried down through generations from ancient times when history began.

Those who had already endured the devastation of floods, droughts, and locust plagues were further burdened by man-made disasters—relentlessly exploited by cruel warlords. In some regions, it was said that certain warlords collected taxes forty years in advance, giving a sense of the sheer extent of their atrocities. One can only imagine how harsh the exploitation by landlords must have been in addition to this.

To these peasants—already torn and trampled—the brutalities inflicted by the Japanese army during eight long years of occupation were nothing short of unendurable torment. It was said that wherever the Japanese army stationed themselves—or even merely passed through—everything would be burned and looted, leaving the local population to starve for the next three years. Truly, Chinese peasants were among the most pitiful and impoverished people in the world.

What made things worse for women was the cruel practice of foot binding (纏足), a sign of how completely women's rights were ignored in China. Foot binding began during the Southern Tang dynasty of the

Five Dynasties period, and this oppressive custom ruled over women for more than a thousand years.

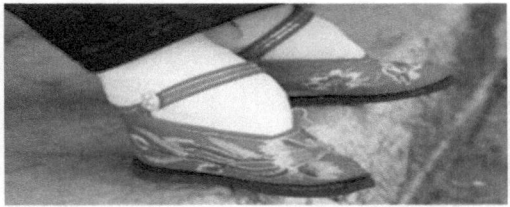

Figure 38: Foot binding, a traditional Chinese custom.

Villages in the Huabei (華北) Region

As we walked through the Communist guerrilla zone, we passed through yet another village. This village had a road running through the center, with shops and houses lined up closely on both sides. We came upon a shabby little eatery shaded by an overhanging eave that blocked the sunlight. Beneath the eave were some rough wooden benches and a few scattered chairs.

Following the guards' instructions, we sat down to rest, expecting nothing more. But to our surprise, food was brought out. The dish consisted of boiled pig's ears, fried in oil—only the ear parts were used. The chewy cartilage embedded in the pig's ear gave it an incredible texture, and the flavor was indescribably good. It was early evening, and we were hungry—so you can imagine how delicious it tasted. I truly felt that I had never eaten anything so delicious in my life.

Even now, I can't forget that taste. Whenever I pass through a market, I often find myself sitting on a wooden stool, happily enjoying steaming pieces of boiled pork—reminiscing about that unforgettable meal.

Figure 39: Crispy fried pig ears.

According to the escorts, we were heading towards the 4th Zone of the New Fourth Army (新四軍). There, the Korean Independence Alliance - Huazhong Branch (華中分盟) was located, along with many independent volunteer forces and even former military students who had already escaped from the Japanese army. Walking quietly along the rural path behind these escorts, I often found myself lost in deep contemplation. It was clear that we had found hope amidst despair. I shuddered at the thought of what our situation would be like if we had been captured by the Japanese troops who were searching for us. It was a chilling scenario to even imagine.

As I walked across the mainland with hope, heading towards the Korean Independence Alliance, how could I possibly describe the joy and gratitude I felt? I once again offered thanks to God. It felt as though God had led us, just as my father's prayers had said, with pillars of fire and clouds of smoke. It seemed that people often turned to God when

114

they were either extremely joyful or in despair. In truth, I had lived without truly realizing God's grace in my everyday life. However, as I faced difficult challenges while being led by the Japanese army and miraculously escaped to reach this point, I felt a constant sense of closeness to God. The words from Psalm 46 were the most empowering for me.

"God is our refuge and strength, an ever-present help in trouble."

As I got closer to the base of the New Fourth Army, my joy increased even more. However, while walking, I witnessed a strange sight. It was the sight of Chinese peasants lining up, each carrying about three kilograms of pork without any packaging, just walking along the dirt path. I wondered why they were all carrying the exact same amount of pork. Soon, I learned the reason – in this socialist society, residents received the same distribution and carried it home. Working the same way, eating the same amount, wearing the same clothes, spending money the same way, without exploitation or being exploited – a world where everyone could live equally. Who wouldn't long for such a world? I pondered whether the Chinese Communist Party could truly build such an ideal society on Earth as I hastened my steps.

Once again, we passed through a village situated on a hill. This village seemed to have an unusually high number of communist soldiers, possibly serving as a gathering point for them. Suddenly, memories of the Henan (Hanam) Operation came to mind. At that time, the Nationalist Army had repeatedly fled without putting up much of a fight, which had been quite embarrassing. In contrast, the communist forces, despite lacking the strength to directly assault cities (城市) occupied by the Japanese, had effectively harassed the Japanese forces by conducting guerrilla actions during the night. They focused on tactics such as destroying strategic bridges or cutting communication lines, giving the Japanese forces a hard time. In response, the Japanese military conducted brutal "scorched earth" tactics known as the "Three Alls Policy (三光政策) ," which involved burning everything, killing everyone, and looting everything.

As a result, the local residents realized that in order to live without fear, they needed to actively support the communist forces, who were willing to fight against the Japanese forces to protect their lives. Furthermore, the residents remembered that it was the communist forces who had expelled the exploitative landlords and redistributed land among them. This created a strong sense of unity between the local population and the communist forces.

During that time, there was a common saying: "The people are the water, and the Communist Party is the fish." Just as fish cannot survive without water, the idea was that the Communist Party couldn't grow without the support of the people. As I walked through the guerrilla area, I witnessed firsthand how the communist forces had garnered unwavering support from the local residents.

Japanese prisoners of war

That evening, when we arrived at the designated village as planned and entered the prepared house, a surprising event awaited us. Inside the house, there was a young man dressed in Chinese clothing, warmly welcoming us. Without hesitation, he said in Japanese, "I am Nakano (中野), a Japanese person. Welcome. Please come in." From his demeanor, it was evident that he had been anticipating our arrival. He continued, "I am a member of the Japan Liberation Alliance led by Nozaka Sanzo (野坂參三) in Yan'an. You will soon be heading to the Korean Independence Alliance (朝鮮獨立同盟)." Hearing his words, we were able to calm our astonished hearts and gradually find inner composure. It was heartening to realize that despite being a Japanese person, at least communication was possible. Over the next three days, we spent time together and engaged in many conversations.

He was the son of a farmer from Kyushu (九州) region and had become a prisoner of the Communist forces around two years ago near Sukhyun (宿縣) in central China (中支). He mentioned that Japan would soon face downfall and continued, "It was morning. Three of my comrades and I left the garrison to catch chickens in a nearby village, but we didn't return by nightfall. I went up the hill alone to survey the area. Suddenly, someone grabbed my legs from behind and another person choked my neck, leaving me unable to move as I was seized." He recounted his experience of being captured as a prisoner.

He described that the Communist forces treated him with leniency. They did not subject him to painful measures like chaining his legs or confining him in a prison cell. Over time, they facilitated his entry into

117

the Japanese Liberation Alliance, treating him as a fellow human being. He spoke of being genuinely welcomed and treated as an international comrade.

When I asked him why he was alone, he explained that once the work here was done, he intended to head for the coast. However, he mentioned that Yan'an was distant and far away, so he wasn't sure what would happen. I also inquired about the nature of his work here, and he told me that he was involved in producing propaganda materials in Japanese. He wrote letters in Japanese to his former colleagues in the Japanese military unit he was a part of, encouraging them to defect and come here, explaining the situation. He added that another part of his duty involved interrogating Japanese prisoners of war.

Listening to his words, I couldn't help but think to myself, "In truth, am I not also in a similar situation as a former prisoner? He was once a member of the Japanese military, potentially engaging in harmful actions towards the Chinese people. However, the Eighth Route Army has worked to reform and influence him, ultimately leading him to fight against his own country, Japan." At the same time, the concept often cited in China, known as "using the barbarians to control the barbarians" (以夷制夷), came to mind. As I conversed with him, I didn't perceive him as a typical Japanese person. Perhaps that was because he had already distanced himself from his own homeland.

He confidently continued, "Look! Japan will inevitably collapse before long, and afterwards, a socialist regime will emerge in Japan. Consider this: The German army suffered a crushing defeat at Leningrad, sealing Germany's fate. The U.S. forces have occupied Iwo Jima

(琉璜島), signaling Japan's impending downfall. The Soviet Union, which already occupies one-sixth of the world's land, is a socialist state. China, with the third-largest territory on Earth, will eventually be won by the Communist Party. When you combine China's quarter of the world's population with the Soviet Union's two hundred million, half of the world's population is already under socialist rule. It's undeniable that after Japan's defeat, militarism will recede, making way for a government representing the oppressed workers and peasants, just like fire illuminates the darkness."

Will the global revolution he speaks of actually come to pass? I couldn't help but feel a sense of fear about the Communist Party's indoctrination efforts. How could such words come from the mouth of a wicked Japanese individual, I wondered in amazement. Once again, I found myself unable to underestimate the political work of the New Fourth Army. Furthermore, he continued by admitting that he, too, regrets his role as a forerunner of Japanese imperialism, causing suffering to the Chinese people. Hearing his story left me dumbfounded. I, too, am a prisoner of war belonging to the Communist Party. If I were to undergo some years of indoctrination, could I also end up professing to be a staunch advocate of communism like him? I couldn't help but contemplate these thoughts.

Parting with him was bittersweet. It wasn't so much that I had grown fond of him, but rather, I pitied him for being coerced into becoming a communist against his will. Did he truly become a genuine communist? Perhaps, it was more a matter of him having no choice but to disguise himself as a communist in order to survive. I felt an indescribable mixture of emotions. In fact, on the day Japan collapsed, it was said that many of the Japanese prisoners of war in the communist party chose to end their own lives.

Chapter 6

Korean Independence Alliance

Reunion

In life, the joy of meeting and the sadness of parting are experiences that everyone undergoes. The act of being born into the world by splitting from one's parents' bodies is a joyous meeting, and forming a family by meeting a spouse is also among the foremost joys of meeting. On the other hand, death in life is the ultimate separation from everything in the world, making it the greatest sorrow. However, no one born into life escapes the return to dust, so we have spoken of this as the natural order. Furthermore, in life, youth does not last forever, so the writer of Psalms sang (Psalms 90: 5-6),

"You sweep them away as with a flood; they are like a dream, like grass that is renewed in the morning:

in the morning it flourishes and is renewed;

in the evening it fades and withers.

After escaping from the Japanese military camp and walking through the New Fourth Army guerrilla zone for about 20 days, I arrived at a remote outpost in a city called Bansheng (半城) near Hongze Lake (洪澤湖), which is the base of the New Fourth Army (新四軍) Zone in Jiangsu Province (江蘇省), around mid-September of 1944. The blazing sun was descending into the western plains as I arrived. Here, I experienced the joy of a miraculous encounter. Many Korean student soldiers had already escaped from Japanese military units and come here ahead of us, so when they saw us, they greeted us with joyful cheers and welcomed us with open arms.

They were all student soldiers who had gathered in Xuzhou (徐州). They had bravely escaped from Japanese military bases near Xuzhou, such as Suhyeon (宿縣) and Hwaeum (淮陰). Additionally, there were many student soldiers from North Pyongan Province who had formed a strong bond near Xuzhou. Most of the student soldiers knew each other's faces, as they had dispersed to various Japanese military camps around Xuzhou. Now, being reunited in the guerrilla zone, seeing those familiar faces must have been an explosion of joy and excitement!

Among them were familiar faces like Shin Sang-cho (申相楚 from my own hometown Jeongju, a graduate of Tokyo Imperial University), Han Myeong-sam (韓命三, a graduate of Yonhi College), Bang Hwi-je (方暉濟, a graduate of Japanese University), Shim Young-soon

(沈榮淳 from Gwaksan, a graduate of Meiji University), and Park Hang-gu (朴沆九, a graduate of a Japanese University). In addition to these individuals, there were around 20 more familiar faces.

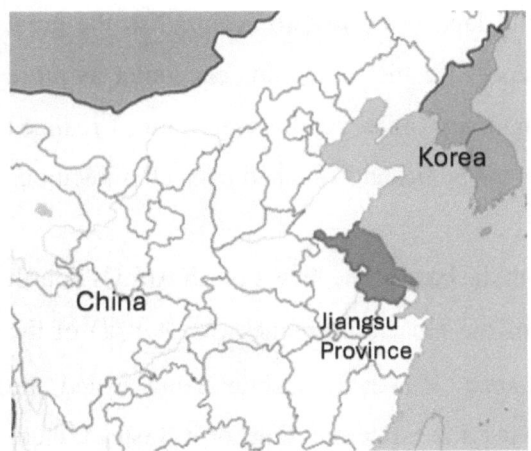

Map 40: Location of Jiangsu Province (江蘇省)

Figure 41: Commanders of the New Fourth Army.

We embraced each other and shed tears of joy for a while. Never had I imagined that such a reunion could happen in this world. I felt that I could now die without regret. Resolving to join forces with them and fight against our enemy, the Japanese army, to accomplish the great cause of Korean independence, I came to see this encounter as more meaningful and valuable than any other. At the same time, I realized how the course of one's life can be instantly shaped by such miraculous meetings.

This place served as both the base of the New Fourth Army's Fourth Division and the location of the Huazhong branch (華中分盟) of the Korean Independence Alliance. However, despite being called the Huazhong branch, there wasn't a separate building for it. Instead, there were 4-5 older individuals than us in a house within the local village. Of course, there were no signs indicating its presence. While I spent several excited days getting accustomed to the new environment amidst the joy of our reunion, I soon realized that the faces of the fellow student soldiers who arrived earlier weren't as cheerful as expected. Moreover, I could sense that they were filled with discontent.

Most perplexing of all was the fact that the Korean Volunteer Army, claiming to be an independent force, didn't even possess a single rifle. I couldn't help but feel disappointed. Soon, I came to understand their grievances. It was a reality we all had to accept – that we had been brought here as prisoners of the New Fourth Army, regardless of anyone's intentions. In fact, our escape from the Japanese military was driven by the zeal to join forces against them and fight to the end. Yet, arriving here, we found ourselves practically coerced into becoming prisoners of the communist party, compelled to adopt communist beliefs. While we weren't physically imprisoned, our intellectual and behavioral freedom was restricted. Furthermore, it became evident that the New Fourth Army's provision of food was less about striving for Korean independence and more about utilizing us as part of the global communist movement.

Figure 42: Shin Sang-cho (申相楚)

Figure 43: Shim Young-soon, at Tapgol Park, Seoul.

Enemy Operations Division of the New Fourth Army

One of the persons in charge of "Huazhong branch (華中分盟)" was Sun Dal (孫達). He was responsible for propaganda and ideological work in the Korean anti-Japanese resistance organization operating in Chinese-controlled Huazhong region. One day, he led us to a place where New Fourth Army officials were welcoming us, but it turned out to be the "Enemy Operations Division " (敵工部) of the New Fourth Army, which was essentially a branch responsible for screening and handling Japanese prisoners of war. The New Fourth Army provided substantial rewards for capturing Japanese prisoners, and it was this department that supervised the prisoners and distributed the rewards.

Upon entering the Enemy Operations Division, there was a large room with earth walls adorned with a single Map hanging on them. There were only a few large desks for conducting work and several wooden chairs placed around. The head of the department was a man named Oh (吳), so we addressed him as Director Oh. He claimed to have attended the Tokyo Imperial University in Japan and appeared to possess a refined demeanor, suggesting his traditional background as a committed member of the communist party.

With a smiling face, he welcomed us and began by acknowledging our journey of escaping from the Japanese army and reaching this place. He mentioned that Japan's imminent defeat would lead to victory for our country as well, and he spoke optimistically about the prospect of Korean independence. He continued by mentioning the presence of captured Japanese soldiers in this area who were affiliated with the Japanese Liberation Alliance, engaged in Enemy Operations activities freely. We listened to his words in silence, expressing our gratitude with bowed heads. Soon, a meal was brought to the table, and we could tell that it was a carefully prepared feast, filled with sincerity.

After the meal, Director Oh led us to a nearby room. Inside, the room was filled with various spoils of war, including letters intended for Japanese military units and diaries of captured Japanese soldiers. Among the letters written by Japanese prisoners to their fellow soldiers was a recurring message:

"Here in the New Fourth Army region, the New Fourth Army treats Japanese prisoners with favor and will not harm them. Our enemy is not the New Fourth Army, but the Japanese military imperialism. The New Fourth Army is located just 10 *li* (5 km) away from the Japanese military camp. Do not hesitate; escape without delay."

In one of the diaries, there was an entry that read:

"September 1938, we spent several days engaged in slaughter, plunder, and rape. Once again, we were dispatched for a crackdown of the New Fourth Army. We occupied the villages and conducted house-to-house searches to find women. The search lasted for about two hours. We dragged out hidden women, satisfying our lust as men, and then stabbed them to death with bayonets. This was done to prevent any evidence of Japanese soldiers' rapes from coming to light."

In another diary, the following story was written:

"We captured five villagers as captives. After torturing them, we extracted confessions that they were members of the New Fourth Army and then stabbed them to death on the spot with bayonets. The newly enlisted so-called 'new recruits' initially looked on with fearful eyes, but they will soon become accustomed to killing people and become desensitized to it. We captured another village, but all the residents had fled, leaving no cooking pots to prepare food. Since they had escaped completely, we set fire to their houses without hesitation."

From this, I realized that the "Enemy Operations Division " in the New Fourth Army not only managed the captives but also induced them to participate in psychological warfare.

Divided Student Soldiers

During the several days I stayed there, I came to realize that the student soldiers in this place were divided into three groups. Shim Yeong-soon and Bang Hwi-je, and others were firmly confronting the branch (分盟) leaders, declaring,

"The reason we risked our lives and escaped from the Japanese military camp was to join the Korean Liberation Army under the provisional government of the Republic of Korea led by Kim Gu (金九), and to fight with rifles and bayonets. Therefore, from a humanitarian and nationalistic standpoint, we must be sent to Chongqing (重慶)."

While there were comrades of the 'Chongqing faction' who insisted they must go to Chongqing no matter what, like this, there were also people like Shin Sang-cho who argued that, after the war, the global trend would shift toward socialist ideology. Therefore, since this place was also an organization striving for the independence of our people, we should remain here and cultivate the strength of our nation.

In this way, the student soldiers from various backgrounds were completely divided in their ideologies. Apart from that, most of the student soldiers, including Han Myeong-sam, who had gentle and sincere personalities, and were meticulous in everything, did not strongly assert their opinions. While they may not have been in favor of the situation here ideologically, they had an attitude of waiting, as they had already escaped from the Japanese military and saw no other alternative.

However, as time went on, Shim Yeong-soon and Bang Hwi-je became more irrational and resorted to aggressive actions, demanding to be sent to Chongqing at all costs. The leaders of the Branch were increasingly perplexed, assuring them that when the right time came, they would find a way to send them, even if it meant crossing through Japanese-occupied areas. But Shim and Bang did not believe these promises. Among ourselves, we even said that if the Chinese Communists were to grant them clemency and send them to Chongqing, it wouldn't actually be sending them – they would likely be killed en route. This was a time when Japan's defeat was imminent, and a sharp internal conflict was unfolding between the Nationalist (Kuomintang) and the Communists.

Leaders of the Huazhong branch

The organization of Huazhong branch (華中分盟) was a secret communist organization linked vertically through loyalty, making its true identity unknown to anyone. It was referred to as a regional faction of the Korean Independence Alliance based in Yan'an, but it seemed to have no connection with Yan'an and rather appeared to follow the directives of the Enemy Operations Division of the New Fourth Army. On the surface, there were three individuals referred to as leaders, and there were around 7-8 civilians. According to one leader, there were many secret operatives in the Japanese-occupied areas, but the exact number was unknown, and this claim was not necessarily believed to be true. One of the leaders with close ties to the Enemy Operations Division of the New Fourth Army was Sun Dal (孫達).

The individual known as Sun Dal appeared to be in his early 50s, but no one knew about his background. He only boasted about being from his hometown, Yeongdeok (盈德) in Gyeongsang Province, having received no education, and being a former factory worker. Nobody knew when he joined the Huazhong branch or became one of the leaders, as he never spoke about it. Despite maintaining close contact with the leaders of the Enemy Operations Division and fervently praising communism, he endeared himself to people by accommodating the preferences of the soldiers, who had little education. However, the

130

soldiers did not view him as a seasoned independence activist due to his lack of revealed experience. It is evident that he was not highly regarded for his public contributions within the Korean Independence Alliance, considering his later involvement in naval affairs in North Korea after liberation.

There was an individual named Kim who served as an assistant behind Sun Dal. He appeared to be in his early 60s and never revealed his real name. Like others, he never spoke about his past experiences, making it impossible to know how and when he joined the Huazhong branch. He disliked being in the public eye and often stayed confined to his residence, where his activities remained unknown. He interacted with the soldiers very kindly and kept his distance like an elderly figure, which is why we referred to him as Elder Kim.

Another officer was named Lee Deok-mu (李德武). He boasted that he had graduated from a military academy in China and served as one of the commanders in Chiang Kai-shek's Nationalist Party army. He also claimed to have participated in the Korean independence movement under the provisional government in Chongqing, stating that he joined the Huazhong branch after leaving the provisional government due to factional infighting and a lack of progress towards the Korean independence. His personality was cheerful, and he exhibited a soldierly demeanor, but when interacting with the soldiers, he maintained a very humble attitude, perhaps to gain their favor.

In addition to these three, there were a few civilians, one of whom was named Lee Yong-cheol (李容哲). It was said that he had been an operative for the provisional government, engaged in intelligence activities in enemy-occupied areas—namely, regions under Japanese control—before infiltrating into the New Fourth Army's territory. However, the truth of this could not be confirmed. Judging from his close association with comrades Shim Young-soon and Bang Hwi-je, it was clear that he was a distinct or unusual figure within the Huazhong Branch.

Among the other civilians, there was someone who had been involved in opium trading in the Japanese-occupied areas and sought refuge here after being exposed. Additionally, there were comrades who came here as a couple and helped provide our meals. Organizing meals was a revolutionary endeavor, highlighting their significant influence and resources. We often witnessed the three high-ranking members of the Huazhong branch gathering under dim lantern light, engaged in deep discussions. Most decisions within the Huazhong branch seemed to be made primarily by these three individuals, and it appeared that they collectively assessed the beliefs and contributions of each and every soldier.

Origins of the Korean Independence Alliance

The Korean Independence Alliance was a nationalist independence organization formed by Korean communists in the Huabei (華北, North China) region in August 1942. It included an armed military unit called the "Korean Volunteer Army." After the March 1st Movement (1919), many independence activists converged in Shanghai (上海), where the provisional government of the Republic of Korea was established. Among them were individuals who had already embraced socialist ideas.

132

Shanghai, often referred to as the "cradle of the East Asian communist movement," played a significant role in the emergence of the Korean communist movement.

Korean communists, unable to establish a foothold for communist activities in Korea due to Japan's oppression, joined the Chinese communist revolution under the spirit of proletarian internationalism, with the belief that 'the victory of communism in China would directly bring about Korea's liberation and independence.' During the 1928 Nationalist-Communist civil war, as many as 200 Koreans reportedly took part in the 'Guangdong (Canton) Commune', and most of them are recorded to have died. Among those who participated in the Chinese communist movement and achieved notable accomplishments—earning the deep trust of the Chinese communist party and rising to senior cadre positions—was a Korean figure named Mu Jeong (武亭).

Mu Jeong was born in 1905 in Gyeongseong (鏡城), North Hamgkyeong Province, Korea. After attending Joong-ang high school, he went to Beijing. There, he graduated from the Northern Military Academy and was appointed as a captain in the artillery unit. With his exceptional military talents, he quickly rose through the ranks and became a major in the artillery unit by the age of 22. The reason he gained a high position within the Chinese communist party was due to his participation in the arduous Long March (大長征 1934-1935), a significant journey for the Chinese communists. To quote Sun Dal, there were only two Koreans who successfully completed this march, one named Pistira and the other being Mu Jeong.

Figure 44: General Mu Jeong.

Figure 45: Prominent leaders of the Korean Volunteer Army. From left: General Mu Jeong (on horseback), Unit Commander Park Hyo-sam, Political Commissar Kim Hak-mu, Lee Cheol-jung, Yi Ik-sung, and Lee Chun-am.

It was said that Pistira, unfortunately, was killed in action during the Eastward Anti-Japanese Campaign shortly after the Long March, during the operation to cross the Yellow River. After successfully completing the Long March, Mu Jeong became the commander of the only artillery regiment in the Chinese communist forces, which shows how significant his position was within the army. He was said to have had close ties with Zhu De (朱德), the commander-in-chief of the Chinese communist forces, and Peng Dehuai (彭德懷), the deputy commander. Notably, Peng Dehuai would later become the commander-in-chief of the Chinese People's Volunteer Army dispatched to Korea during the Korean War (June 25, 1950 - July 27, 1953).

Figure 46: Prominent leaders of the Eighth Route Army. From left: Peng Dehuai, Zhu De, and Deng Xiaoping (on the far right).

Figure 47: Peng Dehuai (彭德懷).

Figure 48: Zhu De (朱德).

During the Sino-Japanese War, Mu Jeong fought against the Japanese army. In 1942, while serving as the commander of the Eighth Route Army's artillery division, he established the Korean Independence Alliance, a political organization that united Korean communist activists operating on the Chinese mainland, primarily in Yan'an. Subsequently, he took on the role of commander of the Korean Volunteer Army, leading the establishment of the Korean Volunteer Army Military

Academy in the Oji Mountains of the Taihang Mountains Range (太行山脈). This marked a shift away from direct collaboration with the Chinese communist forces, as he focused on engaging in revolutionary activities for the homeland's liberation. His efforts were particularly directed towards preparing for liberation in anticipation of Japan's impending defeat, which became more apparent by 1944.

Another group that formed the Korean Independence Alliance consisted of communist activists and radical young individuals who had fled to China to engage in independence movement activities. Key figures among them were Choi Chang-ik (崔昌益) and Han Bin (韓斌). They had been early members of the Korean Communist Party and were also officials in the communist party organized by M.L. (Marxist-Leninist) faction. They had previously been apprehended by the Japanese police. In 1926, Choi Chang-ik, along with Han Bin and Heo Jeong-suk (許貞淑, wife of Choi Chang-ik), went into exile in China. They even made contact with Kim Won-bong (金元鳳) at one point. However, after the fall of Wuhan (武漢) to the Japanese army in October 1938, Choi Chang-ik moved to Yan'an. In 1942, with the establishment of the Korean Independence Alliance, Choi assumed a leadership position as its vice-chairman.

Han Bin was born in Vladivostok and graduated from Moscow Communist University. He infiltrated Korea to work towards the reconstruction of the Korean Communist Party but was arrested by the Japanese police. Similar to Choi Chang-ik, he fled to China and became involved in revolutionary activities. He later went to Yan'an and also became a vice-chairman of the Korean Independence Alliance in 1942.

The third group that formed the Korean Independence Alliance consisted of nationalists who were graduates of military academies established by the Chinese Nationalist Party (Kuomintang). Central figures among them included Park Hyo-sam (朴孝三, a graduate of Hwangpo Military Academy, Commander of the Central Army Division) and Yang Min-sam (楊民三, from Gyeongbuk). After arriving in Yan'an (延安), they also played active roles as leaders within the Independence Alliance. Besides them, there were many other independence activists who had graduated from military academies and participated in anti-Japanese activities. Among these individuals, Kim Woong (金雄, Commanding Officer of the North Korea–China Border Defense Command during the Korean War) stood out prominently.

Figure 49: Choi Chang-ik (崔昌益).

There was also Kim Du-bong (金斗奉), who came to the Independence Alliance from the provisional government. He was a renowned scholar of the Korean script and from Kimhae (金海) in

Gyeongnam Province. He studied under Chu Si-kyeong (周時經), a prominent scholar of the Korean language. After participating in the March 1st Movement (1919), he went into exile in Shanghai and took part in the establishment of the provisional government. Following the outbreak of the Sino-Japanese War, he moved to Chongqing. Disillusioned with the factional struggles within the provisional government, he left Chongqing in 1942 and came to Yan'an (延安).

Figure 50: Kim Du-bong (金枓奉)

Figure 51: Han Bin.

139

On August 15, 1942, key figures of the communist movement on the Chinese mainland, mainly from Jidong, played a central role in officially establishing the Korean Independence Alliance in Yan'an. They formed armed groups under the name of the Korean Volunteer Army (朝鮮義勇軍). Kim Du-bong was chosen as the chairman of the Alliance, and the central executive committee included members such as Mu Jeong, Choi Chang-ik, Han Bin, and Kim Chang-man. The decision to appoint Kim Du-bong as the chairman likely stemmed from his long and active history as a Korean independence activist. Additionally, given the ongoing cooperation between the Chinese Nationalist Party (Kuomintang) and the Communist party, the Independence Alliance also appeared to be seeking cooperation with the provisional government outwardly. This context, along with Kim Du-bong's notable presence and reputation as a prominent scholar, likely influenced his selection by the provisional government.

In addition, Mu Jeong, who was elected as vice chairman, continued to hold significant responsibilities within the Korean Volunteer Army, making his role valuable to the Independence Alliance. Naturally, the Alliance received various forms of assistance from the Chinese Communist party, including weapons and provisions. This support was a given, considering that the political objective of the Alliance was to oppose Japanese imperialism and achieve Korea's independence. This alignment of goals between the Independence Alliance's pursuit of political objectives and the Chinese Communist Party's advocacy for anti-Japanese resistance and independence was a fundamental reason for the support provided.

Indeed, the fact that the Independence Alliance was affiliated with communist organizations while outwardly presenting itself as a unified front without overtly displaying communist ideologies is a noteworthy event. They proclaimed the establishment of a democratic republic, which not only allowed nationalist-minded individuals to join the Alliance but also welcomed them. However, they were also stringent in monitoring those who infiltrated from enemy-occupied areas to Yan'an and even imposed efforts to enforce ideological transformation.

When I moved to Taihang Mountains, the location of the Anti-Japanese Military Administration School, I heard that Kim Sarang (金史浪) had infiltrated there via Manchuria, aiming to participate in revolutionary activities as liberation was approaching. At that time, a person named Yi Ik-sung (李益星), who was present at Taihang Mountains, told us, "There is someone named Kim Sarang here, and he is currently in a secluded state, writing autobiographical documents every day." This information provides further insight into the situation.

The leaders of the organization were strictly committed to the ideology of communism, and they lived a disciplined organizational life to realize a communist society. Under the strong leadership of Mu Jeong, who was the practical leader, they remained tightly united. The reverence for Mu Jeong seemed almost like a religious faith. When I visited the Military Administration School in Taihang Mountains after liberation, I had to hear the members of the two companies singing a song called "Comrade Mu Jeong" every day. It was as if they were singing a hymn in his honor.

The lyrics of the song went, "Comrade Mu-jeong's guiding path is the path to national liberation and independence..." The members of the Volunteer Army praised Mu Jeong day and night, and I witnessed their firm belief that he would surely take power in Korea after liberation. I believed that the government of a liberated homeland should and would arise from the will of the people. But seeing the soldiers idolize Mu Jeong so fanatically, I couldn't help but feel bitter, sensing that they were all consumed by a lust for power.

(Editor's Note: The North China Korean Independence Alliance (朝鮮獨立同盟) was a Korean independence organization that operated until Japan's defeat in World War II. It was formed in July 1942 in the Taihang Mountains region of North China, led primarily by Korean socialists and members of the North China branch of the Korean Volunteer Army.

In 1941, Korean communists active in the North China area had initially established the North China Korean Youth Union, which was later reorganized into the North China Korean Independence Alliance in the following year.

In July 1942, the Youth Union held its second representative congress at the foot of the Taihang Mountains, during which it was reorganized as the North China Korean Independence Alliance, and the Korean Volunteer Army's North China branch was restructured into the North China Korean Volunteer Army.

At this congress, the Alliance elected 11 central executive committee members: Kim Du-bong (金枓奉), Mu Jeong (武亭), Choi Chang-ik (崔昌益), Park Hyo-sam (朴孝三), Kim Hak-mu (金學武), Chae Guk-beon (蔡國蕃), Kim Chang-man (金昌萬), Han Bin (韓斌), Lee

Yu-min (李維民), Jin Han-jung (陳漢中), and Lee Chun-am (李春岩).

In 1943, the Alliance also established the Special Northern Manchuria Committee in Harbin, sought to build a united front with the Provisional Government of the Republic of Korea, and pursued cooperation with domestic groups such as the Korea Reconstruction Alliance.

After Japan's defeat, the Alliance was disarmed by Soviet forces and returned to Korea (North), where it was reorganized as the Korean New People's Party. https://encykorea.aks.ac.kr/Article/E0078258)

Anti-Japanese Military and Political Academy

There were eight regional branches of the Alliance. Yan'an, Shandong, Jin-Cha-Ji (晋察冀), Hebei-Shandong-Henan (冀魯豫), Huazhong, and others. These branches largely corresponded in territory and administrative divisions with the base areas of the Eighth Route Army. The Huazhong (華中, Central China) branch of the Alliance, which I joined after escaping from the Japanese army, was located in the Huazhong region and was thus the farthest from the Alliance headquarters in Yan'an. It was also cut off by vast areas occupied by Japanese forces. Although the cadre claimed to be in radio communication with Yan'an, the truth of that was unclear, and it appeared that all matters were discussed with and directed by the Enemy Operations Division of the 4th District of the New Fourth Army.

To encourage our trainees to embrace communism, the Huazhong branch established the Anti-Japanese Military and Political Academy,

143

centered around the trainees themselves. On the day when the sign "Hangdai (抗大)" was hung on the house surrounded by earthen bricks, measuring just over 10 *pyeong*, the Director Oh from the Enemy Operations Division spoke to us about the origin of the "Hangdai" with the assistance of Sun Dal (孫達) as an interpreter.

"Hangdai refers to the renaming of various Red Army military schools as "Anti-Japanese Military and Political Universities" after the conclusion of the Chinese Civil War in 1927. The Hangdai in Yan'an utilized scattered caves as classrooms, and by 1939, the student population reached 2,000. The Hangdai in Shanxi Province (山西省) had as many as 8,000 students. Nationwide, these universities annually produced around ten thousand leaders who completed the military and political training courses, with a primary focus on Marxist principles. The core of education was to integrate the directives and policies of the communist party with the united front and 'the three principles of the people (三民主義)'. Many comrades hoped to nurture revolutionary spirit through education at Hangdai."

Furthermore, Director Oh continued to mention that there was also a Women's Hangdai in Yan'an. The teachers and students there all wore plain military uniforms, covering their faces with makeshift masks or straw-woven veils, and they didn't wear makeup. They sported short hair and military caps. This made it difficult to distinguish whether a student was male or female from a distance. About 60% of the students were

144

young people in their early twenties. It was noted that a graduate from the Women's Hangdai in Beijing was planned to take on the role of a Chinese language teacher at this Hangdai. At this point, Sun Dal emphasized his role as the person in charge of the Hangdai in the Huazhong Branch (華中分盟).

Figure 52: Anti-Japanese Military and Political University.

The establishment of the Hangdai (抗大) was a plan aimed at capturing the enthusiasm of the student soldiers. It was clear that in the future, when we entered society, having the experience of graduating from Hangdai would undoubtedly expand our horizons in a communist society. The curriculum included Chinese language, political debates, and political rectification. To teach us Chinese, as Director Oh mentioned, a very attractive young lady from Beijing came. She wore a blue military uniform of the New Fourth Army, a leather belt, and a pistol at her waist. Her charming appearance captivated all of us.

Seeing her carrying a pistol, we could deduce that she held a high-ranking position in the communist party. Although she and we were fundamentally distant from each other, she, as an enthusiastic party member, earnestly tried to teach us Chinese according to the party's orders. However, we had come to engage in the anti-Japanese struggle, not to learn Chinese. Thus, her efforts to teach us Chinese at Hangdai did not yield fruitful results. Eventually, the situation led to her departure.

The political discussions were not lectures but rather free-form debates aimed at helping us understand communist theories such as historical materialism, class struggle, and dialectics. The sessions were led by Sun Dal, who acted as the chair. Since he was not someone who had studied leftist theory in an academic sense, he would first have us talk about the ideas of Eastern and Western philosophers, and even aspects of capitalist economics. After allowing us to engage in open discussion, he would then guide us to recognize that such ideas were, so to speak, counter revolutionary.

In the political debates, there was a remarkable student Shin Sang-cho from a student soldier background who exhibited exceptional skills in critiquing capitalist society from various angles. His logical arguments left us all amazed, and he often engaged in debates with Choi Il-Woon (崔逸雲), who was a philosophy graduate from Waseda University. Particularly, when the student from the military background discussed Marxist and Leninist theories, it was a novel experience for many of us and left a deep impression.

Comrade Shin, on the other hand, had already been drawn to leftist ideology during his studies at Tokyo Imperial University's law school. He was known as a radical figure and had faced police surveillance and even imprisonment due to his beliefs. His background impressed not only us but also Sun Dal. As a result, some of us jokingly referred to him as a "true red" (communist), and a few comrades were cautious and critical of him.

Rectification Movement

At the Anti-Japanese Military and Political Academy (抗大), the most important focus was the rectification movement (整風運動). This movement was essentially an ideological reformation campaign—a process aimed at shaping dedicated communist revolutionaries. It was a nationwide campaign launched by the Chinese communist party under Mao Zedong's directive in anticipation of Japan's defeat.

In simple terms, it involved self-criticism of one's past thoughts and actions—evaluating whether they had contributed to or hindered the revolutionary movement from the perspective of the masses. Participants would also be subjected to criticism from their comrades. Moreover, it required individuals to examine whether any remnants of capitalist thinking still lingered in their current thoughts or behaviors, which could unknowingly weaken their revolutionary spirit. From the standpoint of the working masses, they were to criticize themselves and be corrected by fellow comrades for their ideological shortcomings. This rectification movement was divided into three categories: Dangpung (黨風), Hapung (學風), and Munpung (文風).

147

Dangpung aimed to rectify inappropriate practices and divisive tendencies within the Party; Hapung sought to correct subjectivist tendencies and faulty thinking not in line with concrete conditions; and Munpung aimed to overcome formalism and shift away from elitist thinking to engage with the masses.

The purpose of this movement was to acknowledge that each of us, having lived in a capitalist society, could unknowingly carry traces of capitalist influence. Therefore, it was necessary to expose and cleanse oneself from these influences through self-critique and by accepting criticism from comrades. During this process of self-reflection, any trace of falsehood would result in receiving harsh criticism from fellow comrades.

Anyone, especially those who were considered educated or "intelligentsia", would naturally dislike exposing their past mistakes in front of the public and would struggle to accept direct criticism of their wrongdoings from others. However, as students of Hangdai, we had no choice but to participate actively in the rectification movement. Each of us had to take turns reflecting on our past lives and, consequently, had to accept criticism from our comrades.

So, even though we had fought against the Japanese army and escaped from their barracks, we found ourselves facing each other, sharing stories of our past experiences, and willingly subjecting ourselves to criticism from our fellow comrades as part of this rectification movement. There was no room for us to shy away from participating wholeheartedly in this process.

During the rectification movement, there were even some bizarre scenes like this one: Comrade Han Myeong-sam came in holding a piece of white paper stained with feces and demanded to know who had used this special white paper in the latrine. According to him, using paper specially rationed to us by the New Fourth Army as toilet paper was an act of wastefulness and lax discipline, and such behavior stemmed from an unpurged remnant of capitalist thinking. Therefore, the person responsible should step forward and criticize their own actions.

Han Myeong-sam was a comrade who had lost his parents at a young age, grown up alone, and graduated from Yonhi College through self-supporting study. He had a large build, a gentle and sincere personality, and was well-liked by his comrades. Since the latrine was used only by us, we had a fairly good idea who the culprit might be.

However, he remained silent and gave no response. The matter ended there, but this incident became the catalyst for growing hostility between Han Myeong-sam and the person involved. The problem was that the individual in question had the most aggressive temperament among the comrades and would confront the leadership daily, demanding to be sent to Chongqing. On the other hand, Han Myeong-sam, though not a leftist, leaned toward a moderate stance—believing that, given our practical situation as virtual prisoners, we had no choice but to follow the orders of the New Fourth Army for the time being. Therefore, even before addressing who was right or wrong in the matter, the emotional rift between the two comrades had inevitably deepened.

During the course of the rectification movement, as mentioned earlier, the relationships between the three groups of soldiers became even more distinct. <u>First</u>, there was a group armed with strong communist theories, surpassing the level of current cadre members, led by Shin Sang-cho. <u>Another group</u> consisted of individuals like Shim Yeong-soon and Bang Hwi-je, who essentially denied their status as captives and persistently demanded to be sent to Chongqing. <u>Third group</u> embraced the idea that since they were already here, they should reluctantly accept the situation and wait for the future, while becoming Communists.

At the time, the cadres of the Huazhong branch would often lament how the provisional government in Chongqing was plagued by so many factions that it resembled a situation of "one person, one party". They would sigh in frustration, saying, "Even if all the people striving for independence united, it would still be uncertain whether independence could be achieved—so how can it ever be won when they are divided into factions and at odds with each other?"

Now, witnessing with my own eyes the deepening divisions in opinion among the student soldiers within the very Huazhong branch to which I belonged, my heart ached. However, our discord did not amount to factionalism. It was purely a difference of opinion, since no one tried to force others to agree with or follow their views.

Consideration of the New Fourth Army

I thought that the New Fourth Army showed us special consideration. They referred to us as international humanitarian workers and treated us accordingly, providing us with appropriate military uniforms, clothing, shoes, and other daily necessities. Food rations included ten cigarettes

150

per day, one pig's worth of pork per week, flour, vegetables, and oil. We attempted communal cooking with the allotted food, but since the meal quantity was always limited, we were constantly left hungry.

Still, we managed to make and eat dumplings with the flour, and sometimes we even made and enjoyed knife-cut noodle soup. Our way of eating formed a unique scene, with the knife-cut noodle pot placed in the center, and we would gather around, spinning around it, picking up knife-cut noodles with our own rice bowls. If there were pieces of pork floating in the knife-cut noodle broth, we would skillfully scoop up the meat first, engaging in a playful competition to get our share.

One day, the villagers picked up a discarded dog from the field, skinned it, boiled it, and made a delicious '*boshintang*' (dog meat stew), providing a rare satisfying meal. However, the villagers' lives at that time were truly pitiable. They barely managed to have two meals a day, and even those meals were meager. The porridge they ate was made with watercress and sweet potatoes, and it was so humble that one of the significant reasons for people to join the New Fourth Army was the hope of getting to eat watercress porridge and dumplings made from flour.

Furthermore, the Enemy Operations Division of the New Fourth Army took great care to win our favor. They provided us with a basketball court and even went so far as to buy several basketballs for us in the Japanese-occupied areas. Every day, we divided into teams on the basketball court and enjoyed the game. Basketball was almost a national sport in China, so it gained popularity within the New Fourth Army as well. Our team and the Enemy Operations Division often engaged in friendly matches.

Because of this, we were determined to win in our matches against the New Fourth Army, to proudly represent our homeland's honor. We dedicated ourselves to practicing with unwavering determination. During our workouts, we could jump and run freely, uniting our hearts as we passed the basketball back and forth. Not only did this help alleviate the built-up stress, but it also erased the conflicting emotions that had existed among us.

However, the problem arose after the exercise was over. There was no water available to wash off the sweat and dust that covered our bodies. In China, there was no readily available water for personal use. Women were said to have boiled water in a jar to wash themselves once in their lifetime before getting married. Even the water we used for meals wasn't from a well; we had to go about a kilometer away to a puddle and collect stagnant water to use. Water needed for meals was also a struggle. We had to take turns carrying water buckets tied to bamboo poles all the way to Cheonpyeong Peak (天坪棒), which was approximately 1 kilometer away. Given this situation, the idea of washing the sweat off our bodies after exercising was simply beyond imagination.

Since water didn't come directly from a well in China, it was customary to always boil water from springs or other sources before drinking. Drinking untreated water was unheard of. To improve the taste of water, people had been using tea for a long time, boiling water to make it suitable for brewing tea. This practice led to the development of pottery craftsmanship, as teapots and vessels became essential for preparing and serving tea. The term "China" that Westerners use to refer to porcelain or ceramics actually signifies "the land of ceramics," as China had a rich tradition of pottery and ceramics.

During the matches against the New Fourth Army, the high-ranking officers of the Enemy Operations Division of the New Fourth Army, including the head, would come out and cheer with joyful faces. However, we were consistently defeated in these matches. Nonetheless, our comrade Han Myeong-sam was recognized as the top player and received a small prize. On such occasions, during the evening meal, Han Myeong-sam used his prize money to provide white liquor (白酒) and boiled meat, arranging a celebratory drinking session. The aroma of a sip of liquor and the succulent boiled meat brought us unparalleled joy. At times, we indulged in drinking to the point of becoming slightly intoxicated.

The presence of alcohol as a form of sustenance was indeed refreshing, but after a long time without drinking, we became not just open but daringly outspoken. All the accumulated grievances and discontent that had built up over time suddenly burst forth. Comrades who used to ask for being sent to Chongqing in the past, once intoxicated, began openly criticizing the officers. They shouted that they were willing to face death on the way if necessary and insisted on leaving this place no matter the circumstances, carrying their belongings with them. They might have expected us to discourage them, but the more we tried to dissuade them, the more resolute and defiant they became, to the point of becoming audacious and reckless.

It was an attitude of refusing to take responsibility for one's own actions. Upon hearing the commotion we were making, the officers hid themselves, while some of us stormed into the officers' quarters. At that moment, Son Dal quickly hid himself in a pile of barley straw and narrowly escaped harm.

When morning came and we faced each other with clear minds, all we could feel was awkwardness. Though the disturbance ended as just a commotion, one could sense that an invisible wall and a sense of estrangement were steadily growing among the comrades.

Those who couldn't suppress their emotions and resorted to actions often ended up suffering losses. Most of the comrades probably wished deep down to go to Chongqing. However, in a communist society, is there really freedom of choice? Ironically, those who caused a disturbance by declaring their intention to go to Chongqing might have felt even more isolated.

In such times, there were those who gained favor in a communist society. These were the cowardly individuals who secretly provided information about their comrades' daily actions and ideological tendencies to the Party officials. They were essentially informants, betraying their fellow comrades. Interestingly, in a communist autocratic society, such people were praised for having strong Party loyalty and were even protected by the Party.

Among our comrades, there emerged someone who engaged in backbiting and informing on us to the officers, creating a division among us. This individual was named Park Hang-gu. He lamented in front of us, claiming he was a descendant of the gentry and therefore couldn't be accepted in a communist society due to class ownership. However, behind our backs, he would complain about our alliance, attempting to curry favor.

In such a communist society, those who betray their comrades for their own advancement are often acknowledged. Park Hang-gu eventually rose in rank significantly in North Korea and reportedly appeared in Seoul as a battalion commander during the Korean War.

Counterintelligence Mission

No one could stop the hands of the clock.

After spending about a month at Hangdai (the Anti-Japanese Military and Political Academy), we received our certificates of completion from the section chief Mr. Oh of the Enemy Operations Division. Then, each of us was assigned operational missions from the higher-ups and had to depart for our respective locations.

I was grouped with Shim Young-soon and Yu Gil-seong (柳吉成). Yu's background as a civilian was unclear, but after liberation, I personally saw him serving as the chief of the security division at the public security department in North Pyongan Province. The three of us were assigned to go to a place called Dongsan (銅山), located about 50 *li* (25 kilometers) from the city of Xuzhou, and carry out enemy-area operations in the Xuzhou region.

As mentioned earlier, Shim Young-soon was a comrade with a fiery temperament who had previously demanded to be sent to Chongqing. The cadres probably paired him with me because of my mild nature, thinking our personalities would balance each other. The team leader was Yu Gil-seong.

Following the order of the party, we left for the Xuzhou area escorted by the New Fourth Army, which was occupied by the Japanese army from which I had escaped. Since it is a Chinese land where no Map can be obtained, I was just passing through the vast plains. I was retracing the path I had taken four months earlier when I escaped from the Xuzhou military unit and was captured and taken away as a prisoner by the New Fourth Army.

It was late autumn, so harvesting crops such as corn and sweet potatoes was in full swing in the fields. Now I feel so happy to think that I have been transformed into a so-called revolutionary and am heading to Xuzhou to fight the Japanese army as part of winning the independence of my country.

Early winter in the Huazhong (華中) region was bitterly cold and dreary. A private house where the three of us arrived and stayed was a shabby farmhouse, a run-down house where you could see the stars through the ceiling if you lay down. I couldn't even imagine heating, and I slept on a thin blanket, but it was so cold that I couldn't stand it. If it could contribute to independence, I thought that such hunger or cold was nothing I couldn't endure.

Since this was the front area of the New Fourth Army, I could see many Chinese soldiers. They wore military uniforms lined with cotton, and all wore tin cans and spoons around their waists. Some of them had backpacks on their backs. It was to put the meals distributed in the morning and evening in a tin can and eat it with a spoon. However, they sang happily and took pride in fighting the Japanese. They approached us and shouted "victory" and "welcome".

Figure 53: Officers and Soldiers of the New Fourth Army with Identification Tags and Insignia

Here, under the lamplight, we wrote many propaganda messages and letters to the Japanese garrison barracks and civilians. A propaganda material under the heading "Information to compatriots living in Xuzhou" was prepared. If I wrote a letter to the officer and sergeant of the Japanese military unit to which I belonged and handed it over to the operative of the New Fourth Army, he would go out to downtown Xuzhou and send it. In addition, if Koreans and Japanese soldiers were taken prisoner, they were reviewed, and Koreans were sent to the Korean Alliance, and if they were Japanese soldiers, they were handed over to the New Fourth Army.

Sometimes, it was called the 'megaphone broadcast' operation, and in the middle of the night, they approached the Japanese army's underground bunker located in a remote place and conducted a propaganda operation shouting in Japanese with a hand-held speaker so that the soldiers would have the idea of anti-war. Thinking that the propaganda materials I had written were being posted on the streets of Xuzhou and that the letters I had written were being delivered to the Japanese military barracks and being read by someone, I was excited to say that I was in charge of a part of the independence movement.

One day, I had a chance to accompany a high-ranking official of the New Fourth Army. It was not clear who he was because it was rare for communist party members to reveal their identity, but it was clear that he was the commander of the 4th Division of the New Fourth Army, judging from all the circumstances. At that time, the division commander's name was Chang Ping Zhang (張愛坪), and he served as the Minister of National Defense for a time after the establishment of the People's Republic. He was dressed in a clean military uniform and wore a pistol for self-defense and a silver spoon slung from his rice bowl. Now I want to talk about what I saw and felt while walking with him.

He and I passed through a village around noon and came to the door of a large and straight mansion, which is rare. It was clear that it was the mansion of a so-called absentee landlord who had fled to the Kuomintang district. A middle-aged old woman in the house welcomed him. Judging from the serious exchange between the two, it could be intuited that the Chinese Communist Party is now implementing a moderate policy, the family members who fled to the enemy territories are discussing the issue of returning home. When their close conversation was over and we were about to leave, the old woman seemed to offer to treat us to lunch.

After we responded and waited for a while, the old woman came out of the kitchen with some food, which was a pancake made of ground corn. Although that house was in ruins, I thought it was the landlord's house so they could have treated communist officials with plenty of food. However, what surprised me was the fact that they treated the officer with meager pancake. And even more surprising was that he, a high-ranking officer of the New Fourth army, ate deliciously without hesitation and expressed his gratitude.

I thought again. How can the Chinese people's livelihood be so poor! Since the life of an absentee landlord is like this, is it not worth mentioning the life of a commoner? So, I thought the communist party had no choice but to play the game. It was taken for granted that there were frequent peasant revolts in Chinese history and that there were many examples of peasant revolts, leading to the creation of new dynasties.

Another day, in the evening as the sun was sinking to the western horizon, we passed through a small village. When we arrived at the entrance of the village, children followed us and gathered shouting that they were welcome. When we reached the center of the village, the villagers were gathering, each carrying a chair and a rug, but at least 30 people could easily see it. It seemed that they had been informed in advance that we would be there.

Then, the senior officer of the New Fourth Army naturally began to address the crowd. Applause broke out here and there, and cheers of Sudi (是的: That's right) and Hoho (好好: Good) broke out. The senior officer of the New Fourth Army seemed to say that Japan would soon fall, and the victory of the communist party was imminent. Also, after the speech, the senior officer of the New Fourth Army left the village in peace. As I followed him, I couldn't help but picture them again. I felt that the satisfied and bright expressions of the crowd and the attitude of the New Fourth army cadre who gave a speech naturally and sincerely without any form or bravado were truly admirable. Communists have always said this.

"The communist party is a fish, and the crowd is water.
Just as a fish cannot live without water,
the New Fourth Army cannot grow without the people."

In fact, the residents seemed to believe that they could live comfortably there because the New Fourth Army prevented the Japanese from brutal sweeping battles. During the Anti-Japanese War, the Chinese communist party did not implement a socialist economy, but sided with the peasants, distributing the land of absentee landlords to the poor peasants and implementing the three-tier system, and the village administration was also a united front in which the communist party, the Kuomintang, and independents participated equally. That was the policy.

Before I knew it, the year 1945 had arrived, and after passing the Lunar New Year—the most important holiday for the Chinese—the fifteenth day of the first month, the Lantern Festival, had come. Climbing a hill and gazing at the bright moon, I felt a deep loneliness. Watching the New Fourth Army members gather for the holiday, cooking food, singing songs, and being merry, I couldn't help but feel a sense of envy. As I looked at them, I was struck once again by the truth that

"No matter how poor one may be, true contentment lies within the heart. No matter how hard I looked, there were no landlords or capitalists in this society—everyone was living in poverty.
Yet how could they live with such profound satisfaction?"

"But at what point am I now?
When I return to my homeland after liberation, will I be armed with communist ideology and serve the people devotedly?
Am I now a member of the communist party, even if I am compelled to do so?
My future has already been decided, and Japan's defeat seems imminent.
So, will the people really welcome me when I appear as a communist in my independent country? "

Everyone around me must have looked at me with wonder. No matter how much I thought about it, I couldn't become a communist party member because of my experience or way of thinking. It is ideal to build a society where there are no classes and people do not exploit people and everyone lives equally, as the communist party says. It was also something that seemed out of place to me. Thinking that my becoming a communist was nothing but self-deception, I returned to my residence to find Shim Young-soon and Yu Gil-seong in a deep sleep.

New conscripts

Our counterintelligence operation ended in March 1945, and by order we returned to Bansheng (半城), the base of the New Fourth Army. When I left the Xuzhou, the New Fourth Army there expressed their gratitude to me and presented me with a set of Chinese clothes made of plain cotton. When I took off the faded New Fourth Army uniform and wore civilian clothes for the first time, I felt lighter at heart, and I also looked more like a Chinese person. This time, coming to the New Fourth Army base was easier than it had been eight months ago when I first came—because in the meantime, the situation had changed significantly, and Japanese military security had become laxer.

When I arrived at the Huazhong Branch, I was truly delighted to reunite with the comrades I had parted with. They told me that they, too, had been sent to other regions where they carried out propaganda work for the New Fourth Army, similar to what I had been doing.

Our gathering at the stronghold this time was the total gathering of all the Koreans scattered in the New Fourth Army ruling district, and the number reached about 60 people. Among them, there were many young Koreans who enlisted in the Huazhong region as the conscription system was implemented in Korea and those subject to conscription were dispatched to China. However, they, like our student soldiers, escaped from the Japanese barracks and were brought here as prisoners of the New Fourth army. It was said that a brave conscript soldier jumped into the Yangtze River to escape the Japanese bullets, swam and fled to the New Fourth Army area before being led here. When they came to the Huazhong branch, they jumped with joy, saying that they felt reassured because there were many senior student soldiers.

We were glad to see many draft dodgers joining, which significantly expanded the strength of the Huazhong branch—but more than that, meeting fellow Koreans who shared our blood was a great joy in itself.

Now, it seemed no empty boast to believe that, if only we had weapons, we could even seize Japanese army pillboxes. However, there was not a single rifle in the Huazhong branch. The only thing they had to offer was *jeongpung*—that is, ideological reformation. So, for the brave, passionate young men, there were no weapons to be given—only the indoctrination of communist ideology.

Political education and cultural education were conducted to educate these former draftees in the Huazhong branch. In the morning, there was a political lecture by Comrade Shin Sang-cho, and in the afternoon, there was a cultural education class led by me. I put a lot of effort into dealing with them. We had to begin to teach them the Korean language. Among them, there were illiterate people, and there were many people who did not know Korean writing because they had finished elementary school at most. I selected texts that promoted class consciousness among the history of the communist party of the Soviet Union or the Chinese communist party that I had, translated them into Korean, and copied them to use as textbooks.

In other words, they talked about events such as the "Bloody Sunday" incident of 1905 in the Soviet Union and the "Five Four Movements (五四 運動)" in China. Their interest was great. It was also because the stories I heard here were things I hadn't heard in my home country in the past. Moreover, all the student soldiers they dealt with had college degrees, so they trusted and respected them as human beings. They seemed to have even the humblest hope that if they learned many new things here, they would occupy a high position in the future after Korea became independent. Since most of them were children of poor farmers, it seemed that they could acquire communist ideas quickly.

Figure 54: Five Four Movement (五四運動), 1919.

As the number of members in the Huazhong branch (華中分盟) rapidly increased, the New Fourth Army also began to pay more attention to us. Our living conditions improved somewhat, and they even provided us with various types of sports equipment. They secured a space for us to play soccer and bought us a ball, and they also provided a full set of baseball gear. It must be said that this was a special gesture of consideration on the part of the New Fourth Army.

In truth, amid our frustrating living environment, sports not only strengthened the bonds of camaraderie among the comrades but also helped clear our minds of idle thoughts. About sixty young men of similar age had gathered in the name of revolution yet were forced into communal living without a single weapon among them—naturally, this led to much discontent and complaints. But during sports, we returned to a simpler state of mind, focusing solely on the game and competing with one another in good spirit.

Demand for free election

In the spring of 1945, the number of members of the Huazhong branch increased rapidly to more than 100. It was because the so-called first draftees risked their lives to escape the Japanese military barracks. At that time, the Eighth Route Army and the New Fourth Army operated based in the rear of the Japanese occupied areas in Central China and North China, so most of the conscripts who fled the Japanese military barracks flocked to the Eighth Route Army or the New Fourth Army area. Most of the newly transferred comrades from the conscription were simple farmers who had not been stained by the sect and were mostly graduated from elementary schools.

Moreover, they deeply trusted and respected former student soldiers who escaped from the Japanese army in the same situation rather than the leaders of the Huazhong branch and wanted to follow the student soldiers' thoughts. In this way, the Huazhong branch was divided into a group of senior civilians, a group of newly formed student soldiers, and a group of former conscripts, and in terms of numbers, the newcomers were by far the dominant.

However, one big change occurred among the former student soldiers, and that was that comrade Shin Sang-cho, who had been trusted by the student soldiers and guided their thoughts, suddenly turned to the right wing and fiercely criticized the leaders of the Huazhong branch. Originally, there is a saying that the difference between a genius and an idiot is a piece of paper, and he, who had been closely attached to Sun Dal as a leftist extremist, turned to the right and advocated that the organization of the Huazhong branch should be reorganized by electing leaders through democratic elections.

He also changed the stance he had long upheld and now declared that the only honorable path for our people—the true path to independence—was for all of us to go to Chongqing, take up arms, and fight against the Japanese. Furthermore, he fiercely criticized the Enemy Operations Division of the New Fourth Army, lashing out with razor-sharp words:

"Don't treat us as mere prisoners. Grant us our freedom. What we are striving for now is national independence, not the construction of a communist society. Why won't you send us to Chongqing? I urge you to quickly carry out democratic elections and establish a proper system."

166

The comrades who followed Shim Young-soon and Bang Hwi-je—both of whom had been advocating for going to Chongqing—raised their voices even louder once Shin Sang-cho joined their cause, demanding to be sent to Chongqing. In response, the Alliance cadres, who were numerically in the minority and lacked the trust of the conscripted members, were at a loss and could do nothing but stand by helplessly.

The group I belonged to, including Han Myeong-sam, held the position that heading to Chongqing at this point was nothing more than opposition for opposition's sake, ignoring the realities on the ground. We agreed to stay and observe the situation here until Japan was defeated. However, this stance was seen as pragmatic self-preservation and complacent passivity, leaving no room for it to gain traction.

As a result, the prevailing opinion became dominated by the belief that going to Chongqing was the only way forward. The Huazhong branch soon fell into a state of gloom, mired in mutual blame and suspicion.

When there was no prospect of carrying out their opinions any longer, the student soldiers formally demanded that if the New Fourth Army could not send us to Chongqing, new officials of the Huazhong branch should be newly elected by anonymous elections. This problem could not have been a more serious problem for them. It was because they had behaved so far, saying that all organizations and administration in the New Fourth Army were carried out through free elections centered on the communist party, so the dictatorial cadres could not find any other justification to reject the student soldiers' demands. Furthermore, as long as the Independence Alliance put forward the establishment of a democratic republic as its platform, there was no theoretical basis to oppose free elections.

Shin Sang-cho and Shim Yeong-soon personally visited the chief of the Enemy Operations Division and obtained consent to elect leaders of the Huazhong branch through elections after a single decision, and the timing was decided in consultation with the officials of the Huazhong branch. It was clear that once the elections were held, the incumbent officers would step down and the former student soldiers would take the initiative. If elections are held and student soldiers take the initiative, will the New Fourth Army approve the system? I thought that it was unlikely that the officers at the Enemy Operations Division, who treated us as prisoners of war, would entrust the student soldiers, who were considered the liberals and had not washed away the poison of capitalism, with the Huazhong branch.

The leaders of the Huazhong branch have always criticized the Nationalist (Kuomintang) for a one-party dictatorship and said as a habit that the liberated districts of the New Fourth Army are a democratic centralized system and that the opinions of each faction are reflected in the administration after free elections. As a last resort, they bluntly said that they would hold an election if they contacted the headquarters of the Korean Independence Alliance in Yan'an (延安) and received approval. The student soldiers had no choice but to wait because they could not reject it head-on, even though they knew that their words were a mere delay and a desperate measure to overcome the immediate crisis. At this time, the Huazhong branch said that it was contacting Yan'an by radio, but it is doubtful whether it communicated by radio.

168

In the midst of this, in early June 1945, Sun Dal gathered all the members in the branch and made a major announcement. It was an order from the headquarters of the Yan'an Alliance of Peoples Republic of Korea obtained by the Communist Army. On July 29, 1945, to mark National Humiliation Day (國恥日), the 3rd Representative Congress of the Korean Independence Alliance was scheduled at Yan'an, and the Huazhong (Central China) branch also decided to send five executive representatives to attend. In addition, the majority of members of the Huazhong branch were to be sent north to enroll in the Korean Volunteer Army Military and Political Academy, located in the Taihang Mountains (太行山). Sun Dal (孫達) delivered these instructions, saying that the date of the northward visit was set for June 20, 1945 and requested the election of five representative officers. Sun Dal's announcement was enough to clear away the dark clouds hanging over the Huazhong branch.

Figure 55: Entrance to Luojiaping Village in the Taihang Mountains.

Map 56: Taihang Mountain Range.

As representatives to attend the 3rd National Assembly of the Independence Alliance in the Huazhong branch, three former student soldiers were Shin Sang-cho, Shim Yeong-soon, and me (Uhm Young-sik , 嚴永植), and the other two were Wang Shin-ho (王信虎); Kim Woong (金雄, Commander of the 1st Army front at the time of 6.25 Korean War) and Hwang Mo (黃慕).

At this time, it can be said that it is a very noteworthy event that Wang Shin-ho appeared in the Huazhong branch and commanded the representatives going to Yan'an. As mentioned earlier, the communists did not reveal his identity, so I could not know Wang Shin-ho's career or position, but it is certain that he graduated from the Guizhou (貴州) Military Academy and was active as a regimental commander in the

Kuomintang army as a member of the Korean Independence Alliance. Looking at the age of 40, he had a nimble body, indicating that he had a lot of combat experience. I later heard that he was a classmate of President Park Chung-hee (朴正熙) at Daegu Teacher's College.

Now, as the members of the Huazhong branch are busy preparing for their northern advancement, the comrades who are set to join the Military and Political Academy were excited in their own way. They were delighted to receive the opportunity to undergo training at the Military and Political Academy established by comrade Mu Jeong and to join the Korean Independence Army, where they would carry guns and fight against the Japanese forces.

Even the enlisted soldiers who were selected to represent the group on the coast were also quite thrilled. On the coast, there were excellent revolutionaries with vast experience, such as Kim Doo-bong (金枓奉) and Choi Chang-ik. Furthermore, as they were chosen to participate in the Third Conference to be held at Yan'an, they considered leaving this place and moving to the stronghold of the Alliance a fortunate event. So, most of them headed north, leaving a few Huazhong branch members, including Han Myeong-sam, who had to establish a new system and face a new phase as they bid farewell to the northern expedition force.

Chapter 7

The New Fourth Army

Organization of the New Fourth Army

Let me explain the nature of the situation. When the communist forces—that is, the Eighth Route Army—were unable to withstand Chiang Kai-shek's first encirclement and suppression campaign in October 1934 and embarked on the Long March, a remnant force of about 20,000 soldiers, left behind due to illness or other circumstances, remained in the area. These troops, led by Chen Yi (陳毅) and Xiang Ying (項英), roamed the surrounding mountainous regions, fending off relentless attacks from the Nationalist Army and managing to preserve their existence.

On the other hand, the leadership that had gone on the Long March had no choice but to believe that the remnant forces had been annihilated by the Nationalist Army. Even after the full-scale war between China and Japan broke out in July 1937, the Nationalist forces continued their attacks on the remnants of the communist forces.

Remarkably, however, these remnant forces not only withstood attacks from the Nationalists but also successfully resisted assaults from the Japanese army.

During this time, the Second United Front (國共合作) was established, bringing the Nationalist Party and the Communist Party together to fight against the common enemy, Japan's invading forces. It was only after this collaboration that the remaining guerrilla units were able to establish communication with the Yan'an communist forces.

Consequently, the remaining troops were incorporated into the National Military Council of the Nationalist Party and were newly organized into the National Revolutionary Army. In January 1938, they were officially named the New Formation Fourth Army (新編第四軍). They were also referred to as the New Fourth Army (新四軍), named in reference to the so-called "Iron Army" that Ye Ting (葉挺) led as the 4th Army of the National Revolutionary Army during the Northern Expedition in 1926, which advanced with great momentum.

The remaining guerrilla units were conducting guerrilla warfare in the vast regions in China. To reorganize these units, it took about two to three months to gather them at designated locations in the north and south of Anhui (安徽) Province. The total number of assembled soldiers was approximately 15,000, with the majority gathering in the southern part of Anhui Province and the rest in the northern part of the Yangtze River (長江). Among them, around 13,000 soldiers were reorganized into the New Fourth Army and divided into four regional units.

173

Map 57: Route of the Long March (長征)

As a result, the New Fourth Army was composed of four regional units:

1. The 1st Regional Unit led by Chen Yi (陣毅), who had a prominent role in the establishment of the Republic of China.

2. The 2nd Regional Unit led by Zhang Xiancheng (張縣承).

3. The 3rd Regional Unit led by Zhang Yunyi (張雲逸).

4. The 4th Regional Unit led by Gao Qingting (高慶亭).

Among these units, only the 4th Regional Unit operated guerrilla warfare in the rear areas of the Japanese occupation north of the Yangtze

174

River. On the other hand, the 1st, 2nd, and 3rd Regional Units stayed in the southern region of the Yangtze River, where the Japanese forces occupied the heartland of China, and conducted guerrilla operations near areas such as Wuhu (蕪湖) and Zhenjiang (鎮江).

In the beginning, under Chiang Kai-shek's Nationalist Party government, the soldiers of the New Fourth Army were initially provided with similar amounts of money, ammunition, and uniforms as the other Nationalist Army units. However, they were not allocated the most crucial weaponry for combat.

When the scattered troops, who had been conducting guerrilla warfare alongside the Nationalist forces in various regions, were called to gather at designated assembly points to be reorganized into the New Fourth Army, many civilians living in the Japanese-occupied rear areas also joined them to provide support and enlist in the New Fourth Army. This influx of civilian recruits required significant expenses to train them as new soldiers. However, the Nationalist government did not offer any assistance in this matter and did not provide financial support for the recruitment and training of these civilian volunteers.

As a result, the New Fourth Army had no choice but to divide and use the initial funds they received to raise these new civilian recruits as soldiers. Unlike the Nationalist government forces, the New Fourth Army did not have significant differences in salaries between commanders and soldiers. Soldiers received around 1.5 yuan (元) per month, while commanders received between 2.0 to 4.0 yuan, and divisional commanders received 4 yuan. While the army provided rations and uniforms, other personal items such as shoes, underwear, toothbrushes, soap, and so on, had to be purchased by the soldiers themselves using their stipends.

(Editor's Note: In the 1930s–40s during the wartime period in China, 1 yuan (元) could buy a large sack of rice or support a modest living for a few days. It could be worth anywhere from $10 to $100 USD in modern terms.)

Indeed, the expansion of the New Fourth Army by training local civilians into soldiers was not well received by the Nationalist government. When the New Fourth Army recruited new soldiers and requested budget allocations, rifles, and ammunition, the Nationalist government was hesitant to provide full support. They argued that the budget should be used to improve the living conditions of soldiers within their existing forces and not solely for expanding the New Fourth Army.

From its inception, the New Fourth Army faced friction and disputes with the Nationalist government forces. Although the Nationalist government saw the New Fourth Army's resistance against the Japanese as a positive development, they also secretly wished for the New Fourth Army to be annihilated by the Japanese during their joint struggle.

The strained relationship between the Nationalist government and the New Fourth Army continued throughout its existence. Despite their shared goal of resisting the Japanese invasion, ideological differences and the competition for power between the Nationalist Party and the Communist Party created ongoing tensions.

Activities of the New Fourth Army

The New Fourth Army's commander, General Ye Ting (葉挺), was a very honest soldier. He did not hide the growing strength of the New Fourth Army in the slightest and reported everything in detail to the Nationalist government. When the government criticized the expansion of the New Fourth Army, he responded by asserting that only through mobilizing and arming the masses could China achieve victory.

General Ye had originally been a member of the Kuomintang (Nationalist Party). After studying in the Soviet Union and returning to China, he became a member of the Communist Party. He was a man firmly convinced that only through cooperation between the Nationalists and Communists could China be saved.

In July 1927, when the first split occurred between the Kuomintang and the Communist Party, Ye was serving as a division commander in Chiang Kai-shek's National Revolutionary Army. However, he joined Mao Zedong in launching the Nanchang (南昌) Uprising. When the uprising failed, he later participated in the failed Guangzhou Commune in December 1927 and then went to study in the Soviet Union.

After Japan launched its invasion of Manchuria in 1931, Ye Ting returned to China with the goal of realizing the Nationalist-Communist cooperation once again. However, his efforts were in vain due to the Nationalist Party's focus on anti-communist campaigns during the period known as the Encirclement Campaign (1930-1934).

Ye Ting's remarkable activities can be attributed to his leadership, particularly after the Japanese invasion of China's mainland in 1937. The New Fourth Army's impressive performance and its development into a formidable and intellectually superior force while operating in the rear areas of Japanese-occupied territory can be largely credited to General Ye Ting's achievements. Vice Commander Xiang Ying (項英) came from a background of working on railroads and became involved in labor movements before joining the Communist Party.

The operational base of the New Fourth Army was in the southern coastal region of the Yangtze River. This area was under Japanese occupation and comprised a network of roads, rivers, lakes, canals, and railways connecting Shanghai and Nanjing. As such, it was strategically important and advantageous for the well-equipped Japanese forces, with their aircraft and mechanized units. When the New Fourth Army was assigned this area as their operational zone by the Nationalist government, they were faced with formidable Japanese forces, with Japanese trucks and mechanized vehicles patrolling the roads and Japanese warships controlling the waterways, canals, and lakes.

Despite these challenges, the New Fourth Army, under Ye Ting's leadership, carried out operations in this difficult region, demonstrating their resilience and determination to resist the Japanese invasion and contribute to the Chinese resistance efforts.

The advanced units of the New Fourth Army began infiltrating the region in April 1938 to conduct operations. The intelligence operatives worked in small teams of two or three people, moving from village to village, covertly investigating the Japanese military positions, equipment, and movements. The residents warmly welcomed and sheltered them, aiding in their covert activities.

Figure 58: Commander Ye Ting (葉挺), 1939.

Figure 59: From left: Xiang Ying, Zhou Enlai, and Commander Ye Ting in 1939.

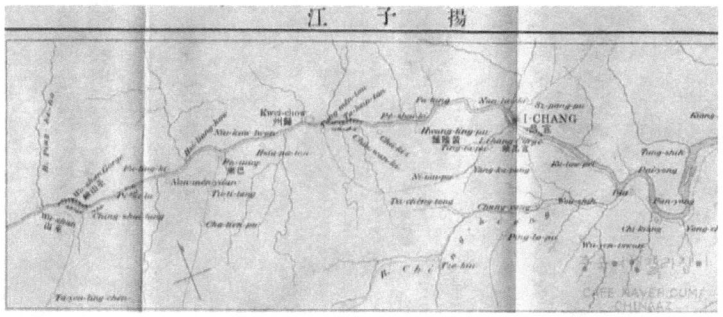

Map 60: A Map of Yangtze River (Changjiang) created by Japan in 1915.

After completing about a month of intelligence gathering, when the operatives returned to their headquarters, the guerrilla units swiftly launched attacks based on the gathered intelligence, destroying various Japanese military facilities throughout the region. Following these actions, political operatives followed suit, infiltrating numerous villages to organize the residents into anti-Japanese political groups. This network of anti-Japanese political organizations aimed to resist Japanese occupation and further the Chinese resistance efforts.

The guerrilla units of the New Fourth Army indeed put significant effort into seizing weapons, including rifles, from the Japanese forces. They also focused on sabotaging infrastructure such as railways, roads, bridges, and communication lines. In conducting guerrilla warfare, the New Fourth Army received absolute cooperation from the residents, which played a crucial role in their success.

One of the most critical activities against the Japanese forces was the capture of their rifles. This was a major focus because while killing one Japanese soldier could end with that action, seizing their rifles meant they could use those weapons to take down many more Japanese soldiers.

180

It was a highly effective strategy to undermine the enemy's strength and posed a significant threat to the occupying Japanese forces.

The New Fourth Army's ability to gain the trust and cooperation of the local populace was vital for their guerrilla operations. With the support of the people, they could move freely, gather intelligence, and launch surprise attacks against the Japanese forces, further enhancing their effectiveness in resisting the occupation.

The New Fourth Army placed great importance on education. Despite being poor peasants, many were drawn to join the New Fourth Army because it offered them three meals a day made from flour, a significant improvement from their previous diet of only two meals of watery corn porridge. As a result, a considerable number of the recruits were illiterate.

Recognizing the significance of education, the New Fourth Army established literacy classes as a priority for the new recruits. These classes taught them how to read and write, simultaneously enlightening them about the root causes of their poverty, which were often linked to the exploitation by landlords and the aggression of the Japanese forces. By educating the recruits, the New Fourth Army aimed to empower them with knowledge and awareness of their social and political circumstances, fostering a sense of unity and purpose in their resistance against the oppressors.

Figure 61: Weapons Treasured by Manchurian Anti-Japanese Fighters.

Every three months, a group of political operatives was selected to undergo retraining at the training centers they had established. As instructors, they recruited university graduates, artists, and intellectuals who had managed to cross the Japanese blockade from enemy-held areas. During the training, a significant emphasis was placed on military issues, which comprised 70% of the curriculum for military commanders, while

182

political and cultural matters accounted for the remaining 30%. For political operatives, 30% of their training focused on military issues, while the rest of the time was dedicated to political and cultural subjects.

Among the important lectures on political matters, there was a focus on tactics related to unification fronts, and other topics included methods of mass mobilization. In terms of cultural subjects, the curriculum covered geography, music, and especially emphasized the importance of writing and composition.

New Fourth Army's 4th Detachment Unit

When I escaped from a Japanese military camp in August 1943, I was taken as a prisoner of war and escorted to the New Fourth Army's 4th Detachment without any relation to my original intentions. As a guerrilla force, the New Fourth Army had to constantly relocate their base depending on the situation. The location I arrived at was a small fortress situated on the northern outskirts of Bansheng (半城), near Hongze Lake (洪澤湖), which is the border area between Jiangsu Province (江蘇省) and Anhui Province (安徽省).

The 4th Detachment's base was not a typical military camp with large concentrations of troops, nor did it have proper headquarters or buildings. Instead, it consisted of humble cottages in the fortress, serving as barracks for the soldiers and the office for the commander. The commander's office had little more than a large table and chairs, with a Map hanging on the wall. It was a simple setup in that regard.

The New Fourth Army did not use insignias to indicate ranks, and there was little distinction in clothing between commanders and soldiers, making it challenging to differentiate them from one another. The only notable difference was that soldiers did not possess their own weapons, but aside from that, if you were to ask the soldiers what they wanted to have, everyone would say they wanted a rifle, just like those used by the Japanese soldiers.

Before the outbreak of the Sino-Japanese War, the New Fourth Army's 4th Detachment engaged in sporadic conflicts with the Nationalist army in the southern mountainous regions of Anhui province while actively mobilizing the local population. In 1938, when Ye Ting became the commander of the New Fourth Army, he gathered around 3,000 scattered guerrilla fighters in the area and established them as the 4th Detachment of the New Fourth Army, with Gao Qingting (高慶亭) as the detachment commander.

However, in May 1938, the Japanese forces moved to this region to launch an operation against Hankou (漢口). In response, Chiang Kai-shek ordered the 4th Detachment to guard the roads within Anhui Province that connected Tianjin and Nanjing, which were occupied by the Japanese troops. As a result, the 4th Detachment lost contact with the main forces (1st, 2nd, and 3rd Detachments) of the New Fourth Army, which were operating guerrilla warfare south of the Yangtze River.

As a result, Gao Qingting, the detachment commander, found himself in a position similar to a local warlord, effectively ruling over a particular region. Unfortunately, he behaved just like the warlords of the past, disregarding his Communist Party membership and succumbing to corruption and abuse of power. He took advantage of his authority,

184

engaging in immoral behavior by taking multiple young women as his concubines. Furthermore, he showed no respect for dissenting opinions and went so far as to arrest and execute anyone who opposed him.

He even sold the medicine received from the Nationalist government to make money and urged the central command for more medical supplies, all for his own financial gain. When the Nationalist government became aware of his misconduct, they investigated Gao Qingting's actions and decided that a reorganization of the 4th Detachment was necessary to effectively combat the Japanese forces, as his behavior was hindering the New Fourth Army's mission.

As a result, Gao Qingting was replaced as the commander of the 4th Detachment by Zhang Yunyi (張雲逸), who was originally from Guangdong province, participated in the Northern Expedition, and later became the chairman of the Guangxi (廣西) people's government after the founding of the People's Republic of China. However, Zhang faced significant challenges due to the strong influence of Gao Qingting's faction within the 4th Detachment, making it difficult for him to maintain control and facing many restrictions.

In 1939, when Ye Ting learned about the internal situation of the 4th Detachment, he crossed the river from the main base of the New Fourth Army in the south and arrived at the 4th Detachment's location to conduct an inspection. Upon hearing about this, Gao Qingting deployed a special guard force consisting of his loyalists around the detachment and adopted a threatening posture towards Ye Ting. However, Ye Ting, who was unarmed and with only a personal bodyguard, fearlessly walked into the headquarters of the detachment and reportedly shouted that he was arresting Gao Qingting.

At that moment, Gao Qingting was taken aback by the fact that his deployed guard force did not fire a single shot, even though Ye Ting was entering the detachment's headquarters. What surprised him even more was when Ye Ting, as the commander, publicly put Gao Qingting on trial before his subordinates, and they demanded his execution. Finally, in June 1939, Ye Ting executed Gao Qingting.

After Gao Qingting's execution, it was reported that both of his mistresses were raising his children. The New Fourth Army continued to provide financial support to his children as they did before. The reasoning behind this was that the children bore no responsibility for Gao Qingting's crimes; thus, the punishment was solely directed at him. While some may criticize the Communist forces as being lawless and barbaric, this incident shows that they followed a modern system of military law and justice.

Wannan Incident

In January 1941, the New Fourth Army faced an extremely difficult tragedy known as the "Wannan (皖南) Incident." That happened because the Nationalist Military Commission had ordered the entire New Fourth Army to move from south of the Yangtze River, where its main forces were stationed, to the region north of the Huánghé (黃河, Yellow River).

As the army followed the order and began the relocation, the 3rd Division faced challenges in moving wounded soldiers due to their base hospital. As a result, they could not complete the relocation within the given time frame. Seizing this opportunity, more than 8,000 troops from the Kuomintang government surrounded the 3rd Division and launched an encirclement attack, leading to the tragic annihilation of the entire division, which consisted of around 3,000 personnel.

During this distressing event, political operatives and nurses from the 3rd Division were reported to have been brutally killed, with some of them hanged from trees, meeting a gruesome fate. General Ye Ting, the commander of the New Fourth Army, was injured and captured, subsequently facing a military trial under the command of Gu Zhu Dong (顧祝同), the commander of the Nationalist government's 3rd Theater Command. Vice commander Xiang Ying (項英) narrowly escaped capture but was later found and killed. The New Fourth Army referred to this incident as the "Wannan (皖南) Incident."

Regarding the Wannan Incident, the Nationalist government offered an explanation that the New Fourth Army's 3rd Division initiated a rebellion and attacked the government's forces first. They also claimed that Ye Ting and Xiang Ying had conspired against the government, intending to occupy Guyong (句容) and Danyang (丹陽) in Jiangsu Province (江蘇省), along with the strategic triangle point connecting Nanjing, Shanghai, and Hangzhou, to use them as operational bases against the Nationalist government's forces.

However, this justification seems highly implausible since the strategic triangle point connecting Shanghai, Nanjing, and Hangzhou was already under Japanese occupation, serving as their operational base in the Huazhong region. Additionally, Guyong and Danyang were heavily fortified strongholds of the Japanese forces located just south of

Nanjing. It is doubtful that the New Fourth Army, no matter how strong, would have dared to occupy such points. Therefore, the Nationalist government's explanation appears inconsistent with the facts.

Indeed, the Nationalist government had valid reasons for issuing the order to the New Fourth Army to move its troops to the Northeast region of the Huánghé (黃河). After occupying the Wuhan three towns (武漢三鎮), the Japanese forces realized that they could not conquer China by military means. They sought to find a way to engage with the Nationalist government in Chongqing and explore possibilities for negotiations. To achieve this goal, they encouraged Wang Jingwei, who was in opposition to Chiang Kai-shek, to break away from the Nationalist government and establish the Puppet Reorganized National Government in Nanjing, hoping to negotiate a peace treaty with Wang Jingwei's government instead of confronting Chiang Kai-shek.

However, Japan became disappointed when their puppet government, the Nanjing Puppet National Government (偽南京政府), failed to gain the trust and support of the Chinese people as they had hoped.

In the mid-1940s, the British blockade of Burma Road disrupted the transportation of aid materials to China, effectively cutting off the supply route. Taking advantage of this situation, Japan made demands on the Nationalist government. Japan proposed severing ties with the Wang Jingwei puppet government (Nanjing Reorganized National Government) and recognizing Chiang Kai-shek as the leader of China. They also promised to withdraw their occupation forces from Hubei and

Hunan Provinces, granting Japan the right to maintain control over the north of the Yellow River (黃河, Huánghé).

What Japan effectively demanded from China, even to the point of launching a full-scale Sino-Japanese war, was the land north of the Yellow River. This area was not only rich in industrial resources that Japan desperately desired—such as food, coal, and iron—but also strategically essential as an operational base against both China and the Soviet Union. Some corrupt elements within the Nationalist government responded favorably to Japan's peace overtures. However, this created a problem: the New Fourth Army, growing stronger with its base in the rear of the Japanese-occupied territory south of the Yangtze River, became a major concern. As a result, an order was given for them to relocate to the land north of the Yellow River.

Moving the New Fourth Army to the Huánghé-Northeast region would place them under the pressure of the formidable 500,000-strong force led by General Ho Chong-nam, known for having the best-equipped troops within the Nationalist Army. This army was encircling the Eighth Route Army. In fact, since the Battle of Tai'erzhuang (台兒莊) in the spring of 1938, Ho Chong-nam's forces had refrained from firing a single shot at the Japanese and had focused solely on blockading the activities of the Eighth Route Army. By this time, the Nationalist government had already broken its promises to provide resources, ammunition, and medical supplies to the Eighth Route Army. The situation had become dire, with the Eighth Route Army engaged in constant battles both against the external Japanese forces and the internal blockade imposed by their fellow Nationalist Ho Chong-nam's army.

189

Figure 62: Battle of Taierzhuang — National Revolutionary Army
Soldiers Deployed in the Battle, Spring 1938.

The clashes between the New Fourth Army and the Nationalist
forces occurred when the government issued an order for the New
Fourth Army to move from the lower reaches of the Yangtze River to
the Huánghé-Northeast region. At that time, the Huánghé-Northeast
region was facing severe food shortages due to an unprecedented and
prolonged flood, and even the stationed Eighth Route Army was
suffering from hunger. Despite the difficulties, the New Fourth Army
decided to comply with the Nationalist government's orders. However,
they requested the necessary resources to move to the Huánghé-
Northeast region, including winter clothing for the harsh climate and
ammunition to overcome the Japanese blockade in that area. The New
Fourth Army believed that the Nationalist government's command to

move to the Huánghé-Northeast region was a deceptive ploy for peace negotiations with Japan.

According to the orders, the First and Second Divisions of the New Fourth Army crossed the Yangtze River and infiltrated into the coastal areas on the opposite side of Nanjing, while the Third Division, which had many wounded soldiers and a base hospital, faced difficulties in moving quickly and stayed there temporarily. It was this Third Division that came under attack from the Nationalist forces, resulting in the tragic loss of around 3,000 soldiers, both men and women. This incident not only cast a shadow over the Second United Front between the Communists and Nationalists but also foreshadowed the harsh internal conflict that China would face in the future.

The Communist Party presented an ultimatum to the Nationalist government as a final measure. The demands included ceasing the attacks on the New Fourth Army, providing compensation for the fallen soldiers, and releasing General Ye Ting. Additionally, the Communist Party called for the introduction of a democratic system where all parties would have equal speaking rights. They also notified that in the future; the Communist Party would independently appoint its own commanders.

At that time, the Nationalist government announced that the New Fourth Army had already disbanded, but in reality, the New Fourth Army scattered and began to regroup to launch guerrilla warfare. Disregarding the government's orders to move north of the Yellow River, the New Fourth Army intensified its activities in the central part of Anhui Province and the eastern part of Jiangsu Province, where the Fourth Division was operating. The Communist Party declared that the

New Fourth Army would continue to engage in combat with the Japanese army and the collaborating Nationalist government forces. They further stated that if the Nationalist government forces attacked the New Fourth Army, they would firmly fight back to defend themselves.

Confrontation between Nationalist and Communist Parties

The deep-rooted mistrust and power struggle between the Nationalist Party and the Communist Party did not disappear even after they formed the United Front to face Japan's invasion. The specter of civil war lingered everywhere. The ruling class, especially the landlords, viewed the Eighth Route Army and the New Fourth Army with terror, as the Communists were mobilizing and educating the people and arming them. Landlords who had fled to the remote western regions (areas not occupied by Japan) or Nationalist-controlled areas knew that their former tenants were receiving education and training under the Communists and fighting against the Japanese with weapons. They wondered whether these armed peasants, imbued with Communist ideology, would simply return and resume obediently tending the fields for their landlords after the war ended. The absentee landlords believed that their former tenants would never return to their old ways and would not continue to toil the land for their benefit.

The political department of the New Fourth Army had long claimed that China could not be built into a socialist society without first going through a stage of democracy. They did not confuse capitalism, in which the means of production are controlled by a small capitalist class, with democracy. However, the democracy advocated by the New Fourth

192

Army was one that was based solely on the working masses, excluding landlords and capitalists — thus, it was not genuine democracy either.

During the struggle against Japan, countless members of the New Fourth Army died. They believed they were dying for the people — in other words, for democracy — but in truth, they were dying for the construction of a socialist society.

The New Fourth Army, like the Eighth Route Army, faced challenges in acquiring weapons when fighting against the Japanese. There were no weapon manufacturing facilities in their bases, and they had to constantly move and adapt to Japanese attacks in the occupied areas. Establishing weapon factories in such circumstances was unimaginable. However, they managed to produce crude hand grenades. As for rifles, they obtained them mainly by disarming enemy forces, including Japanese troops and other traitorous groups. They also acquired rifles from the local populace through contributions or purchased them from merchants.

Hence, the primary source of the New Fourth Army's weapons was through capturing them from disarmed enemy forces or procuring them from the local population or merchants. As a result, the origin of their weapons was often attributed to the Yawata (八幡) weapons factory in Kyushu (九州), Japan. Although some people may assume that the communists received weapon supplies from the Soviet Union, examining China's geopolitical situation and military circumstances reveals that this is not likely to be the case. The New Fourth Army relied more on their resourcefulness and the weapons they captured from enemy forces rather than significant military aid from the Soviet Union.

Indeed, the communist party of China's operating area was located far from the Soviet Union, separated by desert regions, and blocked by the Nationalist Party's military forces on the mainland. As a result, any direct smuggling of weapons from the Soviet Union was practically impossible. Before the Soviet Union came under attack from Germany in 1941, the Soviet government had signed non-interference agreements with the Chiang Kai-shek government and provided significant military support to the Nationalists. However, it is highly unlikely that the same weapons supplied to Chiang Kai-shek's forces were directly transferred to the communist forces.

The rifles carried by the members of the New Fourth Army were quite shabby and old, yet they cherished them more than their own lives. Moreover, the New Fourth Army employed a method of providing two rifles to three soldiers. Among the three soldiers, the one without a rifle either died in battle or received a rifle from a fallen comrade to carry out their mission. According to their beliefs, one rifle could kill many enemies, making it more valuable than a person's life.

On July 7, 1942, during the 5th anniversary of the Sino-Japanese War, the commander-in-chief of the communist party, Zhu De (朱德), reported the truth of the war as follows:

"For the past 3 years, the communist party forces received no support in terms of weapons or funds from the Nationalist government. However, from 1941 to 1942, both the Eighth Route Army and the New Fourth Army engaged in combat with 24

Japanese divisions, which accounted for 44% of the total Japanese forces stationed in China.

During this period, the Eighth Route Army suffered 23,034 casualties and had 40,813 soldiers wounded, while the New Fourth Army had 6,775 casualties and 10,856 wounded. The fact that 75% of these casualties were of high-ranking officers indicates the intensity of the battles they fought.

Furthermore, during the same period, the communist forces inflicted more than 24,000 casualties on the Japanese and puppet troops, capturing 38,985, mostly belonging to the puppet forces. The New Fourth Army captured 15,721 rifles and 301 light machine guns, along with a significant amount of other war material during this time."

Although it is difficult to fully accept the New Fourth Army's actions at face value, there is no denying that they posed a significant challenge to the Japanese occupation forces. On the other hand, the growing strength of the New Fourth Army was undoubtedly a major headache for the Nationalist government. Therefore, they chose to cut off all support to the New Fourth Army, claiming that the aid would be used to organize and agitate the masses rather than improving their military capabilities.

Spirit of the New Fourth Army

The New Fourth Army, despite having inferior training, equipment, and salaries compared to many other Chinese military forces, was able to defeat the formidable Japanese forces in actual combat due to their unwavering determination and conviction in the anti-Japanese struggle. They were united in battle by qualities such as endurance, cunning, courage, exceptional leadership, and an indomitable spirit. Moreover, they embodied a strong sense of revolutionary consciousness within their military organization.

After the New Fourth Army entered into an agreement with the Nationalist Party and the United Front, they stopped wearing rank insignias. However, the veteran soldiers did not completely discard their red-star-shaped rank insignias but kept them carefully inside the left pocket of their military uniforms.

Figure 63: The insignia of the New Fourth Army (Xinsijun).

The training in the New Fourth Army was characterized by a 40% political component and a 60% military component. From squads to regiments, all unit formations included both military and political leaders side by side. During combat, the military leaders had full command responsibility, but for other activities, both leaders worked together as one.

At the company level and above, soldier committees were elected, ranging from company-level committees to regimental-level committees.

These committees worked in collaboration with political leaders to engage in activities beyond the military scope. This included teaching illiterate soldiers to read and write, cultural clubs, sports competitions, choir singing, propaganda efforts aimed at the civilian population, and the publication of the "Eight Points of Attention" (八軍紀), which was a record of their activities.

The "Eight Points of Attention" refers to the following eight principles that the Red Army soldiers used to demonstrate that "the Red Army is the army of the people" while marching:

1. First, when staying in civilian homes, always seek permission from the homeowners, and ensure there are no issues when departing.
2. Second, keep the homes clean.
3. Third, show kindness to the people.
4. Fourth, repay borrowed items promptly.
5. Fifth, repair anything that has been damaged.
6. Sixth, always pay for things obtained.
7. Seventh, construct latrines in safe locations away from civilian homes.
8. Eighth, do not kill prisoners or engage in looting.

These principles reflect the Red Army's commitment to treating the civilian population with respect and ensuring that their actions did not harm the people they were supposed to be protecting.

A military that adhered to such rules was unprecedented in Chinese history at the time. Failure to comply with these rules would result in being reported to the soldier committee and facing execution with the accusation of being an enemy of the people.

Furthermore, regardless of their humble origins as peasant laborers, as long as they demonstrated capability, individuals could be selected and receive education at political and military schools, ultimately becoming commanders. However, whether a commander or a soldier, their lifestyles were essentially the same.

This approach highlighted a commitment to social equality and the importance of adhering to principles and discipline within the New Fourth Army.

The New Fourth Army may have been abandoned by the Nationalist government, but they were brimming with confidence that they would lead the anti-Japanese war to victory. They were convinced that their prospects were bright, believing that the international expansion of the anti-fascist front, especially after the German defeat at Stalingrad, would ultimately result in victory for the people. The New Fourth Army also declared that they would cooperate with the Nationalist Party (Kuomintang) and other political factions until the Japanese forces were defeated and a democratic republic was established. They expressed their willingness to cooperate with all freedom-loving nations and peoples.

The anti-Japanese sentiment among the local population in the New Fourth Army's area was indeed strong. The residents had experienced repeated Japanese atrocities, with their families being massacred and their property looted during Japanese raids. They were in dire straits, realizing that the only way to survive was to fight and defeat the Japanese.

They were aware that the army protecting them was not the Nationalist government's forces that had retreated westward, nor was it the warlord armies that had exploited them. It was only the New Fourth Army that was there to protect them. Therefore, they willingly sent their sons to enlist in the New Fourth Army and paid taxes to support it.

Chapter 8
Road to Yan'an

Farewell Sentiment

Eight months ago, when I joined the Huazhong branch (華中分盟) and first met the comrades who had arrived here before me, I truly experienced what the joy of reunion meant. Having left my homeland, parted from my parents and wife, I encountered the faces of comrades I had never dreamed of seeing again on the vast expanse of China. It felt as though my life was beginning anew. But now, the thought of once again parting from these dear comrades filled me with an overwhelming sorrow. Still, since I was leaving under the orders of the organization, it was something I could not avoid. And because I was headed to Yan'an—the red capital of China and the cradle of Asian communism—I tried to depart with a hopeful heart, looking forward to new possibilities.

Nevertheless, the thought of leaving behind comrades, including Sun Dal and around ten others, who had chosen to stay here as per the organization's orders, left a heavy and melancholic feeling. In reality, those comrades who remained behind due to the organization's orders were usually the ones who obediently followed the whims of the local authorities without causing any trouble. It was the troublemakers who were all sent northward on their journey.

We were scheduled to depart on June 10, 1945. On the evening before our departure, the Enemy Operations Division of the New Fourth Army hosted a grand farewell banquet in our honor, calling it a "farewell celebration." The table was filled with an abundance of food, and suddenly, Han Myung-sam—despite his large and imposing build—began to shed tears, saying to those of us who were leaving that once we part ways, there is no telling when we might meet again. He asked that if there had ever been any misunderstandings or hurt feelings in the past, we forgive one another. His tears made me feel, once again, just how deeply painful parting can be in the human experience.

He came to me and handed me a single bullet as a farewell gift, telling me it was a parting gift. He said that since we were about to embark on a long and perilous journey, and we didn't know what emergencies might arise ahead, he wanted me to use this bullet to shoot down the enemy if necessary and ensure that I would survive and return to our hometown so we could meet again. He cried uncontrollably. I, being older than him, had always regarded him like a younger brother, loving and respecting him deeply. He had a humorous and warm personality, despite having two protruding front teeth, which led him to humorously call himself "*Tian Erbai*" (田二百, two hundred fields), encouraging comrades to use that name when addressing him.

He surely knew that our northbound unit didn't have a single gun—so what use was a bullet without a gun? When he had escaped from the Japanese army, he had hidden and carried that bullet with him, treasuring it like his own life and wearing it at his waist for self-defense. Now, giving me that bullet as a farewell gift, his gesture moved me so deeply that I embraced him and we wept together. Isn't this what true friendship is? After returning to Korea on August-15 liberation, I unexpectedly heard news of him—from a jail cell in the North Pyeongan Provincial Security Department. It was a strange twist of fate indeed—he and I were both imprisoned there under the same charge of counterrevolution, forced to undergo ideological re-education.

The next morning, before our departure, Sun Dal came to me, firmly grasped my hand, and said with a bright smile, "Use the knowledge you have for the benefit of the proletariat." Then he looked at me warmly. Following him, Lee Deok-moo also expressed his desire, "Let's return to our homeland and meet again to fulfill the revolutionary tasks." (It is said that Sun Dal and Lee Deok-moo held important positions in North Korea after liberation.)

The northbound unit was divided into three divisions under the command of Kim Woong. Each division consisted of 18 members, totaling around 50 people, who carried their bags and set out. The five individuals heading to Yan'an also joined the northbound unit and were organized to travel together until they reached Taihang Mountains, where the Military and Political Academy was located. As I watched

Kim Woong lead the way, I could sense his satisfaction. It was only natural for him to feel pride in leading a vanguard unit of 50-60 revolutionary comrades, who were the seeds of the revolution. Furthermore, his physical appearance was refined and dignified, likely the result of his long military and revolutionary experience. I wondered if I could become like him through training and discipline here. It seemed that both Shin Sang-cho and Shim Young-soon also trusted Kim Woong. Anyone could feel the revolutionary passion emanating from him.

The appointment of squad leaders for the three squads was clearly made with political considerations in mind. Shim Young-soon was appointed leader of the 1st squad, Shin Sang-cho the 2nd, and I was appointed leader of the 3rd. Giving intellectuals a title or position was the only way to keep them from complaining. In fact, titles were the most effective way to bind intellectuals. Comrades Shim and Shin, who had been loudly demanding to be sent to Chongqing, stopped complaining entirely once they became squad leaders, and instead began urging us to hurry on our way to Yan'an.

At that time, we believed that a new holy land would open up only if we went to Yan'an and Taihang Mountains. There was no atmosphere of discipline and learning as in Huazhong branch. We believed in fighting against the Japanese as volunteer soldiers with guns. Kim Woong probably knew a lot about the Military Academy in Taihang Mountains, but he didn't explain much. He simply encouraged us to take pride in becoming soldiers of justice. He took care of us with the utmost convenience and did not spare words of encouragement. He even referred to us as comrades in the revolution.

Map 64: Chinese Communist Forces Marching Toward Yan'an (1934-1935).

Liberation of Korea

On the way to Yan'an, many Japanese military blockades had been set up, so we had to be escorted by the Eighth Route Army when passing through this area. During these times, we had to march under the cover of darkness, hiding in local villages during the day and waiting. Sometimes we would take detours through rural roads to avoid Japanese checkpoints. Kim Woong handled these situations skillfully with his fluent Chinese, which only strengthened our trust in him. During the march, our meals mainly consisted of noodles we made ourselves using the flour, salt, and forage provided by the local communist party.

Preparing meals and finding a place to sleep after a day of marching was quite challenging. This responsibility fell entirely on the shoulders of the platoon leaders. Providing meals three times a day while on the move was indeed a strenuous task. Furthermore, finding suitable sleeping arrangements was equally important. After arriving at a village, some of us would work on securing food while others sought out a place to sleep.

The most comfortable option was to remove the front gate of a local house and use it as a makeshift bed frame, elevating us above the ground. We could then lie on top of it, looking up at the sky. However, not all villages had suitable gates to use, so in some cases, we had no choice but to sleep directly on the bare ground.

Despite these challenges, we were prepared to endure mosquito bites during the summer, and, above all, the most painful part was the inability to wash off the sweat and dust that clung to our bodies while marching. Nevertheless, we faced these hardships with a positive attitude. After all, Yan'an was not just any place in communist China; it was the headquarters of Korean Independence Alliance and the home of experienced revolutionary leaders. Thinking about this made our journey to Yan'an feel lighter and more enjoyable.

On the way to Yan'an lay the Taihang Mountains, where the Military and Political Academy was located. We were told that going there was truly an honor. However, if we encountered Japanese blockade lines along the way, we had to wait several days depending on the situation of the Eighth Route Army troops escorting us. If we came upon a river during the march, we often had to wait several days before crossing. We also had to rest when it rained—since it was summer, if it rained for days, we had to wait until the weather cleared. Gradually, we grew weary from it all.

However, the most painful aspect of our journey was the constant thirst. Walking under the scorching sun made us sweat profusely and left us parched with thirst. Yet, in Chinese territory, we couldn't drink water freely wherever we wanted. We could only drink water when it was provided during mealtimes, and we couldn't carry water containers with us during the march. So, we often found ourselves without water.

These hardships were physical in nature, but our passion for independence and our determination allowed us to endure them. We were filled with hope that by reaching Yan'an or the Taihang Mountains, we could contribute meaningfully as revolutionary comrades.

On the night of August 13th, Kim Woong urgently summoned the three division leaders. He had received reports from the Eighth Route Army that the movements of the Japanese forces near Kaifeng (開封) were unusual. It appeared that the Japanese were gathering in Kaifeng. Based on this information, Kim Woong decided that we should move about 20 *li* (10 kilometers) to the rear of the enemy lines, toward the village where the headquarters of the Eighth Route Army was situated, before sunrise the next day.

We began our march at 3 a.m. the following morning, cutting through the dawn air. As we neared Kaifeng, we could see many Eighth Route Army soldiers maintaining vigilant guard positions.

It was here that we experienced the long-awaited liberation of August 15. Due to the lack of proper communication facilities, we spent August 15 itself unaware of what had happened. Only on the morning of the 16th did we learn through a broadcast that the Emperor of Japan had unconditionally surrendered. How long we had waited for this moment! What joyous news it was! On this day, surely our fellow countrymen back home were raising the Korean national flag (太極旗, Taegeukgi) high in their hands, shouting cries of freedom. I could almost hear the triumphant chants of "Manse!" echoing in my ears. We, too, gathered together and shouted 'Long live Korean independence!' three times with great vigor.

Now that the long-awaited day had finally come, it felt as though there was much work ahead of us. That day, we were treated to a generous meal.

Figure 65: Hirohito's surrender speech.

Word came that two Japanese prisoners of war belonging to the Japanese Liberation Alliance in the Kaifeng area had committed suicide. Kim Woong, showing no emotion on his face, calmly said,

"Our homeland has been liberated. The Japanese will retreat from our land, but a new war is about to break out on the Chinese mainland. Chiang Kai-shek has issued a statement declaring Wang Jingwei's puppet troops to be part of the Nationalist army and has ordered that Japanese forces surrender only to the Kuomintang. Meanwhile, Lin Biao's Communist troops have entered Manchuria—civil war has already begun in China. The delegation bound for Yan'an will leave tomorrow, and those going to the Military and Political Academy should depart for the Taihang Mountains."

There was no joy of liberation visible on his face—only a solemn determination, as if he were preparing for the beginning of yet another struggle. That night, I couldn't sleep. I truly felt like

"I had been born again into a new world.
In the midst of this historic upheaval, where am I headed?
Am I supposed to go to Yan'an and become an unlikely communist?"

At this moment, it felt like

"I couldn't escape the destiny that lay ahead of me as a communist."

Passing through the Loess Plateau

As we headed north, we entered the Shanxi Province (山西省), and we encountered the Loess Plateau (黃土地帶). Loess is fine sand carried by the wind from Central Asia's desert regions, accumulating over time to form what's known as the loess layer. The houses in this area were all cave dwellings, dug into the hillsides with openings shaped like a dome and windows at the front to let in sunlight. Due to the sedimentary nature of the loess, these caves were sturdy and resistant to collapse, keeping dust at bay and maintaining a clean environment. Here, we used wooden beds, and a corner of the cave served as a kitchen. Kim Woong mentioned that even Mao Zedong lived in a cave dwelling in Yan'an. Kim Woong stressed that we must arrive in Yan'an by August 29th, so we hastened our journey to Yan'an.

Now, on the road ahead, there were no more Japanese army pillboxes; instead, all the areas were base zones of the Eighth Route Army, so we were able to walk 70 to 80 *li* (about 35–40 km) a day with ease. Everywhere we went, there were nothing but crumbling mud-brack houses or cave dwellings dug into hillsides. Occasionally, a donkey would pass along a path between fields, carrying bundles of harvested barley. Once, while crossing a mountain ridge, I was surprised to see unusually large jujubes growing on a jujube tree — they looked as big as small apples in our country. I tried one or two, and they tasted excellent. China is so vast that I hadn't known there were famous jujube-producing regions like this.

The impoverished living conditions of these peasants were no different from what I had witnessed in Huazhong. Given their low productivity and underdeveloped circumstances, it was understandable that they had no choice but to embrace communism as a means of survival. Consequently, many rebel groups in China advocated policies such as tax exemptions or the equitable redistribution of land, gaining control over regions for a time. Hong Xiuquan (洪秀全), for instance, had distributed land to peasants, promising to build a society where they wouldn't go hungry and could live comfortably, leading to the establishment of the Taiping Heavenly Kingdom (太平天國) at one point. Once again, I realized that China's future lay in addressing this issue of impoverished peasants.

Figure 66: Hong Xiuquan (1814–1864),and the imperial jade seal of the Taiping Heavenly Kingdom (太平天國).

(Editor's Note: Hong Xiuquan was a religious figure and revolutionary of the Qing Dynasty. Born in Guangdong Province (廣東省), he founded the Taiping Heavenly Kingdom (太平天國)—a theocratic state influenced by Protestant Christianity—and led a rebellion against the Qing regime. Hong Xiuquan studied the Bible and Christian doctrine under Isaac Roberts, an American Baptist missionary.)

As we passed through a somewhat larger village, I noticed a line of vendors selling "*soji*" (小鷄: a dish made by deep-frying whole chickens in oil) along the road. Kim Woong bought some of these *soji* and handed one to each of us. At that moment, I thought of that greasy *soji* as one of the joys brought by liberation, and I savored it so deliciously that I can't forget that memory even now. Also, it was the first time I had walked along such a big road since fleeing from the Japanese army. I thought, "Now that we're liberated, can't we stroll through the city?" I questioned, deeply experiencing the joy of liberation.

Korean Volunteer Army

Kim Woong, who had been honing his body as a revolutionary in China for a long time, urged us to expedite our journey to Yan'an. However, he remained completely silent. Communists did not discuss their past experiences, likely because it could expose them, and also because the communist movement valued secrecy in organizing above all else. We only discovered Kim Woong's high rank in the Korean Independence Alliance when we arrived at Taihang Mountains. As the time to reach Yan'an was pressing, he proposed that we first visit the Taihang Military and Political Academy, which was situated along the way.

Our delegation of five members arrived at the Taihang Military and Political Academy on August 26th. Upon our arrival, we learned that the Korean Volunteer Army of the Military Academy was set to march towards our homeland in commemoration of the "National Humiliation

Day" on the August 29th. The atmosphere was highly charged and enthusiastic. Additionally, the representative conference originally scheduled to be held in Yan'an was naturally postponed indefinitely due to the liberation. Consequently, the five of us became part of the Korean Volunteer Army on that day.

In Taihang Mountains, there were many high-ranking officials and seasoned members of the Military Academy, but Kim Woong stood out without a doubt. He often appeared to be the foremost figure, even carrying himself like the leader. With a gentle smile on his face, he spoke proudly about his illustrious history in the revolutionary movement, as if he were showcasing his shining past. We learned that Mu Jeong and Choi Chang-ik were staying in Yan'an, and they had likely already departed on their mission to return to our homeland.

The next day, we were to set out as members of the Korean Volunteer Army toward our newly liberated homeland. That evening, Yi Ik-sung came to the cave dwelling where we were staying. With a very cheerful expression, he praised our efforts and confidently asserted that "the Korean Independence Alliance would surely take power upon returning to Korea." He also said that our leader, Mu Jeong, had made great contributions to the Chinese communist party through his long revolutionary activities in China, and thus, it was only natural and just that he would be entrusted with power with the support of the Chinese communist party. He went on to say that our journey from Huazhong (Central China) to this place and our enlistment in the Korean Volunteer Army was a stroke of luck, and we had seized a great opportunity.

Then, he mentioned that a man named Kim Sarang (金史良), the writer, had recently arrived here and was currently under house arrest, writing a statement of self-reflection. Yi criticized him as an opportunist.

That night, I couldn't help but ponder over his words. It was clear that they regarded us as stepchildren and criticized us as people who showed up at a well-prepared dinner table with only spoons in our hands. Furthermore, it became evident that there had been no actual communication between the headquarters of the Korean Volunteer Army and the Huazhong Branch. Yi mentioned that Kim Woong from Huazhong had led us, four student soldiers, to Taihang Mountains. I wondered who these people were and why they were looking for us.

The glances of the other members towards us were also quite chilly. They seemed to be questioning whether we, who had joined the Korean Volunteer Army without any training and at the last moment, were just trying to reap the benefits of their hard work.

It was here that I first began to think about the concept of "power." Until then, under Japanese colonial rule, I had always believed that "our path to independence and revolution was a matter of conscience, a way to fulfill our duty to our nation." The idea of seizing political power had never crossed my mind, not even in my dreams.

However, the members here, without exception, were convinced that power was now in the hands of Mu Jeong, and they were all excited about finding a place for themselves in this new regime. I couldn't help but feel a sense of disgust. "What exactly did it mean to seize political power?" To me, political power should naturally arise from the will of the people, and the idea of an individual seizing it by force was incomprehensible.

Among the volunteers preparing for the expedition, there were both former soldiers and civilians. Their reverence for Mu Jeong reached a level of personal devotion, and they referred to him as the "Great leader Comrade Mu Jeong." The first lines of the Volunteer Army's anthem, sung daily, began with "With one heart and one mind, firmly united, fighting for the nation... Comrade Mu Jeong shows us the way to the liberation and independence of our homeland..."

It was evident that they were all suffering from severe malnutrition, and their faces showed signs of exhaustion, with a yellowish complexion.

Although the Military and Political Academy provided military knowledge and political education, it was said that the focus at the time was on productive labor activities.

A severe drought that swept through the Huabei (North China) region in 1943 significantly reduced agricultural output in Communist-controlled areas, making it extremely difficult even for the Eighth Route Army to supply its growing combat forces.

Therefore, the school believed it was not right to rely unconditionally on food supplies from the Chinese communist areas. As a result, the Korean Independence Alliance launched a large-scale production campaign to solve the food problem independently.

Figure 67: General Mu Jeong – A Tragic Korean Revolutionary.

These instructions were, of course, determined by Mu Jeong, who had a good understanding of the communist situation. Furthermore, the reason for Mu Jeong and his group's strong emphasis on production campaigns was to cultivate the communist party spirit among the members. They believed that in an environment where they couldn't engage in direct combat against the Japanese army but had to struggle against nature, achieving victory in this natural struggle was essential for strengthening their party spirit. In other words, they thought that without a strong party spirit, they wouldn't be able to endure the rigors of agricultural activities. Therefore, Mu Jeong and his group adopted the slogan "Labor Heroes" and began clearing and cultivating the hills behind the Military and Political Academy, known as Oji Mountain .

Oji Mountain was a type of rocky mountain commonly found in the northwestern regions of China, with an elevation of about 800 to 1,000 meters. The members of the Korean Volunteer Army cultivated this rugged mountain using primitive farming tools, with the same fighting spirit they used to defeat the Japanese army. They planted potatoes and corn to meet their own food needs. As a result, they were able to be entirely self-sufficient in food, without receiving a single grain of barley from the Eighth Route Army.

This would have been utterly impossible without the burning passion of revolutionary zeal. By accomplishing this task, the soldiers were able to personally experience the hardship of the revolutionary path, and it deepened their conviction that only by winning this struggle could the revolution be achieved.

I soon came to understand that the firm revolutionary determination among the members of the Korean Independence Alliance stemmed not only from their absolute trust in Mu Jeong, but also from the victory they achieved through this campaign of productive labor.

In this way, they were clearly worn out from intense labor and deprived of proper nutritional support.

And yet, didn't we, who came from the Huazhong Branch, simply eat whatever the New Fourth Army gave us, and even complain and clamor for more when it wasn't enough?

I realized then that there was a fundamental difference in attitude between them and us when it came to accomplishing the revolution. That was why they looked down on us with contempt and regarded us as shameless newcomers who had joined their honored ranks at the last moment.

They considered the "Victory of Oji Mountain Cultivation" to be their own proud achievement, just as the Chinese Communist Party boasted of the 25,000-*li* Long March.

I came to the Military and Political Academy at Taihang Mountains with a single hope, but as I observed the atmosphere and the comrades at Taihang Mountains, I began to feel that this might not be the right place for me. I realized that the path of revolution involved extreme hardships such as personal devotion, seizing power, mutual criticism, mutual surveillance, and ideological transformation. It became clear to me that I could not become a revolutionary. I even feared that I might eventually be coerced into something I did not desire. Mu Jeong's rise to power had no connection to me. The people at this place appeared to be all opportunists who followed Mu Jeong's orders, hoping to take positions of authority one by one when he came to power.

I found the atmosphere at Taihang Mountains to be repulsive. However, I couldn't find an alternative place to go. My destiny had already turned towards the path of revolution, and all I wanted was to act in a way that wouldn't bring shame to my nation and conscience. I didn't want to betray my people or the honor of being a Korean, and if the only path to achieve that was through communism, I didn't want to betray communism either. But no matter how hard I thought about it, the correct path didn't seem like the path of communism to me.

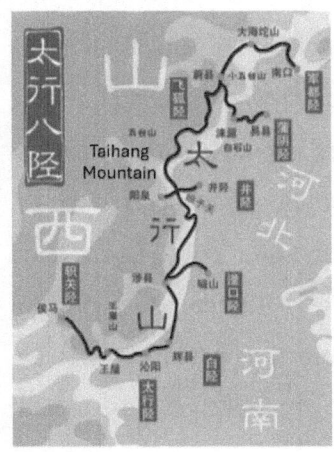

Map 68: Taihang Mountain Range

217

Chapter 9

From Taihang Mountain to Fengtian

Towards Manchuria

The Korean Volunteer Army set off towards Taihang Mountains on September 29th, 1945. The Volunteer Army was organized into two battalions. The commander of the 1st Battalion was Yi Ik-sung (李益成), and the political director was Park Il-woo (朴一禹, who later became a prominent figure during the 6-25 Korean War). The organization of the 2nd Battalion was not known. The 1st Battalion was divided into three platoons, and each platoon was further divided into three squads, making the total strength of the battalion around 80 soldiers. I was part of the 1st Battalion, 3rd Platoon, 3rd Squad, along with Shim Young-soon. Each squad was armed with a machine gun and rifles. Additionally, there were elderly civilians and non-combatants who joined us when we departed from Taihang Mountains, so the total number of people was close to 200.

Moreover, we were informed that various detachments from different regions were also launching expeditions into Manchuria.

My squad leader was a man named Hwang (黃), a former student soldier, who had attended the preparatory course at Waseda University, my alma mater. He was four years younger than I was.

Given that he had risen to the position of squad leader as an intellectual, one could easily infer how strong his loyalty to the Party must have been. From the beginning, however, his attitude toward me was cold and watchful, as if he were constantly monitoring me. He persistently gave me a hard time and treated me like a thorn in his side, though I had no idea why.

Our squad had a single machine gun, and it was almost always Shim Young-soon and I who had to carry it during the grueling marches.

Figure 69: Yi Ik-sung   Figure 70: Park Il-woo

At this time, it seemed that Kim Woong was the overall commander of our advancing Volunteer Army. Kim Woong would occasionally look at Shim Young-soon and me while we were marching and let out a mocking laugh, clearly indicating that this place was different from Huazhong, and we should be prepared for some hardships. Kim Woong informed us that Manchuria had already been occupied by Soviet forces.

Additionally, General Ju De (朱德), the overall commander of the Eighth Route Army, had initiated an advance toward Manchuria, and all Volunteer Army units were to assemble in Fengtian (奉天, now Shenyang). Despite the challenges, I encouraged myself to endure and make it to Fengtian, as the present place was relatively close to both Fengtian and Korean territory, no matter what challenges lay ahead.

The Volunteer Army chose a route that would avoid conflicts with the Japanese army, which still held control over Beijing and Tianjin. The Volunteer Army planned to cross the railway connecting Zhangjiakou (張家口) to Fengtian, bypassing Beijing, and enter Manchuria via Chengde (承德). However, when the Volunteer Army reached a village near Xuanhua (宣化), they found that Japanese army units from Zhangjiakou were using the railway to move toward Beijing, making it impossible for them to cross.

The Volunteer Army stayed in the area for about ten days, hoping for an opportunity to cross the railway, but the Japanese army maintained strict security, and no chance presented itself. They realized they couldn't delay any longer and decided to change their course, heading southward into Hebei Province (河北省).

Map 71: Formation, Movements, and Anti-Japanese Activities of the
Korean Volunteer Corps, and Their Post-Liberation Routes to
Manchuria and Korea

During our stay in the village near Xuanhua for about ten days, we
studied Mao Zedong's "New Democracy" or "United Government
Theory" and "Revolutionary Theory" while waiting. We received news
that during this time, Japanese Army General Anami Korechika
(阿南惟幾), who represented the Japanese military dictatorship, had
committed suicide. Additionally, we learned that Korea had been
granted independence according to the Cairo Declaration, and Soviet
troops had already advanced into the northern Korean territory.

With the Japanese military's collapse and changing circumstances in
our homeland, we, the Volunteer Army, found ourselves trapped in rural

221

isolation for several weeks, losing our freedom of movement. This situation was a source of great anxiety for us.

Figure 72: General Anami Korechika.

Furthermore, this was one of the most impoverished areas in China, so our meals consisted of narrow grains of rice mixed with sand and dirt. We had to thresh the rice in a courtyard made of mud, and it was so sandy that nearly half of the rice consisted of dirt and sand. We would turn this into a porridge, but at times it was hard to tell whether we were eating porridge or just consuming dirt. During these times, we longed for wheat flour so much. At least wheat flour didn't contain sand.

The Korean Volunteer Army changed its route and headed south instead of entering Manchuria via Inner Mongolia. However, the Japanese forces' pillboxes (bunkers) were completely deserted, and not a single enemy soldier could be seen. Reportedly, some of the Japanese troops who had been stationed in the area had even surrendered to the Eighth Route Army.

The Volunteer Army marched more than 100 *li* (about 50 km) a day through uninhabited zones, pushing through the area between Beijing and Tianjin, and then hastened toward Manchuria via Sankakuan Pass.

At times, they were able to enjoy the taste of freedom by catching and eating roasted pigs, thanks to the kindness of the Eighth Route Army. On some days, they even received distributions of Chenmen (high-quality British cigarettes). The southern part of Hebei Province (河北省) was relatively affluent as an agriculturally productive area in China, and it had long been under the rule of the Communist Party, which might explain the generous distributions provided to the Volunteer Army. They received supplies such as military uniforms from the Eighth Route Army, as well as everyday items like toothpaste. They were even given a type of cigarette called "Ukko (旭光)" that the Japanese soldiers used to smoke.

Like many Eighth Route Army soldiers, some of the Volunteer Army members were also heading towards Manchuria through Sankakuan. One day, I received a summons from my squad leader. On that night, our mission was to perform a propaganda operation near the Japanese guard station at pillbox.

With the protection of fellow Volunteer Army members, I approached within 50 meters of the guard station. It was a quiet midnight, and I could see the guard station illuminated by the moonlight. I dug a trench to hide my body, and the Volunteer Army soldiers who were providing cover were positioned 20 meters behind me. I shouted loudly toward the Japanese guard station, of course, in Japanese.

"Dear Japanese soldiers! Your homeland, Japan, has surrendered. If you wish to return to your home alive, drop your weapons and come out to us. This place is under the jurisdiction of the Korean Independence Alliance, and we will treat you warmly as fellow countrymen. If you stay there, you will be subjected to attacks by the Eighth Route Army. We hope you will surrender to us as soon as possible."

However, there was no response from the Japanese soldiers in the pillbox.

The following night, captain Hwang Bun-deok convened a platoon meeting for the third platoon. The platoon leader suggested self-criticism, which meant that one would reflect on whether their thoughts and actions were aligned with the interests of the masses, and this reflection would be subjected to criticism from comrades to determine its objectivity and whether it was truthful or counter revolutionary.

The comrades were sitting around me under the candlelight, and I could feel all sharp eyes focused on me. It was then that the platoon leader instructed me to engage in self-criticism. I replied that I had nothing to criticize. At that moment, one comrade looked at me and suggested that I should open the ammunition clip I was carrying. Thus, I opened the clip, only to find that the 50 rounds of ammunition that should have been there were missing, and the clip was empty!

I was so surprised by this unexpected turn of events that I could only be bewildered. Losing ammunition, especially something more precious than our lives during the revolutionary struggle, was a grave offense, and I was not only ashamed but also faced the risk of execution for counter-revolutionary charges. I insisted that I had not discarded the ammunition and had no idea when it had disappeared.

At that moment, my comrades cast cold glances at me, criticizing me as a counter-revolutionary element, a typical intellectual, and the one responsible for reducing the fighting strength of the Volunteer Army. I admitted my mistake, attributing it to carelessness, and promised that I would never make such a mistake again, requesting leniency in dealing with the matter.

However, to my surprise, Huang Bun-doek, who had always been harsh and tormenting toward me, now looked at me with a more compassionate expression. He suggested that we consider it a lesson learned and forgive, indicating that he might have realized his own faults. He even proposed not reporting it to the higher-ups.

The incident of the missing ammunition troubled me deeply. I couldn't believe that I had lost the ammunition. It seemed impossible for the loaded magazine to open by itself. Moreover, if it had opened and all the bullets had fallen out, how could I not have noticed it? It was a significant number of bullets, and the weight of the magazine would have felt noticeably lighter.

Furthermore, I questioned how the squad leader could have known about my ammunition loss before I did. It was also unsettling that, despite many comrades who could speak Japanese, why I was singled out for the propaganda mission the previous night. These thoughts left me feeling uncomfortable.

I was not part of the orthodox Taihang Mountains faction within the Korean Volunteer Army. But even so, for them to set a trap and torment me — that is nothing but malicious trickery, not the righteous path of revolution between comrades, is it? In the communist party, there were many cases where they would entrap those, they found undesirable and then purge them.

Thinking about how so many of the early revolutionary comrades were purged in this way during Stalin's dictatorship sent chills down my spine.

On the other hand, I tried to rationalize this incident in a different way. I wanted to believe that it might have been a staged act to test my loyalty, a measure taken to mold me into a dedicated Korean Volunteer Army member. We were on the verge of advancing towards our homeland, and if, as they claimed, Mu Jeong came to power and established a communist state, there was no doubt about it. By facing adversity in my current situation and quietly carrying out my duties, I believed I was contributing to the communist society and adapting to it.

However, before being drafted as a student soldier in January 1944, I had never imagined that my homeland would become a communist state. The Korean Independence Alliance claimed to be building a democratic republic, but it was merely a transitional republic on the path to constructing a communist state, with the leading class of the time holding power in the republic. I was disillusioned by the idea (政綱) of building a democratic republic and working in the Korean Volunteer Army, fearing that I would eventually be heading down a self-destructive path. With a heavy heart and a machine gun in hand, I continued my journey toward my homeland.

Sankakuan

The Korean Volunteer Army chose a route through the middle of Beijing and Tianjin and arrived in Yuktan (Okcheon 玉田), Huabei Province (North China). In Huabei, you could see settlements established by fellow countrymen. These Koreans had emigrated to North China (Huabei) and Manchuria, and through relentless effort, they reclaimed land and converted it into wet rice fields, cultivating rice. Wherever there were Koreans, there were always rice paddies; and where there were rice paddies, there were always Korean compatriots. In the Korean villages, it was harvesting season, and stacks of rice sheaves were piled high — it was clear that it had been a bountiful year. One could only imagine how much hardship they had endured to dig irrigation channels and bring water to what had once been dry fields.

I lived in the border area of the Gyeongui Line railway in Korea when I was young, and I witnessed countless heartbreaking scenes of impoverished peasants being exploited by Japanese colonizers, losing their land and having to leave their hometowns with baskets on their backs to emigrate to Manchuria or the northern areas. Now, thinking that their hard work has paid off and they can enjoy a full meal of white rice, it filled me with a warm and contented feeling.

The Korean Volunteer Army stayed in a Korean village near Yuktan, where they were warmly welcomed with a bowl of freshly cooked rice and kimchi provided by the villagers. I could truly feel in my bones that blood is thicker than water.

The Eighth Route Army gave the Volunteer Army a significant gift in Yuktan — military currency that we could use once we entered Manchuria. It was a considerable amount. At the time, the fixed exchange rate between regular Chinese currency and military currency was 10 to 1, but Chinese civilians refused to exchange at that rate, and the military currency was not widely accepted at all.

With the Nationalist currency, you could buy anything, but the red military currency issued by the Eighth Route Army was generally shunned by the public. This was because many people believed that, although the Eighth Route Army was presently in control at the moment, Nationalist forces would soon take over.

However, if you were lucky, you could exchange it for the currency of the Korean provisional government or even threaten with a gun to make them exchange it for Nationalist Party currency. In any case, we were very pleased that the military currency issued by the Chinese communists could be used as soon as we entered Manchuria. Distributing military currency to us in this way was undoubtedly part of the clever economic policy of the Chinese communists in Manchuria to circulate military currency.

From Yukan to Sankakuan was not a very long journey. As we marched, seeing the faces of our fellow countrymen made us happy, and seeing stacks of rice straw at every stop made us even more content. The officers gathered and expected that once we crossed Sankakuan, we would encounter the disciplined and courageous red army of the Soviet

Union. They hoped that this red army, which had annihilated the Japanese Kwantung Army and liberated oppressed nations, would be an exemplary force with neat appearances. Now, the members of the Korean Volunteer Army not only heard about the red army but also had to learn from them once we met them.

Figure 73: Sankakuan.

However, as we crossed Sankakuan, we encountered the Soviet army that turned out to be one of the most brutal and aggressive forces one could find in the world. The atrocities committed by the Soviet army in various places quickly became evident, and the mouths of our officers were sealed shut. It was a shocking realization that the red army, like the Japanese imperial army, was a military force of a totalitarian state, and there was little difference in their heinous acts of murder, plunder, and rape.

I met Heo Gab (許鉀) at Sankakuan, who happened to be my fellow student from Waseda University's history department. Heo Gab had graduated from Sophia University (上智大學)'s department of arts and had transferred to Waseda as an undergraduate student. Seeing me in the uniform of the Korean Volunteer Army with a gun, he was surprised but also looked at me with admiration. He told me that he had lived in Jilin (吉林), Manchuria, and had managed to evade being conscripted as a student soldier. He had hidden himself and, against his parents' strong objections, escaped to join the Korean Independence movement on the eve of liberation, making his way here in secrecy.

While attempting to pass through Sankakuan, he learned that Japan had surrendered sooner than expected, and with the liberation, he had joined the Korean Independence Alliance there. He was now serving in a position at the Sankakuan (Shanhaiguan) judge office, providing support to fellow Koreans. He spoke emphatically:

"Right now, due to the Yalta agreement, Soviet and American troops have entered Korea and are each conducting military administrations, divided by the 38th parallel. In South Korea, the political landscape is split between the left and the right, and the situation is extremely unstable and unclear. That's why conscientious Korean intellectuals must strengthen their forces within the Korean Independence Alliance and march into the homeland to build a new Korea. Only strength can bring glory to our nation, and that is why I have joined the Korean Volunteer Army, to serve and wait for the right time."

Heo Gab had already joined the Korean Volunteer Army, and he believed that he would eventually be entrusted with a high position and have a bright future ahead. He seemed envious of me. I knew that he originally had a heroic and opportunistic nature. How could I honestly confide in him about the Korean Independence Movement and the dilemmas I was facing now? I could only silently disdain him as an opportunist. I asked myself:

"Did he truly believe that he could dedicate himself to the class interests of the working masses and the construction of a communist society?
Did he understand that the path of revolution is long and arduous, ultimately leading one to dig their own grave?"

These were the questions I silently pondered as we parted ways, being cautious in these times of historical upheaval.

As he turned away, he stopped me and asked me to convey to his parents in Jilin that he had met me at Sankakuan. He even wrote down the address of his parents' home in Jilin for me.

Parting ways with Heo Gab, I walked alone, lost in thought. At the current moment of the liberation, I couldn't be sure if the glorious path for our homeland was indeed the path of the independence movement as Heo Gab believed. However, I couldn't help but wonder when Heo Gab,

231

who mentioned that his father was a Christian elder, had become a communist. Had he been swayed by the independence movement's policy of a united front? I believed that intellectuals embracing communism was merely a temporary illusion.

Emerging from my contemplations, I suddenly found myself before the majestic Great Wall (萬里長城) of China. I couldn't help but wonder how much toil and labor had gone into constructing this wall. It seemed that human effort knew no bounds. How many impoverished peasants must have perished in its construction! It reminded me of the heartbreaking story of Meng Jiangnu (孟姜女), who wept bitterly for her husband's death during the construction of the wall. The section of the Great Wall that stretched from Sankakuan was built during the Ming dynasty (明王朝), and unlike other parts with large gateways, this section allowed entry into Manchuria through a narrow pass right next to the wall. Gazing at the winding structure of the wall, my emotions were overwhelming.

Figure 74: The Great Wall of China (萬里長城).

Indeed, history often presents us with ironic twists. The construction of the Great Wall of China, a colossal feat that endures as a world-renowned monument, started as an endeavor under the emperor Qin Shi Huang (秦始皇). However, due to adverse weather conditions and the strict discipline imposed by Qin (秦)'s rule, the workers, led by Qin general Jin Sheng (陣勝) and his aide Wu Guang (吳廣), found themselves unable to meet their deadlines and faced execution as a result. Faced with this dire situation, they chose to rebel rather than accept their fate, ultimately leading to the downfall of the Qin (秦) dynasty. Ironically, while the construction of the wall contributed to the fall of the Qin dynasty, it remains an enduring symbol of China's rich history and heritage, a testament to the resilience and determination of the human spirit.

Xinfangzi

The weather was getting colder, pushing winter ahead. The march continued from Sankakuan, passing through to Jinzhou (錦州), and we kept hearing and witnessing the atrocities committed by the Soviet forces. Along the way, we saw people being harassed and labeled as Japanese, and we even witnessed Japanese women collapsing and dying on the roadside.

It was in Jinzhou that the Volunteer Army first used horse-drawn wagons for transportation. This was the first time I had used any form of transportation in Chinese territory, aside from when I was taken as a prisoner of war by the Red Army and transported to their base, excluding the donkey I rode on at the time.

In Manchuria, horse-drawn wagons were the main form of public transportation. Originally, wagon wheels were made of wood and made creaking sounds, but I noticed that all the wheels had been replaced with automobile tires. For the coachmen, replacing the wooden wheels with rubber tires on their wagons—their only means of livelihood—had been a lifelong dream. When liberation came, the first thing they did was to loot various vehicles previously used by the Japanese and take the tires to install on their own wagons. Because of this, whenever they looked at the rubber wheels on their wagons, they rejoiced, calling them gifts brought by liberation.

The Volunteer Army split up and rode several horse-drawn wagons, cheerfully listening to the sound of horses' hooves as they set off toward Fengtian (奉天). However, upon arriving in Fengtian, the Soviet military command stationed there did not permit the entry of the Volunteer Army into the city. With no other choice, the Volunteer Army had to stay in a Korean village near Fengtian, called Xinfangzi (新坊子). At that time, Xinfangzi was the last stop on the Jingfeng (Beijing–Fengtian) railway line. Every time a train arrived in Xinfangzi, many Korean refugees would disembark, so the plaza in front of the station was lined with makeshift eateries selling food. There was also a bustling market where all sorts of goods looted from Japanese army warehouses were bought and sold.

Map 75: Railway Lines in the Manchurian Region, 1945.

This was the first time we bought and ate rice cakes, along with some boiled pork. We stayed in this place for three days, during which I exchanged the cheap Eighth Route Army military notes given to us for Manchurian currency and used it to buy a set of thickly woven underwear, which was part of the military supplies for the Japanese Kwantung Army. Having this clothing greatly helped me to endure the severe cold of that year.

The streets of Xinfangzi were very calm. This was because the local self-governing committee, to prevent acts of looting and rape by Soviet soldiers, had collected money in advance from the villagers and purchased Japanese women to offer them as comfort women to the Soviets. I deeply realized once again that history repeats itself. As the Japanese army had invaded Manchuria and China early, committing

235

unspeakable atrocities such as rape that enraged the entire world, now they were facing retribution at the hands of the Soviet army.

When the frail Japanese women were subjected to atrocities by the Soviet soldiers, who behaved like starving beasts, I wondered whether they thought they were paying the price for the sins committed by those who came before them in the war. In any case, I thought to myself that if one goes to war, one must win—one must never lose. Every time I saw those women trembling in the cold by the roadside, forced to serve Soviet soldiers, I couldn't help but feel a sense of pity, even though they had once been the enemy.

Xinfangzi was a place where refugees from various regions gathered, and it was bustling with activity. There was a cafe that employed Korean women to sell alcohol. When I saw Independence Alliance leaders enjoying drinks at the cafe with the women, I couldn't help but be surprised that even these cold-blooded officials had moments of romance. After wandering in remote parts of China for several years, suffering from hunger, I realized that having a drink to ease the accumulated hardships was only natural. I felt deeply moved by the fact that all of this was a gift brought by liberation.

Sim Yeong-soon invited me to have bulgogi, though I wasn't sure how he had managed to exchange military money. He told me not to ask about the source of the money, but it was clear he had likely gone into a Chinese shop and forced the exchange at gunpoint. Together, we had beef bulgogi and plenty of alcohol for the first time, in the main room of a makeshift Korean-run cafe. It felt great to finally have a proper drink after so long. Even more so, because from here, Andong (安東) was not too far. And once you cross the Yalu River (鴨綠江) from Andong, isn't that home soil? Thinking that I would soon be able to set foot in my homeland made me feel as if I could fly.

November 6th, 1945, was the eve of Socialist Revolution Day, commemorating the completion of the October Revolution in the Soviet Union. On this day, the members of the Korean Volunteer Army and the Korean Independence Alliance gathered in the large square of Xinfangzi. There was an improvised stage set up, and behind the stage, a large banner read "[Korean Independence Alliance - 3rd Representative Congress]." The assembled crowd, composed of those who had some connection to the Independence Alliance, numbered roughly around 500 people. Although it was called a representative congress, it was more like a mass meeting rather than an event for elected representatives.

During this congress, it was stated that as liberated members of the Korean Independence Alliance, they would decide on the direction to move forward. However, the decisions appeared to have already been made among the leaders, and the congress served to boost morale and give directives for action. Figures like Mu Jeong and Kim Du-bong were not present, indicating that they had likely already entered Korea. Speeches by individuals like Choi Chang-ik, Han Bin, Kim Chang-man, and Heo Jeong-suk, during this assembly, contributed to an increasingly revolutionary atmosphere. The leaders appeared to be excited as they approached their entry into Korea, and those giving speeches emphasized that the period ahead would be a challenging struggle to complete the revolution.

The directives from this congress included the division of the Volunteer Army into three units. The 1st unit would consist of older veterans who were to immediately enter Korea and engage in revolutionary activities. The 3rd unit would relocate to North Manchuria and work in coordination with the Korean Independent forces stationed there to expand the Volunteer Army's strength. Additionally, the 5th unit would be formed, with this unit primarily composed of former student soldiers from the Taihang Mountains period. It was described as the Volunteer Army's reserve unit. The 5th unit would initially go to Kangdo (間島) to expand the revolutionary forces there before advancing into the homeland, serving as a key force.

In other words, the 1st and 3rd units were primarily focused on political operations, while the 5th unit was primarily involved in military operations. The 5th unit was considered the most elite and revolutionary unit within the Volunteer Army. The commander of the 5th unit was Yi Ik-sung, and the political leader was Park Il-woo. Yi Ik-sung had previously served as the commander of the 1st company during the deployment to the Taihang Mountains. Park Il-woo had once studied in the Soviet Union and had connections with Kim Il-sung's anti-Japanese United Army. Perhaps because of this, Park played the role of the de facto leader of the 5th unit.

Xita (West Pagoda 西塔)

I was assigned to the 5th unit. Disobedience is essentially reactionary, so we had to go to Kangdo (間島). I was not at ease with this decision. I thought I could return to my homeland from Fengtian, but now I had to change direction again and embark on a long journey to Kangdo. How could I be at peace with this decision? However, I consoled myself by thinking that Kangdo was close to Hamgyeong Province, and there were many Koreans living there. Before the congress concluded, we received orders to assemble at the square again before sunrise tomorrow, on November 7th, the day of the Soviet October Revolution Anniversary.

The next day, the Korean Volunteer Army assembled at the square, fully armed and carrying all their belongings. Now, the Volunteer Army set out in the dark of night, awakening the morning streets, and entered Fengtian as the morning sun shone upon them. It was the first time I had set foot in a major city since escaping from the Japanese army. In Fengtian, I headed towards Xita (West Pagoda 西塔), where I heard many Koreans lived. Meeting the faces of my fellow countrymen there was truly heartwarming.

However, in Fengtian, even though there had been no fighting between the Japanese and Soviets, the streets felt desolate. The shops were tightly shut, and the houses looked almost abandoned, with windows falling apart. Seeing street vendors shivering in the cold as they sold rice cakes, taffy, and cigarettes made me feel sorry for them. As I walked through the Xita Street, I finally realized why we had come to this place—it was because that day was the anniversary of the Soviet Socialist Revolution. The victorious Soviet army was holding a major commemorative event in the square in front of Fengtian Station to celebrate the occasion. Our Korean Volunteer Army was not only expected to participate in the event but also to conduct a military parade for the Soviet commander.

Figure 76: The Famous Xita (Western Pagoda, 西塔) in Shenyang and the Xita Koreatown.

At the head of the military parade stood General Shtykov and many other Soviet generals. After the parade, there was an unveiling ceremony of the Victory Monument erected in the square in front of Fengtian station. When the cover over the monument was removed, a towering marble obelisk—about 40 to 50 meters tall—was revealed, and thunderous applause erupted. I couldn't help but be astonished as I looked at the monument, for at the very top sat a massive tank with its long barrel pointed toward Japan. I interpreted that tank as a symbol of the Soviet Union's far east policy. The Soviet ambition to occupy Manchuria had begun as far back as the days of Imperial Russia. Now, I believed, they had fulfilled that ambition and were aiming to use that tank to take over Japan as well, almost realizing their goal of communizing Asia.

Figure 77: General Shtykov and his diary, published in Korean.

Tank

Figure 78: Victory Monument Tower at Shenyang Railway Station.

(**Editor's Note:** General Shtykov, while serving as a member of the Military Council of the Primorsky Military District, became the de facto authority in North Korea after Liberation and led the Soviet military administration. His posthumous work, *The Shtykov Diaries*, is considered an important source for studying the history of North and South Korea immediately after Liberation.)

I once had the opportunity to perform a salute to emperor Hirohito (裕仁) during my university days in Japan. At that time, I felt a sense of shame as a Korean, but now, I couldn't help but have mixed feelings about the fate that had placed me in a position where I had to salute Soviet military commanders. I questioned why I should show the utmost respect to them when I had never saluted a Korean king or ruler. These conflicting thoughts left me feeling ashamed and filled with anger.

Figure 79: Military parade celebrating the emperor's birthday at
Yoyogi Parade Grounds, Japan, 1932.

I followed the organization's orders and participated in the
celebration, but I couldn't help but feel angry about why the Korean
Independence Alliance should show the utmost respect to the Soviet
forces, who I saw as acting in a barbaric manner. The reason for this was
that while the Independence Alliance advocated for Korean
independence, it also embraced a communist form of independence,
aligning with the Soviet Union and aiming for the prosperity of Asia.
We spent that night in an inn in Fengtian and set off for Kangdo early
the next morning.

Chapter 10
Road to Kangdo

Cities of Jilin Province

The term "Fengtian (奉天)" indeed means "to offer the heavens" or "to serve heaven." It was named so because Qing (淸) dynasty founder Nurhaci (奴雨哈赤) occupied Shenyang (瀋陽), and the power of the Jurchen (女眞) ethnic group was growing rapidly in that area.

The 5th unit of the Volunteer Army, heading to Kangdo, departed from Fengtian early in the morning and arrived in Fushun (撫順) in the evening of the same day. Fushun was well-known for its coal mines, especially the open-pit mines. Everything visible there was black coal. Because of that, the clothes and noses of passersby were all darkened, and coal dust filled the sky. I couldn't help but feel envious, thinking how wonderful it would be if our country also had such coal mines.

In Fushun, you boarded a train for the first time. Despite the missing windows and damaged seats, riding the train was a significant treat. It was likely due to the consideration of the Soviet army for our participation in the Victory Day parade in Fengtian. While on the train, you observed many freight cars filled with war materials and machinery being shipped back to the Soviet Union. When your train turned into Jilin Province (吉林省) and arrived at Meihekou (梅花口), it was a chilly morning.

As the Volunteer Army disembarked and assembled in front of the station, among the Korean autonomous committee officials who had come to welcome us was Kaneyama (金山)—someone I had once been close with in Tokyo. I thought to myself, "Ah, so his hometown was Meihekou". I wanted to run over and shake his hand, but as I was tied to the Volunteer Army, I didn't have that kind of freedom. He, too, looked glad to see me but only gazed from a distance with a faraway look in his eyes and didn't come closer. Back in Tokyo, he had lived as an extreme liberal, posing as a Japanese to make ends meet—so when had he become a communist? I thought to myself, he must surely be someone with a quick and clever mind.

What could he have felt when he saw me, now armed as part of the Volunteer Army? He must have certainly labeled me a communist. Perhaps he even saw me as an opportunist. I wanted to talk to him about the situation and share what had happened to me, but I couldn't leave the train, and it was about to depart, so I could only watch from afar and mutter to myself before we had to part ways. However, the Korean autonomous committee officials had prepared a lot of food for us. As we had to depart quickly due to the train's schedule, they hurriedly made rice balls (Korean *jumeokbap*) and distributed them to us in great haste.

The freight train loaded with lumber arrived in Banseok (盤石) in the evening. We got off there and were dispersed among local homes to spend the night. The house I stayed in belonged to the local elementary school teacher. The teacher, who appeared to be around forty, welcomed us warmly and with admiration. He said his hometown was Juksan, Gyeonggi Province, South Korea, and that he had been in the area for ten years. He was teaching the children of fellow Koreans, most of whom were farmers. He said it was the greatest honor to host members of the Volunteer Army, who were working tirelessly on Chinese soil to win Korean independence.

He also mentioned that during the Japanese colonial period, since this place was part of Manchuria, he had conscientiously taught the Korean language to the children of fellow Koreans, fostering a sense of national pride. Now that our homeland had been liberated, he intended to return home. He added that the northern part of Korea would likely be influenced by Soviet forces, but he would proudly go to his hometown, Juksan, which had been occupied by the United States, to devote himself to the communist movement. Considering the prevailing socialist sentiments in the region of Kangdo, it seemed only natural for him to become a communist, so I just listened quietly without saying a word.

That night, for the first time, I was able to stretch out my legs under a blanket and fall into a deep sleep in a warm *ondol* room, relieving my fatigue. In the morning, as I sat before a table thoughtfully prepared with tofu soup, I silently wished in my heart that these kind-hearted people of good background would one day be able to make great contributions to the cause they hoped for.

My father

Sitting on the roof of a freight car loaded with machinery bound for Jilin, I gazed out over the endlessly vast plains and thought of my father back home. He had once told me that during the March 1st Movement (1919), he had shouted for independence in our hometown of Osan and was forced to flee from the pursuit of Japanese military police, eventually coming to Tonghua. That very Tonghua was not far from Banseok, where I had spent the previous night.

I had grown up hearing how my father taught at an elementary school in Tonghua while also engaging in the independence movement, so I could vividly imagine him racing through the mountains and valleys of this region in the prime of his youth.

Now, twenty-five years after the March 1st Movement, as I, his son, passed through the liberated lands of Tonghua and Banseok in Manchuria, a powerful wave of emotion overcame me. I couldn't help but think:

"This very land was once where my father had run, and
this air—this very air—must have been the same he once breathed."

The freight train carrying the volunteer army arrived in Jilin the next afternoon. Jilin, situated in the heart of Jilin Province, was a major city, and there were many people gathered at the station. Among them, there was an elderly man with white hair who respectfully bowed and performed a deep bow when he saw our Volunteer Army. He said, "You have worked so hard for the revolutionary movement." I felt that his words were completely sincere and lacked any falsehood. I didn't inquire about his past, but from his humble and earnest attitude, I could sense that he was grateful for our efforts in carrying on the fight for independence that he might not have been able to complete himself.

The urban area of Jilin was in chaos and lacked order. In the distance, occasional gunfire could be heard, giving the impression of a turbulent eve of a storm. Currently, the Soviet army was occupying the city, but it was said that if the Soviet army withdrew, the Nationalist (Kuomintang) forces would enter and take control. Although the Nationalist army hadn't arrived yet, it was clear that their affiliated forces had already secured the outskirts. It was also reported that pro-Nationalist spies had infiltrated Jilin's city center in large numbers, seizing important institutions. Given the deep-rooted rivalry between the Nationalists and the Communists, it was evident that a major showdown between the two was only a matter of time in this area.

In Jilin, the Volunteer Army stayed at a large inn run by Japanese proprietors. In the past, this inn was known for lavish parties with geishas dancing and people enjoying drinks under the chandeliers. However, now most of the sliding doors were missing, and the glass windows were shattered, leaving a desolate atmosphere.

Heo Gap's father

The Volunteer Army stayed for two nights in this *tatami* room. During that time, I remembered the request of my comrade Heo Gap (許鉀), whom I had met at Sankakuan. Recalling the address that he had written down for me, I made inquiries and had a messenger from the inn deliver a letter to Heo Gap's father. His father soon came to the inn and treated me warmly, overjoyed at the news of his son. I, in turn, greeted him with the same joy I would feel if I were meeting my own father.

Heo Gap's father told me that he was serving as an elder at a large church in the area and then began cursing his son, saying he was an ungrateful child. He explained that his son had gone into hiding to avoid being conscripted as a student soldier, and later said he was going to Yan'an. The father had strongly opposed and tried to stop him. He said he knew very well that the Independence Alliance in Yan'an was a communist group and denounced his son as a disgraceful child. I briefly explained the reasons why I had become a member of the Korean Volunteer Army and also shared that my own family had been Christian for generations.

When I asked about the situation in Jilin, he replied that the Eighth Route Army would soon march in. He then offered to treat me to dinner. However, since I could not leave my unit, I politely declined. He left the inn with the words, "May God's protection be with you."

As I had thought, Heo Gap was clearly a minor romantic idealist and a liberal. Despite his parents' opposition, he left for Yan'an, enchanted by the place and mistakenly believing himself to be a communist, and ended up joining the Independence Alliance. I could only hope that his future would be one of success and fulfillment.

However, according to what I heard later, he returned to Korea and took a position as the head of propaganda for the North Korean communist party, but for some reason, he took his own life. When I heard this, I thought to myself: as expected, Heo Gap had dug his own grave through his minor heroism and desire for prestige.

For an intellectual who has not overcome his own class background to claim to fight for the proletariat is nothing but self-deception. The path to becoming a true communist requires one to defeat oneself, to denounce comrades, and to possess the cold-heartedness to kill others without reason. Through Heo Gap's death, I once again deeply realized this harsh truth.

After bidding farewell to Heo Gab's father, I went to the laundry room with my laundry. I didn't expect running water, but water came out smoothly, allowing me to finish my laundry easily. When I turned around, I saw a woman standing there with no expression on her face. She appeared to be in her thirties and looked like a Japanese woman. Perhaps she was doing cleaning or running errands for the inn while residing there. Seeing her, I couldn't help but feel more pity for an unfortunate Japanese woman rather than harboring any nationalistic resentment. I had seen many pitiable Japanese women suffering and dying in Manchuria, so at that moment, my empathy for her plight was stronger than any sense of national enmity.

I couldn't just walk past without saying something, so I asked her in Japanese if she wouldn't consider returning to her homeland. She looked surprised and asked if I wasn't part of the Korean Independence Army, clearly puzzled about my identity. Then, with a melancholic expression, she replied that "when the time comes, I will go back to my homeland." I remained silent, thinking that "she, a pitiable soul, was now bearing the consequences of the sins her fellow countrymen had committed," and then I left that place.

At that time, the Soviet soldiers would open fire indiscriminately whenever the locals pointed fingers at the Japanese as "*Yaponski*" (a derogatory term for Japanese). As darkness began to fall, the outskirts of the city erupted once again with fierce gun battles between the Nationalists and Communists. Gunfire echoed loudly, and tracer rounds illuminated the cold night sky.

Disarmament by Soviet troops

In Jilin, the Volunteer Army boarded a train loaded with Soviet military supplies, bound for Yanji (延吉) in Kangdo. The cold of January in Kangdo was truly brutal. The falling snow piled up and covered the entire landscape. Breathing with masks on was impossible as it froze instantly. The temperature fluctuated between minus 30 to 40 degrees Celsius, and despite not being properly dressed for such conditions and lacking wind protection, we had to sit on the stacked timber on freight cars. This exposed us to bitter winds, resulting in numerous cases of frostbite. Moreover, with the snow falling steadily, there was genuine doubt about whether we would survive this night unscathed.

One midnight, the freight train entered Tonghua station. Suddenly, heavily armed Soviet soldiers rushed in and surrounded the Volunteer Army, assuming a combat posture. The atmosphere was tense, as if they might open fire at any moment. They demanded that we disarm. Facing this unexpected crisis, Park Il-woo, the Political Commissar of the 5th Corps, ordered us to disarm as demanded by the Soviet soldiers.

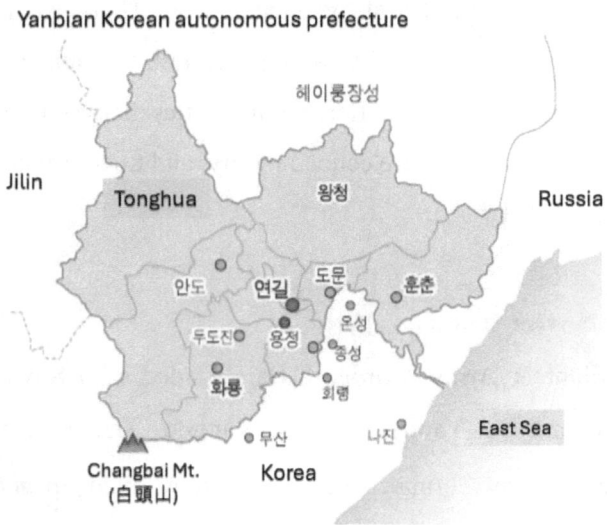

Yanbian Korean autonomous prefecture

Map 80: Yanbian Korean autonomous prefecture Map , 2024.

The Soviet soldiers insisted that even our meager outerwear, which we had bought ourselves, counted as weapons and ordered us to take them off. The Volunteer Army gathered their weapons and clothing in one place as requested. As we complied, the Soviet soldiers cheered and celebrated loudly. High-ranking officers, including Park Il-woo, could only wear embarrassed expressions as they didn't understand the language being spoken.

Fortunately, Park Il-woo, who had studied in the Soviet Union, was able to speak Russian and thus had the opportunity to speak with the Soviet commander. The Soviet forces said they had received orders from their superiors to disarm the Volunteer Army, as it was considered part of the Nationalist forces.

Thus, Park Il-woo had to meet with the Soviet officer who issued the order and convince them that the Volunteer Army was not part of the Nationalist military but rather the liberation army of Korea. It took a significant amount of time for Park Il-woo and others to persuade the Soviet officer, and during this period, the Volunteer Army had to endure the extreme cold while waiting. It was a critical moment where the Volunteer Army could have become casualties of the larger conflict between the Nationalists and Communists.

Later investigations revealed that agents of the Nationalist deliberately spread false information to the Soviet authorities, claiming that Kuomintang troops were on a train headed for Tonghua with the intention of assassinating the Volunteer Army. This false information was intended to provoke the Soviet forces into attacking us. It was further reported that these agents had bribed Soviet officers, both with money and women, to secure their cooperation.

The Soviet forces were hostile to the Kuomintang forces in Manchuria and supported the Chinese communist forces, providing them with weapons confiscated from the Japanese Kwantung Army. The Soviets ensured the safety of the Communist forces in the region while actively opposing the Kuomintang.

After going through this turmoil, the night had grown deep, and we once again boarded the open-top freight train cars and departed. With our flimsy outerwear taken away, enduring the cold became even more challenging. We had to sit among slippery timber, as the snow fell, and spend the night. Falling asleep was out of the question as it would lead to frostbite. We kept rubbing our feet, huddling together, using our body heat to battle the threat of frostbite, and enduring with all the strength we had left.

As the freight train continued its journey and eventually arrived at Chaoyangchuan (朝陽川) Station, the morning sun had risen, casting a dazzling light. We felt a profound appreciation for the warmth of the sun. The weapons were returned, but the winter coats were nowhere to be found. It was said that Soviet soldiers had sold them and used the money to buy women.

The next station after Chaoyangchuan was Yanji (延吉), but the Soviet command refused to allow the entrance of the Korean Volunteer Army into Yanji. They cited a rule similar to what had previously prevented our entry into Fengtian. Consequently, we found ourselves stranded at the railroad station in front of Yanji. The railway quarters were buildings originally constructed as housing for Japanese railway officials. They had stoves installed and running water, so they were livable. I had been selected as part of the advance party and arrived here first; once the main unit arrived, a new assignment would be given to us.

I found a shabby barbershop and got a haircut for the first time in a while. While I was there, the radio was reporting that Rhee Syngman had entered the country in a personal capacity. Additionally, I came across a newspaper, and in huge, bold letters was the list of a provisional cabinet reshuffle of the People's Republic of South Korea. Rhee Syngman was named interim president, and Kim Gu, Yeo Un-hyeong, Kim Il-sung, Heo Heon, and Mu Jeong were appointed as ministers.

Realizing that the homeland was actively moving toward the establishment of a republic, I felt a deep longing to be there myself. Exiled figures from abroad were returning one after another — but when would I ever be able to return to my beloved homeland? In my current situation, there was no way to tell, which only deepened my sorrow.

Nationalist party bandit

The mission assigned to the Korean Volunteer Army at Chaoyangchuan (朝陽川) was to recruit and train new members in Yanji, expanding their influence. It seemed like a never-ending task, and the uncertainty of when we would be able to return home hung over us. If Manchuria became the battleground between the Nationalists and Communists, we would naturally have to fight alongside the Communists against the Nationalist forces. This made the prospect of returning to our hometown even more bleak.

At Chaoyangchuan, I was occasionally called upon by the local autonomous council to undertake sentry duty in the outskirts of Chaoyangchuan. The reason for this was that in the outlying areas, there were bandits aligned with the Nationalists who had established strongholds and were causing great distress to the local residents. This region was referred to as the "*Idogu* (二道溝)" area.

On a bleak day with snow falling heavily, I found myself on a mountain ridge, standing guard with a rifle slung over my shoulder. I couldn't help but think how pitiful my situation was. What on earth did this duty have to do with me — or with my homeland?

Now, in our newly liberated homeland, American and Soviet forces have entered Korea and are confronting each other. In the South, Rhee Syngman is calling for unity, while in the North, Hyun Jun-hyuk (玄俊赫), a leader of the Korean communist party, has been assassinated in broad daylight on the street. When this agony ends, will a unified republic truly be born? And if so, when will that be?

While waiting for the arrival of the main unit at Chaoyangchuan, I once again responded to the request of the local autonomous council to participate in the suppression of Nationalist-affiliated bandits. Our unit was a battalion-sized force, and the battalion commander was a local Communist Party member. He proudly mentioned that he had spent over a decade in prison following the Yi Lisan (李立三) line, an early revolutionary period, which made him a veteran of the cause.

We took a train to Myeongwolgu (明月溝), located near the foothills of Changbai Mountain (長白山 - 白頭山), which had been a key area of activity for our independence fighters in the past. Upon arriving at Myeongwolgu station, we had to walk through deep snow-covered trails for the entire night.

At dawn, as the sky began to brighten, the clear moon was still hanging over the western hills. About 500 meters ahead, a village came into view, surrounded by stone walls with a tall watchtower erected. We were told that we would be attacking that very village. We spread out in skirmish formation and cautiously approached the village. There was no sign of life from within—only silence. Crawling to within 50 meters of the village, we took up battle positions and began firing our rifles, but for some reason, the guns wouldn't discharge.

In response, the enemy began firing rapidly through holes in the wall from the watchtower. Meanwhile, our rifles wouldn't fire—because in the freezing cold of over minus 40 degrees Celsius, the guns had frozen, and the bullets wouldn't discharge. The enemy, on the other hand, kept a fire burning to warm their guns and continued shooting.

In truth, hitting a target in battle wasn't easy. Lying prone on snow piled more than 50 meters, we tried to fire our rifles, but the bullets wouldn't come out. Only the enemy's bullets whizzed past us with sharp, buzzing sounds. Then suddenly, I saw the comrade beside me get hit by a bullet—his red blood spreading across the snow. A voice cried out somewhere, shouting for a retreat. We withdrew to the position from which we had launched the attack.

The morning sun had already risen, and the enemy in the village, realizing we were retreating, came out beyond the walls, shouting at us and firing their guns. We did not engage again and instead retraced our steps, heading back toward Myeongwolgu.

As I walked through the snow, I thought to myself: how pathetic it was that we, calling ourselves a so-called revolutionary army, had to turn back without defeating a band of bandits. But even more heartbreaking was the suffering of the people who had to endure the torment of these bandits because security had not been established.

If we had successfully wiped out the bandits and taken the village, wouldn't those bandits have simply moved to another region? And wouldn't that new place become their base, where more looting would occur? Manchuria was so vast and wide that after the war ended, countless bandits roamed freely, causing hardship for the residents everywhere they went.

When I returned to the lodging in Chaoyangchuan, the autonomous committee, claiming victory in the campaign against the bandits, had gathered many local notables and was holding a celebratory feast to which I was invited. There, I enjoyed a delicious meal made from a large wild boar that had been barbecued.

However, everyone at the gathering proudly praised the "Yi Lisan line" of the 1930s and boasted that they had raised the red flag high. Once again, I realized that Kangdo was indeed a place where communist ideology ran deep.

New Mission of the Korean Volunteer Army

The main force of the Volunteer Army had returned. Since they, like us, chose the Chaoyangchuan railway quarters as their lodging, the quarters became very crowded. As members of the Korean Volunteer Army and of the Independence Alliance, we were assigned new missions. According to what was being said, we would be dispersed throughout the Kangdo Province area to carry out organizational operations and contribute to expanding our influence.

Another piece of information suggested that the 5th unit, being the core unit of the Volunteer Army, would move to the Ando (安圖) region at the foot of Changbai Mountain, which had been a base of the independence fighters during Japanese rule. There, they were expected to establish a military-political academy to nurture revolutionary forces.

The 5th unit was composed solely of former student soldiers, and the idea was that rather than entering the current chaotic homeland, they would further strengthen their capabilities while waiting, and at a decisive moment, advance into the homeland to complete the revolution. Just as the saying goes, "Revolution comes from the barrel of a gun," the Korean revolution would also be resolved through armed struggle, and the 5th unit was considered the elite force responsible for carrying out that mission.

When I heard this information, I couldn't help but feel bewildered. Originally, I had been thinking of leaving the Korean Independence Alliance back in Fengtian, but I came this far because our unit was said to be moving to Kangdo, which was geographically close to my hometown. However, if the unit was not going to enter the newly liberated homeland and instead continued its activities in Manchuria under the pretext of carrying out a communist revolution, then I would only be digging myself deeper into my own grave. I now had to seriously reexamine my current situation once again.

The Alliance is clearly a communist organization. Although I am currently fighting as part of its communist vanguard, it is obvious that at some point, given my class background, I will be purged. In other words, for now, the Alliance sees some utilitarian value in me, but unless I completely rid myself of my class identity, I will inevitably be purged during the period of proletarian dictatorship, which is the transitional phase toward full communism.

"I was now at a crossroad.

To take on the new covert mission and act alongside them, I needed to transform myself into a complete communist.

On the other hand, if becoming a communist meant I couldn't contribute to my homeland, it would be better to escape from this hideout before the new covert mission was assigned."

I heard that the U.S. military had moved into South Korea, and there, true human rights and freedom would likely be guaranteed. Here, while the proletarians might have their own version of freedom and glory, I would likely have nothing but suspicion and surveillance.

Perhaps in the future, I might be given a minor title or position, but that would be merely a temporary measure to make use of me — they would never truly see me as a comrade in the revolution. The longer I stayed in this organization, the deeper I felt I was marching toward my own ruin. That is why I resolved to escape before a new assignment was given to me.

Fellow escapee from the Alliance

I met Jeong Geun-seok (鄭根碩), who had escaped from the Japanese army with me. He was also a Christian and, by nature, someone who could never become a communist. He readily agreed with my opinion that we had to escape — because he had been thinking the same way all along. He went even further, confessing that he had already been mentally prepared to escape, even if he had to do it alone.

Then we met Sim Young-soon. As mentioned earlier, he was a comrade with a fiery temperament who, during our time in the Huazhong branch, had insisted we go to Chongqing, even if it meant dying. Since then, he had consistently acted alongside me as a member of the Volunteer Army. Upon hearing that we were planning to escape, he went even further, insisting that we should flee as early as tomorrow. Though he hadn't said it aloud, his thoughts were clearly the same as mine — he, too, was someone who could never become a communist. All along, he had been under constant surveillance and scorn for his weak party loyalty and free-spirited nature.

Thus, the three of us agreed to escape from the Independence Alliance. We could feel the watchful eyes closing in on us, so we quietly confirmed our intentions a couple of times in the secluded latrine. Then we decided to slip out of the Choyangcheon quarters individually after breakfast the next morning, taking advantage of the usual morning commotion, and pass through the checkpoint.

At that moment, Ahn Guk-ju (安國柱), a fellow student soldier who had been lying down due to poor health, noticed our movements and asked if he could escape with us. He had grown up in a Christian household, and his father was a conscientious nationalist and wealthy man who had served as an elder at the First Sinuiju Church. His father greatly helped Pastor Han Kyung-jik (韓景職, later the senior pastor at Youngnak Church in Seoul), who was ministering at the Second Sinuiju Church. As I thought that if he was left behind, he had to endure a life

261

he clearly did not want, and thus we gladly welcomed him to join us, when he asked to come along.

That left Shin Sang-cho. When we told him about our plan, he too expressed strong agreement and said that he had already made up his mind to escape as well but urged us to go ahead first. He said he would follow us soon after, once an opportunity presented itself. Although he didn't explain in detail why he was postponing his escape, it seemed he was quietly hoping that the Alliance might assign him a new role or perhaps even give him a position of some sort, as there were rumors that new operational tasks would soon be issued. He appeared to be waiting and watching, holding out for that possibility.

We set the date for betraying the Alliance to be tomorrow. I reminded myself once again that I must not look back. This was the very same thing I had firmly told myself when I fled from the Japanese army — because looking back before a decisive act only weakens the heart and risks ruining everything.

Chapter 11

Crossing the Tumen River

Escape from the Korean Independence Alliance

When I escaped from the Japanese military camp, I had a clear sense of justification and conviction, as the Japanese army was a brutal force of aggression. I also felt confident that my actions would be supported and understood by my parents, relatives, and neighbors at home.

Now, regardless of ideology, escaping from the ranks of the nation's independence army was something I could hardly rationalize as justifiable. Since the action lacked clear moral justification, it weighed heavily on my heart. I couldn't help but think that if the Korean Volunteer Army officers had accepted us with even a bit more generosity—like they did during our time in the Huazhong branch—I wouldn't have taken such an extreme step as betrayal through escape.

There was also a lingering sense of regret that if I had simply stayed behind in the Huazhong branch, I might have safely returned to the homeland with them. But more than anything else, what troubled me most was the ominous premonition that 'this act of escaping from the Korean Volunteer Army would surely bring misfortune upon my future' — a feeling that I couldn't shake from my mind.

As they had mentioned, isn't it clear that if they were to establish sovereignty in Korea, we who had escaped would face harsh reprisals? Communists detest those who leave their organization the most because they fear that their organizational secrets will be compromised. However, I had firmly concluded that

"I could no longer continue marching toward my own ruin here.
I should postpone dealing with future consequences and
first choose the best course of action at the present moment."

On January 15, 1946, the four of us finally carried out our escape from the Korean Independence Alliance. Each of us slipped out through the guard post in the morning, but I couldn't shake off the emptiness and sadness in my heart. This was largely due to the thought that even the local residents might come to see us as enemies because of our actions.

Among the four, Jeong Geun-seok had already made up his mind to escape alone if necessary, and during our stay in Choyangcheon, he had already contacted some of the locals. Being a devout Christian, he had visited a nearby church and spoken to the pastor there, explaining his intentions and asking for help.

And so, under Jung Geun-seok's guidance, we went to visit that pastor. The pastor's first reaction upon seeing the four of us was one of great astonishment. It's not surprising considering that Kangdo had deep-rooted communist movements dating back to the Japanese colonial era. By this time, four months after liberation, autonomous committees had been established, and the communist party's cell organizations were spread out like spiderwebs. In such circumstances, churches were under the watchful eye of the authorities, making it a difficult situation. So, it was no wonder that the pastor was greatly taken aback when four escapees suddenly appeared without any prior notice.

He calmed himself and led us into a room. He explained that since the liberation, the church had been under silent pressure, the number of congregants had dwindled, and even those who remained were difficult to care for, so he was now in a situation where he had to leave the area. He cursed the communist party as he spoke.

The pastor was also startled when he saw us in military uniforms and immediately offered civilian clothes for us to change into. He said that when Jeong Geun-seok had first come and shared his plans, he felt in his heart that helping the young man return safely to his hometown was in accordance with God's will. So, he had asked the church members to prepare civilian clothes in advance. I couldn't help but be deeply moved — Christians truly were different.

He advised us to go to Yongjeong (龍井) and mentioned that if we went up to Samseongbong (三上峰), we could cross the Yalu River from there and reach Hoiryeong (會寧). We felt that staying longer would be burdensome for the pastor, so we decided to leave immediately. However, the pastor insisted that if we went to Yongjeong, we should look for Pastor Moon's house and even drew a Map to help us find it.

He guided us to the road leading to Yongjeong. As fugitives, we walked without rest and arrived in Yongjeong that evening, where we were able to find Pastor Moon's house without much difficulty.

In Yongjeong, we learned that Pastor Moon, who was a respected pastor representing the religious community, had already been arrested by the Soviet army and accused of being a right-wing reactionary when they landed in Jinju. His son, Pastor Moon Dong-hwan (文東煥), greeted us warmly. He was the younger brother of Pastor Moon Ik-hwan (文益煥) and had been a friend of Jung Geun-seok during their Y.M.C.A. fellowship while studying abroad in Tokyo. The atmosphere in their home was somber, knowing that their father had been taken by the Soviet army.

Despite the challenging circumstances, Pastor Moon Dong-hwan welcomed us warmly when he heard our story about escaping from the Korean Independence Alliance in Chaoyangchuan. He provided us with dinner and a place to sleep. The dinner table was simple, and there was very little rice left in the rice pot. Pastor Moon scooped out one portion of cooked rice for each of us and repeatedly scraped the pot, but there was no more rice to be had. He apologized, explaining that he had used up all the rice they had at home. Once again, I was touched by the kindness of a Christian's heart, and I felt a deep sense of indebtedness and love.

We left Yongjeong early in the morning and headed towards Jisin (智新). The cold was biting, with temperatures well below freezing, and the snow had piled up, making it a challenging journey as it reached up to our knees. Endurance could overcome the hardships brought by our young bodies, but as the road grew longer and more treacherous, our energy began to wane.

Leaving the Korean Volunteer Army meant that if we were captured, we would face severe punishment from the organization. We had no money in our pockets, and we were constantly under the watchful eye of the local residents. It felt like the world was closing in on us, and we had no place to call our own.

In the midst of a fierce snowstorm sweeping across the Manchurian plains, we found ourselves wondering where we were headed. After all, wasn't our ultimate goal to find the land of freedom? However, would our homeland welcome those who had fled without a valid reason? They say that the U.S. military has landed in South Korea, but is there truly freedom to be found there?

The phrase "No way out" came to mind. As we ventured further, the fear of falling into the surveillance net of communist party members and facing execution for treason loomed large. However, we couldn't simply retreat at this point, so we continued, silently navigating our way through the snow-covered landscape.

The sun had already set on the western horizon, and we wondered where we would spend the night and how we would endure the cold. It felt like a life-or-death situation.

Map 81: Yanbian Korean autonomous prefecture in 2024.

At that moment, once again, the existence of the loving God came to mind. I believed that God would not abandon us this time either. Did He not promise that "He would be with me, even as I walked through the valley of the shadow of death?" I remembered the days when I escaped from the Japanese military camp and how God had been with me, guiding me and extending His saving hand. With that conviction, I bowed my head and prayed,

"O Lord, do not forsake us.
Lead us with pillars of fire and clouds!"

We reached a remote cottage rather than entering the main streets of Jisin. An elderly couple lived there; no young men were in sight. When they saw us, their expressions indicated they had encountered another bothersome guest. We explained that we had come all the way from Jilin and were on our way back home after liberation. We asked if they could kindly provide shelter for just one night. The couple looked at us again and said that so many groups of refugees had passed through and stayed there that they had nothing left to eat and were simply worn out. Still, since the weather was cold and it was getting late, they told us we could stay in the upper room. However, they added that they didn't have a single grain of rice left and would not be able to offer us a meal.

As we lay side by side in the chilly room, looking up at the ceiling, our dire situation once again felt bleak. Nevertheless, we were thankful for being able to sleep indoors tonight and avoid the snowstorm outside. Furthermore, considering this freezing cold night, the elderly couple probably wouldn't be pushing us out to the People's Committee in the middle of the night, we thought.

Then we heard the sound of a fire being lit in the kitchen, and soon the host came in carrying a bowl of pumpkin porridge for each of us, apologizing as if he were ashamed of not being able to offer more. I thought to myself that even in such a truly difficult world, there were still many good-hearted people. The pumpkin porridge tasted like honey. Even now, I can't forget that taste — and whenever I get the chance, I eat pumpkin porridge and recall that moment.

Crossing the Tumen River

"In the morning, we passed through the streets of Jishin and entered the road leading to Domun (圖們). Everywhere we looked, it was covered in white blankets of snow. All that was visible was the piled-up white snow. The mountains were covered in snow, and so were the fields. It was impossible to distinguish the road from the fields. A cart puller, dragging his cart, passed by us. We asked how much farther we had to go to reach Samsan Peak, and he said it wouldn't be much longer.

Samsan Peak was a single hill. When we reached the top, we could see the surroundings clearly. In front of us, the Tumen River was flowing. Since it was winter, we couldn't see the winding waves; all we could see was the frozen ice.

Across the river lay Hoeryeong. With so many chimneys rising into the sky, it looked like a large city. I imagined how, during the Japanese occupation, many of our fellow countrymen must have crossed that river into Kangdo after being robbed of their farmland, carrying their children on their backs and belongings in their arms. Thinking of that, I felt that the silently flowing Tumen River must carry within it the deep sorrows and joys of our people.

Now, just across that river was my homeland — my hometown — and the thought alone stirred my heart beyond control. Though I regretted not being able to see the winding current of the Tumen River, I was thankful that it was frozen over and we could walk across. Had it been summer and we needed a ferry to cross, getting over the border would have been far more difficult.

However, when we looked closely at the Tumen River, there was a guard with a gun patrolling on the icy surface near the path to Hoeryeong (會寧). Fortunately, there wasn't a sentry post building around the guard, and it seemed like only one person was on duty. Now, we had to pass through this guard post. Would this guard let us through safely? He would surely ask for identification, but we had nothing on us. So, the only way was to pretend to be refugees. The question was, would he believe us?

The four of us discussed various options. While it would have been easiest to pose as returning refugees, judging by the numerous refugees we had seen, the guard would likely not let through four able-bodied men without any luggage or children. So, we decided to go with the direct approach. We entrusted everything to Shim Young-soon, the bravest among us who always led the way, and quietly followed him. Shim Young-soon boldly approached the guard and said, "Comrade, it's really cold, and you're working hard. We're government workers on a secret mission returning to our country, passing through here on our way to Hoeryeong people's committee." The guard, without a word, courteously let us pass.

We quickly passed through the area without entering Hoeryeong city and turned onto the road to Cheongjin (淸津), following the Gomusan (古茂山) path. Two years ago, we left our homeland as Japanese soldiers with heavy hearts, crossing the Yalu River. Now, as liberated citizens, we had finally crossed the Tumen River through various hardships, hunger, and deception, and entered the land of our homeland. It left a bitter taste in our mouths. However, at last, we safely set foot on our homeland. A sigh of relief escaped my lips, and a prayer of gratitude welled up from deep within me.

Among the four of us, Jeong Geun-seok, who had majored in economics, was often teased by the others for being a penny-pincher. But now, he took out a carefully folded one-*won* bill he had kept tucked in his waistband and suggested we go find something to eat. At the time, a one-*won* bill was truly valuable — a bowl of cold noodle soup cost only ten *jeon*. (Note: 1 *won* = 100 *jeon*)

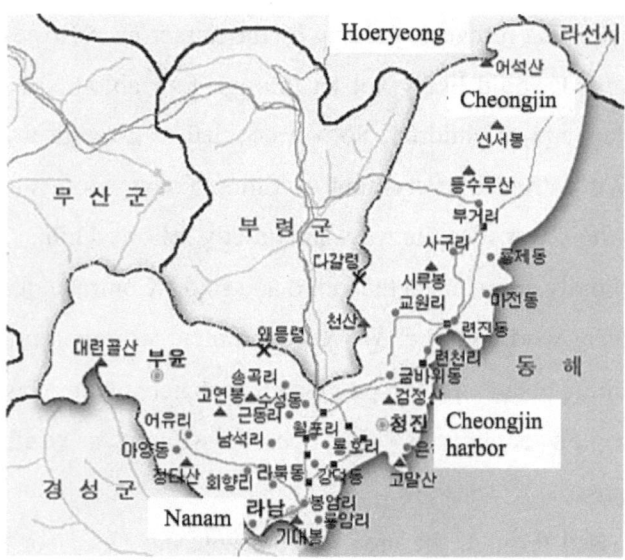

Figure 82: Hoeryeong City and Cheongjin City.

We stepped into a roadside eatery and, with that one-*won* note, were able to buy bowls of soup and rice, spend the night there, and even have breakfast the next morning. The woman who ran the place thanked us,

272

saying most returning refugees demanded food and lodging for free, but our manner was so respectful and proper that it stood out to her.

We entered the mountain road over Gomusan. Although it was a wide road capable of accommodating vehicles—since it connected Hoeryeong and Cheongjin —we were exhausted from trudging through the snow. Gomusan wasn't a particularly tall or rugged mountain. After spending the night in a small mountain hut, we arrived in Cheongjin the next morning.

Cheongjin Port (清津港) was, true to its name, clear and beautiful. The white sandy beach formed a graceful bow shape, and on that day, the usually turbulent East Sea was calm. Perhaps due to the regular ferry route with Japan's Niigata during the Japanese occupation, many Japanese-style houses were still visible.

Seeing occasional Soviet soldiers around town made my heart ache, as I could only imagine the terrible atrocities they must have committed after landing in Cheongjin. It was said the Soviet army landed here on the night of August 16th, 1945.

Figure 83: Cheongjin (淸津) Harbor (2024).

Generous Hospitality

We hurried on the road from Chongjin toward Nanam. I had heard that in Nanam, although distantly related, a relative of Shim Young-soon—an uncle-like figure—was living there, so I thought if we could find his house, we might spend the night in comfort.

In Nanam, perhaps since a division under the Japanese Kwantung Army had been stationed there during the colonial period, military officer residences were lined up in rows. It was now clear that Soviet officers were living in these houses.

Thinking about how the soldiers of the once-mighty Nanam Division of the Japanese Army were taken as prisoners without even fighting and dragged off to Siberia by the Soviets gave me a sense of relief.

At the same time, I deeply felt that war must disappear from the face of the earth, for even here, helpless women must have suffered unspeakable humiliation and been trampled under the boots of the brutal Soviet soldiers.

Soviet forces appeared to be in control throughout North Korean territory. Once again, we found ourselves as their subjects, living in a state of servitude. We keenly felt the plight of our powerless nation under their rule. While some may have welcomed Soviet soldiers as liberators from oppression, we couldn't help but doubt whether they would truly grant our people freedom. It seemed more likely that our nation's destiny was uncertain.

On the other hand, we heard stories of how these same Soviet troops had ruthlessly plundered and caused suffering to Japanese civilians in

Manchuria. But our Korean women reportedly stood their ground and fought off the advancing Soviet soldiers with laundry bats, which was a source of pride and relief in these trying times.

We received a warm welcome from Shim Young-soon's uncle in Nanam. He had only heard that we had escaped from the Japanese army and been part of the Korean Volunteer Army led by Mu Jeong. Despite knowing little about our specific experiences, he held us in high regard and seemed envious of our prospects for a better future.

Nanam was not far from Toijo (退潮), where Mu Jeong was born, so the uncle was well-informed about Mu Jeong. He believed that Mu Jeong would rise to power. He mentioned that there was some initial chaos after the Soviet forces arrived in Jinju, but now the people's committee was gradually restoring order. On the downside, he noted that the cost of living had significantly increased, making life even more challenging.

For dinner, we were served a delicious pollack stew, and its simple yet flavorful taste was beyond words. People often said that you couldn't truly appreciate the taste of pollack unless you were in Hamgyeong Province, and indeed, this pollack stew felt like a genuine taste of Korea. It was a masterpiece of a dish.

Shim Young-soon's uncle suggested that since we had come this far, we should visit the famous Jueul (朱乙) Hot Springs for a bath. So, the next day, our group headed to Jueul. When we arrived at the Jueul Hot Springs and entered the bath, we were astonished by how hot the spring water was. It was so hot that you could have boiled eggs in it. At that time, there was no supply of cold water, so we couldn't immerse ourselves in the bath. We could only scoop water and rinse ourselves, but even that was a luxury. How rare and refreshing it was to bathe like this!

Despite being back in our homeland, enjoying baths and good food, we were still living the life of fugitives, which left a lingering unease in our hearts. We couldn't help but wish for a more natural and free return to our home country without having to flee.

Indeed, who could truly understand the sense of disappointment and the feeling of being chased that we experienced after leaving the Korean Independence Alliance? Who could we confide in? Would anyone sympathize with our thoughts? It often felt like everyone would criticize our rash actions, making the future seem incredibly bleak.

Figure 84: Jueul Hot Springs, North Hamgyong Province, 1945.

Beautiful coastal areas along the East Sea

We turned inland towards the plateau, leaving Nanam behind, and followed the coastline. Looking out over the East Sea, the winter ocean was an incredible shade of blue, just like the sky above. The sky and the sea blended into one beautiful hue, and the pine trees lining the road added to this picturesque scene. When I raised my eyes to look at the nearby mountain, it was covered in a pristine white blanket of snow. The unique rock formations along the roadside, seagulls gliding above the water—all of it harmonized to create a breathtaking natural spectacle.

Walking along the quiet coastal road, where there was not a soul in sight, the surroundings felt not just tranquil but almost eerily silent. As I gazed upon the breathtaking natural beauty that God had bestowed upon our nation, my heavy and stifled heart began to lighten. I started to believe that the days ahead of us would also be guided by the same divine hand that had created this splendid landscape, and my steps felt considerably lighter.

We soon reached Toijo, which was said to be the hometown of Mu Jeong, the commander-in-chief of the Korean Volunteer Army. As we passed through the streets, numerous banners covered the entire town, bearing slogans such as

"Long Live General Mu Jeong's Return,"
"Pride of this Town, Comrade Mu Jeong, Long Live,"
"Long Live the Korean Communist Party."

Not a single one of these failed to surprise us. It became clear that Mu Jeong had already returned and begun his activities. We could only assume that a network of cells had spread across the region under his leadership, and local self-governing committees were likely established and governing the area. Our hearts grew heavy and anxious once again, and our steps felt burdened as we quickly left Toijo behind.

In Gilju (吉州), we were able to board a train, although not in passenger cars. We managed to get onto a coal-carrying top-open freight car. Passing through tunnels, we were choked by the smoke belching from the locomotive. Nevertheless, the freight car, although slow, steadily carried us towards the plateau. Sitting on the coal, I looked out towards the East Sea once again. Along the coastline, I could see rows of dried pollack. With its breathtaking landscapes, distinct seasons, and abundant marine life, this country was undoubtedly a land blessed by God! I was deeply moved. If our liberated homeland truly embraced free democratic politics for the benefit of the people, it could undoubtedly become a paradise on Earth, rivaling any other nation.

As we passed through Heungnam (興南), many factory chimneys came into view. These chimneys stood cold and silent, indicating that the Soviet forces had most likely removed all the machinery from the factories. The Heungnam area had previously been used by Japan as a chemical industrial zone, as they expanded into China. However, now that liberation had come, I believed that it was our duty to operate these factories ourselves and build a prosperous nation with our own hands.

Return to Hometown

The freight train detoured from Gowon and headed toward Sunan (順安), entering the Pyeongwon Line (平元線). The train continued to run through rugged mountainous terrain, but by then the sun had already set, and nothing was visible except darkness.

Eventually, the freight train arrived in Sunan. Pyongyang was not far from there. I had an intense desire to visit Pyongyang, but since members of the Korean Independence Alliance had already entered the country and likely occupied important positions and begun their activities there, I feared I might run into someone on the street. For that reason, I decided not to stop in Pyongyang.

The Kyeong-ui Line (京義線) was still operating properly, so we were able to switch to a train bound for Sinuiju (新義州) directly from Sunan. The journey from Sunan to my hometown station, Goeup (古邑), took about two hours. Looking out the window, I saw fields that had finished harvesting and mountains covered in a light dusting of snow passing by. Now, finally, I was heading home, and my emotions were overwhelming. However, even as my hometown and family's house drew closer, it was hard to believe it was real. Would my parents and relatives warmly welcome my return? I remembered how just two years ago, I had left my hometown station wearing a uniform and with many people there who didn't expect me to return alive.

I had escaped from the Japanese army to survive, wore the uniform of the Eighth Route Army, joined the Korean independence movement, and eventually found myself—unexpectedly—in the ranks of the Korean Volunteer Army. After a long and arduous journey, I was now

279

approaching my hometown station alive, yet my heart felt neither joy nor relief, only turmoil.

I was certain that I would be denounced as "a traitor to the nation and a selfish liberal who deceived the working masses!" It made me feel as though there was no place left for me to stand.

The train was now crossing the Cheongcheon River (淸川江) railway bridge, and the darkness was deepening. I felt somewhat relieved that I would be getting off alone at my hometown station in the middle of the night. As the following thoughts kept surfacing one after another, my heart once again grew heavy with unease.

"Was I truly on the right path, returning home like this?
Should I have headed straight to Seoul, South Korea,
   instead of going toward my hometown from Sunan?
How could a coward like me, who had rejected the revolution,
   face my parents and the people of my hometown?"

The four of us had made a promise. It seemed like we couldn't live in North Korea, so the plan was to briefly visit our hometowns and then contact each other to meet in Seoul. Since Shim Young-soon's hometown was Gwaksan (郭山), and both Jung Geun-seok and Ahn Guk-ju were from Sinuiju (新義州), I was the first one to get off at Goeup Station. From Goeup to my hometown, Osan, it was only about 2 kilometers away, and my house was right next to Osan School. I walked along the moonlit road, following the train tracks, and soon I arrived in front of my house. The house looked exactly the same as when

I left it two years ago. As I knocked on the gate and entered the courtyard, I heard the chime of the wall clock. It was January 20, 1946, the day I returned home, exactly two years after I had been forcefully taken away by the Japanese army. After two years without any news, how must my wife have felt to suddenly see me—alive—opening the front gate and walking in like that!

Figure 85: Kim Deok-yeon, my wife (circa 1954)

Chapter 12

My hometown

Osan after liberation

The village of Osan, my hometown, was centered around Osan School, which had been founded in 1907—just before the fall of the Yi Joseon dynasty—by the enlightened patriot Namgang Lee Seung-hoon (南岡 李昇薰). After hearing a stirring, patriotic lecture in 1905 in Pyongyang by Dosan Ahn Chang-ho (島山 安昌浩), he became convinced that education was the only way to save the nation and used his personal fortune to establish the school.

Because of this, Osan School became a prestigious private institution where teachers and students with a sense of purpose gathered to fulfill their national mission. In fact, during the March 1st Movement (1919), Japanese military police, calling it "a school of the Korean people," set it on fire and reduced it to ashes.

Among the early teachers of Osan School were prominent independence activists like Ye Jun (呂準), Cho Man-sik (曺晚植), Shin Chae-ho (申采浩), and Lee Kwang-soo (李光洙). As for the early graduates, notable figures include Kim Do-tae (金道泰, 1st graduating class), So Woel (素月), Ham Seok-heon (咸錫憲), and the renowned artist Lee Jung-seob (李仲燮).

The village of Osan could be considered a school-centered community, as it was formed around the establishment of the school. With cultural facilities built to serve the roughly 500 students, it was known throughout the surrounding area as a good place to live, and many people from various regions came to settle there. My father ran a shop next to the school.

Figure 86: Lee Seung-hoon (李昇薰).

Figure 87: An Chang-ho (安昌浩).

Figure 88: Osan School established in Jeongju, 1907.

With the arrival of liberation, even Osan—once a peaceful village—began to feel a chilling breeze of unrest. My maternal uncle, Kim Yong-ha (金龍河), had dropped out of Osan School in the third grade and gone to Tokyo to study art. While there, he became deeply immersed in extreme liberal thought and got involved in the socialist movement. When liberation came, he quickly returned to Korea, sensing that his time had come, and transformed himself into a communist. Taking the lead, he organized a people's tribunal on the grounds of Osan School, targeting the Japanese principal named Ito (伊藤). It was said that during the incident, the principal's daughter was handed over to the Soviet soldiers, while Ito was executed after being forced to endure the humiliation of cleaning latrines.

Witnessing all of this, a Japanese instructor named Kobayashi (小林) is said to have returned home, killed his wife with a knife, and then committed *seppuku* (a form of ritual suicide by disembowelment) in his military uniform. This tragic end of the Japanese nationals who had faced defeat could be seen as the inevitable outcome, but when I heard such stories upon returning to my hometown, I couldn't help but feel a deep sense of unease, perhaps because I had fled from the communist army.

I had returned to my hometown—a place I had longed for even in my dreams—but I felt no joy. This was because even in Osan, the conflict between the left and right had become sharply polarized. In Osan, the true leader was effectively Joo Gi-yong (朱基瑢), the principal of Osan School. He was Namgang's son-in-law and had graduated from Tokyo Higher Normal School before returning to Osan, where he took up a teaching position. Until the Japanese took over the school, he served as principal and greatly contributed to its development. After liberation, it was only natural that he was reappointed as the principal of Osan School.

He also had significant political ambitions and served as the north Pyongan provincial committee chairman of the Korea Democratic Party in Seoul. He was vigorously active, turning Osan into a stronghold of the right wing. Thus, in the early days following liberation, the right-wing forces in Osan were unquestionably dominant.

In response to this, there was Kim Jun-sang (金俊相), a member of the hastily formed communist party, who had attended Osan School but dropped out. He had left Osan, dabbled in mining for a while, and then returned to live in Osan. He emphasized that the reason for his departure from Osan was because he was a communist, and he was now rising through the ranks to become a key figure in the communist party, opposing Joo Gi-yong's leadership. At that time, my father was the local leader of the right-wing political organization called the Chosun Democratic Party, organized by Cho Man-sik. My father worked tirelessly day and night, working alongside Joo Gi-yong, with the goal of realizing democracy.

Seclusion

After returning home, I couldn't tell any of my family members that I had escaped from the Korean Independence movement. At that time, considering the political situation, fleeing from the revolutionary forces was not something to boast about. It could even hinder my mental development. As February approached, Ko Han-kwon (高漢權), the director of academic affairs at Osan High School, told me that Principal Joo had proposed me to come to the school and begin teaching at the start of the new semester in March. I declined, citing personal reasons, but Ko insisted that it was the principal's proposal, and he had only come to deliver the message on his behalf. I found myself in a position where

I couldn't clearly state a reason for rejecting it, and I had no choice but to accept the principal's proposal.

In fact, up until I graduated from Waseda university, I had always hoped to become a teacher at Osan School. In our hometown, becoming a teacher at Osan High School was a matter of great pride and admiration. Therefore, my parents, relatives, and neighbors were delighted that I would be teaching at Osan High School. Furthermore, my mother, a traditional Korean woman, spent her life cooking and doing laundry, and her greatest joy was attending church on Sundays. So, my becoming a teacher at that prestigious school in our hometown was an immense source of happiness for her. In this situation, not being able to provide a clear reason and letting down my mother's heartfelt wish was an unbearable pain for me. I decided to wait until March when the school year started to assess the situation and make a decision.

Hesitating the escape to the South Korea, I felt that my space was gradually shrinking during my confinement at home. The communist party had already taken control of all the government offices, and I could sense the watchful eyes of surveillance closing in on me like a spider's web. As time passed, the prospect of leaving my hometown again and escaping to South Korea not only seemed increasingly difficult but also downright impossible.

Running away from here would have been entirely different from fleeing the Japanese military camp or the Korean Volunteer Army. The thought of once again leaving behind my home and family, risking death in yet another escape, was something I didn't even want to consider. At that time, my honest feeling was simply a desire to stay quietly at home and live an ordinary life as a teacher at Osan School. And I tried to console myself with the thought that perhaps such a life might be possible.

I asked myself: Since the U.S.-Soviet Joint Commission is said to be held in Seoul in March 1946 to discuss the unification of Korea, if a unified government is established, wouldn't that mean there's no absolute need for me to go to South Korea? In a unified homeland, the left and right would cooperate, and in that case, going to the South might narrow the scope of my political activity—so I thought.

After much solitary deliberation, I finally mustered the courage and went to the Jeongju security office (equivalent to a police station). At that time, the head of the office was Uhm Mi-seung (嚴美昇), who was roughly an uncle figure to me.

Figure 89: Soviet General Shtykov and American General John R. Hodge at the US-Soviet Joint Commission (Seoul, March 1946)

In his youth, due to poverty at home, Uhm Mi-seung had emigrated to Bansuk (盤石) in Manchuria, where he worked as a principal at an elementary school and participated in the Korean Independence movement. After liberation, he returned to Korea and became one of the founding members of the communist party in Jeongju, eventually rising to the position of head of the security office.

He welcomed me warmly. I spoke to him, frankly, saying that since I had escaped from the Independence Alliance, I was effectively a criminal in this region, and I asked him directly to help facilitate my escape to South Korea.

Regarding this, the police chief firmly said, "Would I arrest my own nephew while I'm in this position? The New People's Party (新民黨) is about to be established, so use your past experiences and contribute to the party."

I was moved by the sincerity of the police chief's words and decided to abandon my plan to defect to the South. Instead, I took part in the founding of the New Democratic Party. Of course, I was aware that as a police chief, he was responsible for executing orders from the communist party, which held real power. The issue was that I didn't want to flee, and I placed my trust in the police chief's words, feeling reassured.

However, at that time, many individuals associated with the Korean Independence movement were already operating under the name of the North Korean Communist Party. They held real power in various fields. My mother's side uncle Kim Yong-ha, who entered the communist party branch in the county, informed me that they were already aware of my presence in my hometown and even knew that I had escaped from the Korean Independence movement. Given this situation, it was clear that I would be arrested when the time came, and after that, nobody could predict what would happen next. Now, it seemed that the only option left for me was to go to South Korea, but I hesitated, feeling trapped in uncertainty.

I didn't want to betray the communist party by fleeing once again. Even if I left my hometown and went to the South, there was no guarantee that I would be able to enjoy freedom there. So, I had some hope of living quietly in my hometown by trying to appease the communist party to some extent.

Divided Osan School

One day, Shin Sang-cho came to my house. He was the one who had asked us to go first when we were leaving the Korean Volunteer Army camp in Choyangcheon. He had followed us shortly after and had now arrived at our hometown. Meeting him was a joy beyond words; it was like meeting a savior. We were in similar circumstances, so we could discuss our situation together. Moreover, he was a quick thinker, and his presence could have a decisive influence on our future actions.

Upon returning to our hometown, he found that his elderly parents were urging him to get married. He desperately asked for my help in introducing him to a woman for marriage.

Shin Sang-cho's marriage happened quite easily. The woman he married was my wife's best friend and came from a prestigious family in Seoncheon (宣川), known for their wealth and reputation. She probably never expected someone like Shin Sang-cho, who was a graduate of Tokyo Imperial University, as her potential partner. I was pleased to think that he would settle down in our hometown for some time with his new family, even if only for a while, because the fate that awaited us would be the same. I told him,

"You have a quick judgment of the situation.
When the time comes to go to the South, don't hesitate to tell me.
I will follow you without question.
It seems that the communist party won't forgive us and will not let us stay here."

He nodded in agreement with my words.

In March 1946, I started teaching at the Osan school. It was my first job, but I wasn't particularly happy about it. Nevertheless, I put my best effort into teaching. However, the atmosphere in the staff room was quite chilly, and I could feel that the staff were completely divided into left and right factions.

Principal Joo Gi-yong seemed busy with political activities, mentioning trips to Seoul to meet with Hanmin Party leader Kim Sung-soo (金性洙) or going to Pyongyang to meet with Choi Yong-geon (崔庸鍵 : Osan alumnus). Physical education teacher Kim Myung-bok (金明福), who later became the vice president of Kyung Hee University, displayed his exceptional skills as he hurriedly traveled to Pyongyang, carrying principal Joo Gi-yong's bag, to contact the prominent figures in both the left and right factions.

Figure 90: Joo Gi-yong (朱基瑢).

Left-leaning teachers were actively enforcing the communist party's directives on both teachers and students, while the right-leaning teachers, unable to openly oppose them, remained in the background, offering only quiet criticism.

This dynamic was especially evident during the morning "newspaper reading sessions" (讀報會) held before classes began. In these sessions, political issues covered in the day's newspaper were discussed, with commentary led by the communist party's cell leader. The right-wing teachers showed little to no interest in participating in these discussions.

In fact, most of the right-wing teachers were preoccupied with only one thing: figuring out how they could escape to the South.

The chairman of the Galsan-myeon (葛山面) people's committee, Kim Jun-sang (金俊相), secretly summoned me to his home. He explained that to capture the stronghold of anti-communism in Osan, which was Osan School, we needed to apprehend the school's principal, Joo Gi-yong. He asked me to secretly report any counterrevolutionary behavior by the principal within the school. I was shocked by this request. While I was in a precarious position with the communist party, I had always considered deceiving others for personal gain as the worst kind of moral corruption. Now, being told to inform on others to save myself left me in disbelief.

Principal Joo Gi-yong was a prominent figure in the right-wing faction of this region and held the position of the Korean Democratic Party's North Pyongan Province leader. However, there were no signs of his being anti-communist in his actions. His belief was that the liberated homeland should achieve democracy by uniting both left and right forces. I heard Kim Jun-sang's words with one ear but chose to ignore them with the other. Regardless of my own situation, I couldn't bring myself to monitor and inform on a person like Principal Joo, who I believed to be a virtuous leader.

As time passed, one by one, the teachers who had shown right-leaning tendencies began to disappear. Each of them had found their own way to head to the South, and those who remained became increasingly cautious with their words and behavior. This was because Kim Jun-sang had successfully planted a new informant within the school, and every detail of the school's internal affairs was being reported to him. That informant was a man named Kim Dong-ho (金東湖), who had been my classmate at Osan School.

When I first met Kim Dong-ho, he had said that with the world now overrun by communists, he couldn't bear the sight of it and just wanted to bury his head and die. He was a small-minded would-be hero filled with an inferiority complex, and for some reason, after transforming into a communist, he began to run wild without any sense of restraint. The other teachers began calling him an "unleashed colt," as he charged recklessly in all directions, utterly blind to his surroundings. Lately, rumors had it that his living conditions had improved dramatically, which made it clear that a significant amount of operational funds had been funneled to him in his role as Kim Jun-sang's informant. As his disruptive behavior escalated, the conflict between left and right within the school grew even more intense.

Conflict

One morning, I heard the news that principal Joo Gi-yong had been arrested and taken to the Sinuiju City Security Bureau. I thought to myself, "So the communist party has finally drawn its sword." Of course, the charge against him was labeled as "reactionary (反動)." At that moment, a thought flashed through my mind — although the principal's so-called reactionary activities had nothing to do with me, I had an instinctive feeling that I, too, would soon be arrested under the same label of "reactionary." The new principal appointed in his place was a man named Jeon Ui-won (全義遠), who had previously been a teacher and had the backing of the Communist Party. He had graduated from a physics school in Japan, but the students, noting his twisted personality, had given him the nickname "Y-shape" (Y 字).

He boasted that he had been involved in underground Communist activities since earlier days and declared that since this was now the age of communism, it was impossible to go against the tide of the times. He went on to boldly claim that if Namgang Lee Seung-hoon were still alive, as a visionary, he would have surely supported communism. With such assertions, he joined hands with people like Kim Dong-ho to drive out the right-leaning teachers. Watching all this unfold, I couldn't help but ask myself once again:

"Can one emotionally accept communism?

To become a communist as an intellectual, I believed, meant not only abandoning everything one had been, but also fully transforming into a member of the proletariat—internalizing the class consciousness of the working masses—and even then, continuing an unrelenting, tearful struggle against oneself."

In the past, I left the Independence Alliance with the conviction that I could not dig my own grave. Now, seeing those leftist teachers who, unaware of their own situation, were inviting disaster upon themselves, I couldn't help but feel a deep sense of pity for them. They did not truly understand themselves and, I thought, were bringing misfortune upon themselves.

The communist party places the utmost importance on class identity. In the early stages, they may give titles and responsibilities to intellectuals to make use of them, but as workers and peasants from the lower levels of society gradually grow and develop class consciousness, it is only natural that those earlier intellectuals are eventually purged. At Osan School, under pressure from the principal Jeon and Kim Dong-ho, communization appeared to be advancing. However, contradictions also deepened, and in 1947, a large-scale anti-communist uprising led by the students broke out, resulting in their expulsion from the school.

The fact that I had walked away from the Independence Alliance might have seemed like a trivial matter to others, but I knew very well that for the communist party—an organization that operates through strict structure—someone who understands the organization and then betrays it is labeled a "reactionary (反動)" and judged as having committed one of the most heinous crimes.

I believed that rather than spending my days at school only to be eventually arrested, I needed to make a decisive move and head south to South Korea. Yet I couldn't bring myself to take that step.

"Was it due to my attachment to my hometown?
Or was it fear of starting a new life?
In truth, even if I escaped to the South, I had no relatives there, no foundation for making a living."

Amidst all this, one day after finishing my teaching duties at school, I decided to go to Gwaksan to check on the whereabouts of Shim Young-soon, who had escaped with me. When I arrived at his home, his younger brother greeted me and told me that his older brother had already gone to the South. He explained the situation: when Shim Young-soon returned home, the family considered it a great blessing and held a village celebration. At that time, encouraged by his parents and wanting to show filial piety, Shim Young-soon even decided to get engaged to a local woman from the village.

However, as the date of the engagement approached and the household was in an uproar preparing for the celebration, news suddenly came that agents from the Jeongju Security Bureau were on their way to arrest him that very day. Upon hearing this, he bolted out the back door and fled into the mountains. His brother said he probably set out on the journey to the South right then. I could understand how desperate he must have been to flee without even sending word, yet I couldn't help but feel a sense of resentment that he had gone alone. After reaching the South, he reportedly became a follower of Kim Gu and joined the Northwest Youth League, where he played a remarkable role in tracking down and fighting the communists.

Father protecting his son

A few days later, I went to Sinuiju. It was to meet Jung Geun-seok and Ahn Guk-ju, who had also escaped with me and with whom I had promised to flee to the South together. Jung Geun-seok's family was running a prominent business in Sinuiju at the time, called Gongshin Trading Company (共信商會), and I arrived there late in the evening. After knocking on the door for quite a while, an elderly man finally appeared. From the moment I saw him, I instinctively knew he was Geun-seok's father. When I told him I had come from Jeongju to see Geun-seok, he replied without the slightest change in expression, "I don't know."

At first, I assumed he claimed not to know because he didn't recognize who I was or what kind of person I might be. So, I explained repeatedly that I had been a student soldier, that I had escaped from the Japanese military camp together with his son, and that we had traveled all the way back to our hometown as comrades. Yet his response remained unchanged: "I don't know." It became clear to me that more than being wary of me as a possible Communist, he was deliberately denying knowledge of his already-defected son in order to protect him. In his mind, insisting he knew nothing was the only way to safeguard his son's safety.

I then asked the father about Ahn Guk-ju, the son of the owner of Anguk Trading Company (安國商會). But once again, he remained consistent in his reply: "I don't know." At that point, I became certain that both Jung (鄭) and Ahn (安) had already fled to the South. I didn't ask any further and quietly turned to leave. How could I even begin to express the emptiness I felt in that moment?

As I made my way home, I guessed that Jung and Ahn had realized that the situation was far worse than we had anticipated—an environment in which the communist party had become so rampant that they couldn't bear to stay even a moment longer—and so they must have fled to the South immediately. In fact, at that time, high-ranking members of the Independence Alliance were entering the country one after another, and since Sinuiju was a key entry point, its security agencies had already been completely taken over by those very officials.

A little house for my wife and me

Thankfully, the school provided us with a cozy little house. After being suddenly drafted as a student soldier following our marriage and then returning, it was the first time my wife and I were able to build a home of our own.

When I was first conscripted into the Japanese army as a student soldier, the Japanese principal of Osan School had placed a placard above my family's nameplate reading, "A Glorious Home of a Soldier Departing for War." He also gave my wife special treatment by appointing her as a teacher at Osan Elementary School.

Having graduated from Ewha Girls' High School and been enrolled at Ewha Women's College, my wife faithfully fulfilled her duties as a teacher and, losing track of time, devoted herself wholeheartedly to educating her students.

However, when the fact that I had escaped from the Japanese army became known at the local police station, the attitude of the school principal changed. He not only removed my wife from her teaching position but also subjected her to various forms of harassment, and surveillance never ceased. Now, after just two years, I was alive and back in my hometown, setting up a home provided by my workplace. It was an unparalleled blessing and joy for us.

My wife also mentioned that she was expecting a baby, with the due date being in December 1946. This made the prospect of traveling to South Korea with my pregnant wife even more daunting. When I escaped from the Japanese army and later fled to the Yalu River as a volunteer soldier, I had firmly resolved not to look back. But now, the situation was entirely different.

Figure 91: Students at Ewha Woman's College after Liberation.

Leaving my wife behind and going south alone felt like committing yet another grave sin against her—and it wasn't something I could bring myself to do. Up until that point, I hadn't told my wife or my parents that I had deserted from the Korean Volunteer Army.

No, more precisely, I couldn't bring myself to tell them—because I didn't want to cause them any more worry or distress on my account.

With determination, I went to see one of my former teachers Kim Ki-seok (金基錫, who later became a dean at the Seoul National University and the head of the Korean Teachers' Union at South Korea), who was known for his strong personality. I confessed to him that I had escaped and that I was in a situation where I needed to go to South Korea.

Mr. Kim, being a man of good character, was likely unaware of class struggle and the harshness of the communist party in those days. The teacher, upon hearing what I said, told me there was nothing to worry about. At the time, the newly forming New Democratic Party was a party meant to accommodate intellectuals, and since he himself was involved with it, he believed lightly that as long as I acted alongside him, nothing serious would happen. Although I knew very well that my situation was something I needed to judge and resolve on my own, I soon regretted having grown weak-hearted, revealing my past to someone else and seeking their advice.

Figure 92: Kim Ki-seok (金基錫).

How could someone who praised Kant's philosophy of concepts understand Marx's communist party declaration or comprehend Lenin's proletarian dictatorship? How could he experience the communist party's cell organization, where one must kill and be killed to survive? His words of reassurance came from his benign character. From his perspective, who could suddenly advise, 'Go to South Korea.'

I realized once again that my affairs were something, only I could decide, and I had to solve them on my own.

Gapsan faction and land reform

The Second U.S.-Soviet Joint Conference ended in failure. The Soviet Union believed that if they could communize even just the northern part of Korea, they would soon be able to bring the entire Korean Peninsula into their sphere of influence, and they had no intention of establishing a unified government for Korea. North Korea intensified its propaganda, labeling figures like Rhee Syngman and Kim Gu as stooges of U.S. imperialism, and banners emphasizing this message were displayed everywhere.

The communist party began military training and established so-called cadre training centers across the country as they dreamt of a forcible unification. Judging by the situation at the time, it seemed that Kim Il-sung's Gapsan faction (甲山派), which advocated military rule under the occupation forces, was in control of politics rather than the Korean Democratic Alliance, which had gained revolutionary experience from the Chinese communist party.

The Independence Alliance, led by Mu Jeong and Kim Du-bong, who had expanded their influence within the Eighth Route Army, possessed both an ideal political ideology modeled after the Chinese communist party's theory of new democracy and a wealth of revolutionary experience. However, they were gradually being pushed aside by the Gapsan faction, led by Kim Il-sung and backed by the Soviet Army. This was evident in the fact that Kim Du-bong instructed the

Alliance's senior members to avoid reckless clashes with the Gapsan faction in various areas of activity.

In March 1946, it was announced that Kim Il-sung would be holding a mass rally in Jeongju, so I went there with my father to observe the event. When my father saw the man in his mid-thirties—Kim Il-sung, whom he had only heard about until then—and witnessed the crowds cheering enthusiastically, even if it was all state-orchestrated, he sighed and lamented that the era had indeed become one of communist rule, and sorrowfully wondered where in this land democracy could still be found.

Figure 93: Kim Il-sung delivering a speech at Moranbong Public Stadium in Pyongyang on October 14, 1945.

I sincerely helped with the establishment of the New Democratic Party organization in Galsan-myeon. Since the New Democratic Party was an affiliate group of the communist party, most intellectuals were indifferent toward it. Some people may have looked at my involvement and suspected that I had converted to communism.

However, I had never received a party membership card from either the Independence Alliance or New Democratic Party. In fact, I didn't even know such identification cards existed. They, too, likely never considered me to be one of their own. In truth, I was merely dancing on the fringes—doing just enough to stay alive without leaving my hometown.

By May 1946, a series of transformations took place in North Korea under the communist party. This was due to the proclamation of the land reform law and the nationalization of industry law. The land reform law defined landlords as those who owned more than five *jeongbo* of land, and stipulated that their land would be confiscated and that they would be expelled to areas over 100 *li* (about 50 kilometers) away.

One day, an elder named Hwang Jang-no (黃長老) came to visit my father and tearfully pleaded his case. He said the land he owned had been earned through years of frugality—going without food and clothing—and he could not bear to have it taken away entirely by the communists.

Hearing this, I thought to myself: "Elder Hwang still doesn't realize that times have changed and with them, so have moral values. This is the era of revolution now." I couldn't help but feel a sense of pity for him.

Owning more than five *jeongbo* of land was not a crime! I had witnessed someone being driven out by sharecroppers just because they had more than five *jeongbo* of land. Seeing the sharecroppers jubilantly burning the tools of their landlords, one of them, who was drunk, shouted on the roadside, 'Ah, this is the life! Get rid of those wicked landlords and take their land, and we should support the communist party.' The peasants were rejoicing at having obtained the land, but it seemed they didn't know that they would have to turn over all the grains they harvested from that land to the communist party. This demonstrated how truly fearful power was, as North Korea was becoming completely ensnared in the chains of the communist party without tasting the freedom of liberation.

(Editor's Note: 1 *jeongbo* is equivalent to 2,934 square meters, which is approximately 890 *pyeong*, Korean traditional unit, or 10 *majigi*, a traditional Korean farming land unit.)

The rejoicing peasants warned that they must crush the antics of counter-revolutionaries while guarding the roads. I once had an occasion to visit a farmers' association one day to meet people. One farmer looked surprised and said, "That person isn't supposed to come here." with a puzzled look, while another farmer greeted me with joy, asking, "Has that person joined our side?" At that moment, I felt deeply ashamed. In reality, I was someone who had no right to be there, no matter what the circumstances.

The peasants were rejoicing in the fact that they had obtained land, but it seemed they were unaware that they would soon have to hand over all the harvested crops to the communist party. Power was indeed a formidable force, and North Korea was to be overwhelmed by the chains of the communist party even before tasting a glimpse of liberation.

Roads to South Korea

At school, the older teachers who had been there for a long time were mostly right-wing, and the newly appointed young teachers were criticized for sympathizing with the communist party during the turbulent times. Baek Nak-min (白樂敏 – a graduate of Waseda University and an English teacher at school), a local landlord who owned about 100 *seok* of land (a traditional unit of land measurement), was a cautious individual and couldn't openly join the communist party but sympathized with communist ideology cautiously.

(Editor's Note: During the Joseon Dynasty, the *seok* unit was used as a taxation measure based on agricultural yield rather than physical size. The *seok* system indicated land area indirectly based on its productivity. For example, fertile land could produce 15 to 20 *seok* per *jeongbo*, while poor land might yield only 5 to 10 *seok* per *jeongbo*.)

He would often say things like, "We must now discard our outdated feudal mindset. With the Soviet army stationed here, there is no going back to the old society. There are reactionary forces lurking in the school, so I want to go to Pyongyang and teach at Kim Il Sung University."

As I listened to his words, I couldn't help but think that he was revealing the typical weakness of an intellectual—someone who had failed to break free from the class character of a petty bourgeois, unable to transcend his small-capitalist mindset.

One day, I heard that Yi Geun-chil (李根七), who had clear right-wing tendencies, had successfully defected to South Korea. He had sent a telegram to a friend in Pyongyang asking him to send a message saying,

'The decision has been made to go to Kim Il-sung University, so come to Pyongyang as soon as possible.' He then presented this telegram to the school principal and received praise for his cleverness before leaving for Pyongyang. Once there, he falsely obtained a medical certificate claiming that his health had deteriorated and that he needed to go to Haeju (海州). He used this document whenever he was searched, and with the guidance of a pre-arranged contact, he safely defected to South Korea.

In the school, Yi Geun-chil's successful defection had a significant impact and was a shocking event that caused a big stir. Kim Dong-ho, who was not only Yi Geun-chil's disciple but also loved him more than anyone else, publicly declared that if he couldn't capture his teacher, he would hunt down and punish the reactionary elements in the school. Right-wing teachers seemed to be exploring various paths to South Korea, inspired by Yi Geun-chil's ingenious idea.

Through this incident, it became clear from Kim Dong-ho's words and actions that, under the communist party, one had to report even their own parents and kill their mentors in order to survive. From then on, both teachers and students discreetly disappeared one by one from the school, and everyone suspected that if they didn't reappear, they had defected to South Korea. Venturing onto the path of defection was not only fraught with the risk of arrest but also meant changing one's way of life, so it required immense courage and determination.

Chapter 13

Detention

Living an ordinary life as an ordinary person
is an extremely happy thing.

Arrest

I sometimes wondered if leading a completely ordinary life, just like ordinary people do, might be an unattainable destiny. There can hardly be anything more agonizing and unhappy than living with secrets, constantly being pursued. While I often thought of going to the southern part of the Korean Peninsula, where they said there was freedom, deep down I cursed myself for not having the courage to leave this place due to my indecisive nature.

One day in June 1946, I was lying in my room. I suddenly felt a presence and when I got up, I saw my old schoolmate from Osan School, Kim Woo-han (金佑漢), standing beside me. I couldn't help but think that the time had finally come! When I met him earlier, he had been fervently opposed to the communist party and had vowed to fight against it even if it meant dying. But somehow, he had become a leading figure in the communist party. He told me that he was now working at the Sinuiju Provincial Security Office, which was a powerful organ of the communist party, and that he had come to find me to escort me to the Provincial Security Office.

No one was home, and strangely, I felt relieved. If my wife had been at home, I would have had to reassure her, and how confused would I have been? With a calm heart, I wrote a note and left it behind as I headed out with him. In the note, I wrote, "Go to Sinuiju. Don't look for me for a while." We took a train from the Goeup Station.

As soon as we boarded the train, Kim Woo-han began to speak. He said that the other colleagues had suggested that I should be brought in wearing handcuffs, but a superior had said that I didn't need to be handcuffed. I thought it was fortunate. If others had seen me being escorted in handcuffs, how much would they have denounced me as a gray capitalist?

Kim Woo-han comforted me with various words as he saw that I was deflated. From the atmosphere at the Jeongju security office, it didn't seem like they were trying to arrest me by force. Perhaps they were just calling me to the Sinuiju Provincial security office to give me a position or for some other reason. In his view, I was probably innocent. He would carry out the orders of his superiors and take me into custody, but he did not think that I had committed any crimes. This was evident from what he said. The order to arrest me was probably handed down from the Sinuiju Provincial security office, not initiated by the Jeongju security office. At that time, the head of the Jeongju security office was no longer my relative, Uhm Mi-seung.

While Kim Woo-han's surveillance of me during the journey to Sinuiju seemed lax, it was a disguise, and I could feel the cold gaze of another observer who was watching both me and Kim Woo-han from the back seat. I had a premonition that something was amiss. We arrived in Sinuiju in the middle of the night, and I had to spend that night in an inn with Kim Woo-han.

When morning came, Kim Woo-han led me to the north Pyongan Provincial security department. After asking around here and there, he took me to the inspection division. The head of the division, Park Chi-rye (a civilian), glared at me and barked, "So, you're the one they call Uhm Young-sik? You're about to learn what suffering really means." With that, he shouted at me in a threatening tone, opened the cell door, and kicked me inside. Although I had now become a prisoner, I thought to myself, "So, at last, the inevitable has come". Strangely, my anxiety vanished, and I instead felt a sense of calm.

The cell I was placed in was Cell No. 101. Among the 12 cells in the North Pyongan provincial security office, Cell No. 101 was the largest and held more than ten inmates. Despite being a cell with iron bars, the toilet was located outside the cell, unlike during the Japanese colonial era. They explained that this was done out of respect for the human rights of inmates. I sat in one corner of the cell all day long. They provided three identical meals of cold rice cakes, but I couldn't bring

310

myself to eat them. According to them, initially, inmates couldn't eat the rice cakes, but after a while, they would eat them all.

The cell was a battleground where interrogators tried to force confessions, and prisoners tried to hide their crimes. Among the ten or so inmates, there was a student named Cha Sun-hak (車淳學), who was my junior at Osan School. I knew that he had led his fellow students during his school days and attacked the communist party headquarters in Galsan-myeon. I felt sorry for him. A young student who should have been devoted to his studies was carrying the burden of his country's tragedy on his shoulders, and it was a pitiful sight. Moreover, when he was scolded harshly by the guards, I couldn't help but feel sympathy for him.

He asked me, "Teacher, for what reason have you ended up in here?" More than anything, he seemed deeply worried that I might be handed over to the Soviet army and exiled to Siberia.

But human beings, in one way or another, find a way to survive. The cell was crowded with many detainees, and despite everything, they all seemed to be getting by. So, I thought to myself that I, too, might be able to endure.

At 10 p.m., after roll call, the lights were turned off. We lay back-to-back, but I couldn't fall asleep easily. The thought of the interrogation and torture that lay ahead made me feel my situation unbearably miserable.

Then, the next morning, the iron door opened—and to my shock, in came Shin Sang-cho, stooping as he entered. I was stunned. Seeing that he had also been arrested like me left me with a sinking feeling. It

311

became clear that, whatever we had misjudged, we had misjudged it gravely.

All I could feel was regret for not having taken the road south sooner. But now, having brought this fate upon myself, there was nothing left to do but endure it and wait—hoping somehow to break through.

Prison Life

After three days had passed, the prison warden called my name loudly, summoning me. He stood me before him and said, "I knew in advance that comrade had come here. One of your comrades, Han Myeong-sam, was imprisoned here for a month until he was released a few days ago. Since then, he has been asking us to assign you to the job of carrying meals."

From that day on, I was tasked with transporting meals from the kitchen to the prisoners. I was once again taken aback by this unexpected turn of events. Han Myeong-sam had stayed behind as a remaining unit when I left Huazhong branch, and the fact that he had been confined here before my arrival was a surprise.

Later, I heard from him that after liberation, he had been serving as an officer in the Eighth Route Army. Driven by a single desire to return to the newly liberated homeland as soon as possible, he escaped from there, boarded a ship in Tianjin, and entered Korea through Seoul—only to be arrested in his hometown of Sunchon (宣川).

After he was imprisoned in the Sinuiju Provincial Security Department, his mother-in-law, who lived alone, managed to bribe the cell warden and secure the privilege of delivering meals to inmates. He had even asked the warden earnestly in advance, believing that I, too, would soon be brought in.

In the prison, being assigned the task of carrying meals was a significant privilege. It allowed me to leave the cell three times a day and not only provided some mobility but also ensured that I received double rations compared to the other inmates, alleviating some of the hunger. I felt grateful to Han Myeong-sam. When I left Huazhong branch, he had given me a bullet as a parting gift, along with his tearful plea to endure whatever came my way and meet him in our hometown when it was safe. Wasn't he the one who, like me, had set foot on the land of our hometown, longed for it, and ended up in the cruel fate of confinement for revolutionary crimes?

It seemed that, regardless of circumstances, people were destined to survive. Many inmates in the prison managed to get by, and I believed that I could survive as well. We, the student soldiers, especially those who had infiltrated the ranks of the independence fighters from the Japanese army, had a fate that was too bitter to comprehend. While those student soldiers who were lucky enough to reach the Korean Provisional Government's side after escaping from the Japanese army became honored patriots, we found ourselves behind bars upon returning to our hometowns. Our destiny filled us with bitterness.

However, when Han Myung-sam was released and I took over the duties he had been performing in the cell, I felt somewhat more at ease, as I became convinced that I too would be released sometime soon.

Three times a day, I was allowed to leave the cell without a guard and walk to the kitchen next to the cell to collect baskets of corn cakes, which I then distributed to the other inmates. The kitchen lady, whenever I came by, would always show me sympathy and set aside a bowl of rice mixed with corn just for me.

She would look at me with pity and say, "What crime could a quiet, decent-looking young man like you have committed to be suffering like this?" When I sat in a corner of the kitchen to eat the corn-mixed rice, she would tell me to take my time and even prepare side dishes for me.

When I had distributed the rice cakes to the inmates, there were still two portions left for me. I handed these to Shin Sang-cho, offering words of comfort and encouragement to endure. It was heart-wrenching to see him sitting alone in a corner, struggling to eat his meager meal.

One day, as I walked towards the kitchen to collect the meals, I collided with Seung Dong-pyo, my former fellow student from Osan School and the school's art teacher. He seemed paralyzed, unable to move, and his astonished eyes locked onto me. I merely nodded and continued walking, not wanting to engage further. Shortly thereafter, he was released and returned to Osan and informed my family and the school that I was imprisoned in the security bureau. Until then, my family had been searching for me, not knowing where I had gone.

Occasionally, the prison warden showed me kindness by giving me a cigarette and encouraging me to smoke. He asked, "Why did you escape from the Independence Army? If you had stayed there, your future would have been secure. Right now, the high-ranking officials in this security bureau are all members of the Independence Army." He expressed sympathy and empathy towards me.

In the communist party, they claimed that they did not extract confessions through torture, as torture was considered a remnant of Japanese imperialism. It involved depriving them of food and not letting them sleep at night. In the same Cell No. 101, there was a person detained on suspicion of having set fire to a military supplies factory in Kanggye (江界). In a communist society, arsonists were treated especially severely, as they were considered criminals who had caused damage to state property. The investigator ordered him to fast and prevented him from sleeping, whether it was day or night.

A guard stood watch beside the iron bars, and if he dozed off even slightly, the guard would strike him with a whip. He wept, pleading that unless the real culprit appeared, there was no way to clear himself of the accusation. From what I could tell by his appearance and manner of speaking, he seemed to be just a laborer at the factory, not someone capable of committing arson. He couldn't endure even two days—he cried out loud and eventually collapsed. He was carried out on a stretcher, and after that, there was no way to know what happened to him.

There was a practice of taking sun baths in the courtyard for thirty minutes after lunch. During this time, the prison guards conducted searches in the cells. One day, while I was sitting and soaking in the sun, a high-ranking security officer unexpectedly passed by and stopped when he saw me. He had not been a student soldier, but he was someone who had been with me in the Huazhong Branch Alliance. Moreover, in the spring of 1944, near Xuzhou in a place called Tongshan (銅山), the three of us—including Shim Young-soon—had carried out enemy counter-intelligence operations together, making him, in effect, a comrade in the revolution. After liberation, he accompanied the Independence Alliance when they entered the country and became the head of the security section in the city security bureau.

He was wearing a large pistol and tall leather boots and exuded an air of authority. He approached me and asked bluntly, "Is it true that Shim Young-soon defected to South Korea?" I had no choice but to reveal my pitiful condition to him, but I did not want him to see any weakness in me, so I responded to his inquiries with cold silence. He seemed to sense something and left after leaving me with the message, "Comrade, you should reflect more."

Although I couldn't help but reveal my miserable state to him due to our past association as fellow revolutionaries, I did not want him to show me any sympathy or compassion. Nevertheless, considering our history as comrades, he treated me kindly and with respect when he met me. Shim Yeong-soon had dismissed him as a mere opium smuggler, and there had been disdain between them. If Shim Yeong-soon had not defected to South Korea and had been arrested, it would likely have resulted in severe retaliation and difficulties for him. After spending about two weeks in the prison, I began to adapt to the rhythm of life there. Human beings had a natural ability to adapt to their environment, even in prison. I realized that I could endure and survive, even in such challenging circumstances.

Interrogation

On the nineteenth day of my imprisonment, the interrogation began. The charge was anti-government activity. The interrogator himself had once been a member of the Independence movement and had returned to Seoul after liberation, but he grew disillusioned with the situation in South Korea. Hungry and disheartened, he had returned to North Korea. Afterward, he had turned himself in, undergone rigorous self-criticism, and eventually found employment with the security agency. He seemed to understand my situation well, perhaps because he had experienced something similar.

As a result, he treated me more like a conversation partner than a suspect. He even mentioned seeing me walking from Taihang Mountains to Fengtian. The focus of the interrogation was to determine why I had left the Independence army. I explained that I had only wanted to return to my hometown after liberation, and there were no other reasons. I pointed out that my quiet life in my hometown since returning was evidence of this. He didn't press further and even hinted that I might be released in about ten days.

Then one evening, I received word that the head of the inspection division, Park Chi-rye, was calling for me. I couldn't help but tremble, as I recalled the fierce glare, he had given me on the day I was imprisoned.

But to my surprise, his expression was unexpectedly warm, even smiling, when he met me—something that caught me completely off guard once again. He approached me and said,

"So it turns out you're Kim Jong-jeong's (金宗丁) son-in-law! Just yesterday, your father-in-law came to see me and scolded me harshly, saying, 'No matter how much the world has changed, how could you possibly throw your own friend's son-in-law in jail?'"

He and my father-in-law were childhood friends from the same hometown and had been extremely close ever since. During the Japanese occupation, they had even done business together in China and were said to be inseparable.

He was also the one who had sent the most generous gift when we got married. Because of this long-standing friendship, my father-in-law had likely spoken to him freely, without reservation, despite Park being the inspection chief. From the moment he realized I was his old friend's son-in-law, it was clear he felt a personal obligation to do whatever he could to save me.

He called me a fool, saying that someone who had escaped from the Japanese army and then joined the Independence Alliance and entered the country with the Korean Volunteer Army would have been guaranteed a path to success. Regardless of the reasons, he lamented that my desertion from the Volunteer Army was a reckless decision.

He also asked me if I knew Park Hang-gu. When I replied that I knew him well, he said that Park had returned to his hometown flaunting a pistol at his side and swaggering around, and that it seemed he now held a high position in the communist party.

Park Hang-gu and I had been in the same squad even after we escaped from the Japanese army, so we had a certain degree of camaraderie. However, he had always been troubled by feelings of inferiority, believing that he wouldn't be accepted in a communist society because of his privileged background. He had openly expressed his grievances, which led us to brand him as a traitor.

Indeed, in a communist society, only those who betrayed their conscience and informed on others to climb ahead could succeed. When he heard from Park Chi-rye that I was imprisoned, he reportedly said, "Please treat Uhm Yeong-sik with leniency." I later heard that Park Hang-gu came to Seoul as a deputy regimental commander in the People's Army during the Korean War.

Park Chi-rye then told me to reflect more deeply and wait patiently in the cell, ending the conversation there.

As I listened to his words, I felt grateful that, even in this harsh communist society, he was treating me with the regard due to a friend's son-in-law. Yet I couldn't help but sense that, whatever connections had brought him to the position of inspection chief, he clearly didn't understand the inner workings of the communist party. His actions were driven by personal sentiment, which made me realize that he was nothing more than a transitional figure in the rapidly transforming North Korean society.

I also felt that, driven by personal ambition, he was unknowingly paving the way for his own downfall.

Release from Prison

On a certain night, well past midnight, as I was sleeping, the prison door creaked open, and a tall man entered the cell with a fearful expression on his face. I couldn't help but be surprised. Wasn't he Bang Hwi-je (方暉濟), a fellow student from Osan school and a former student soldier? He had escaped from the Japanese army before me and had been with me at Huazhong branch. He was known for his fierce and radical personality, often demanding to be sent to the Korean Provisional Government in Chongqing with Shim Young-soon. I had never imagined meeting him again inside this prison cell. I motioned for him to come over, and we spent the night talking.

He told me that after I headed north, he had remained with the Huazhong branch, but after liberation, he had a major disagreement over the issue of the Alliance leadership's return to Korea. He left the group and barely managed to board a ship in Tianjin, eventually arriving in Seoul. After spending several days in Seoul, he returned to his hometown but was arrested as soon as he arrived and brought to the provincial security department.

I sensed that, because he had stayed in Seoul for several days, the security department likely believed he had connections with right-wing political figures and had entered the North with some kind of mission. If so, they would probably assume that I was connected to him as well—which meant they might not release me until his interrogation was complete.

Indeed, despite my confidence that I would be released soon based on the circumstances, the next morning, they transferred me to cell 106, as they considered me and Shim Sang-cho as the same category of prisoners. Not only that, but they also stopped my meal delivery duty and increased their surveillance. Before, I had been told to reflect in a comfortable posture, but from now on, I was required to sit upright and reflect in a disciplined manner.

I examined the prison walls closely and noticed graffiti that read, "I am heading to Siberia. Farewell, my homeland!" Since this prison was located near the border, it had once held many independence fighters during the Japanese occupation. But now, in liberated Korea, it had become a place for imprisoning anti-communist youths — a thought that left a bitter taste in my mouth. But I had only longed to return to my homeland after the liberation. I had no political intentions or affiliations with the independence movement.

Also, since Bang Hwi-je lived in Unjeon, not far from my home, I had simply known him through family ties and neighborhood familiarity, without having any real connection to him. Yet it was clear that unless his case was fully resolved, they would not release me either.

Park Chi-rye, the inspection chief, passed by in front of Cell 106 and, with a sympathetic tone, told me that he had intended to release me but those certain circumstances had caused a delay—and asked me to wait just a little longer.

After two long months, I was finally released. According to rumors, deputy Chief Park had repeatedly appealed for my release to the higher-ups. Although Director Chang Ji-min (張志民), who had been an important officer in the Independence movement, had initially agreed with Park's proposal, the surveillance chief, who was a former student soldier, insisted on strict punishment for defectors. The chief knew me well since we both came from the same region. However, when the chief was away on a business trip, Park seized the opportunity to obtain the director's approval and secured my release.

321

In the morning, the cell warden came to Cell 106 and told us that we would be released that afternoon. I was grateful that I had at last crossed the high mountain that had stood in my way. That afternoon, just as they had said, Shin Sang-cho and I were able to step out of the cell. However, leaving behind Bang Hwi-je weighed heavily on our hearts, so our release was far from joyful.

As we stepped out into the front entrance of the provincial security department, the director, Jang Ji-min, suddenly appeared and extended his hand to shake ours. He said, "You comrades have been through a lot. Now listen carefully to what I'm about to say. Do not, under any circumstances, go to the South. If you do, there will be nowhere left to run. We will definitely march into South Korea." With those words, he vanished into the crowd like a flash.

I could sense director Chang Ji-min's thoughts. He had warmly welcomed us when we arrived at the Military and Political Academy in the Taihang Mountains after liberation. After entering North Korea, he became the head of the north Pyongan Province security command, and it was likely he had me arrested under his orders, thinking that I had betrayed our Alliance. Nevertheless, since we were comrades who had fought together in the revolutionary movement during difficult times, he showed compassion by releasing us.

However, he must have known that we would inevitably defect to the South. Therefore, telling us not to flee south and warning that they would surely invade South Korea was likely his way of expressing a desperate hope that we would stay in the North and cooperate with the communist party—because once we defected, we would become his eternal enemies.

When the communist party official said they would soon invade the South, it was not just a threat to stop us from fleeing; by that time, the invasion of the South was already a firm and unshakable policy of the communist party. Giving thanks to God for having safely endured two months of imprisonment, I returned to my hometown.

Transfer to Jeongju

I have finally returned home and felt relieved that I could put everything behind me. Over the past two months, I tried to erase the memories from my mind, and I didn't mention to anyone that I had been in prison. Prison is a peculiar place, where some people become more resolute upon their release while others wither away. I felt like I remained unchanged.

However, half a year ago, when I first returned home, everyone welcomed me with open arms. Now, it seemed like the welcome had faded, and some people were even giving me strange looks, as if questioning, "Who is this person?" This made me realize that my freedom of movement had narrowed, and I felt uncomfortable.

The school had been taken over by left-leaning teachers. New teachers who had recently arrived also seemed wary of me. Even the older teachers, who used to gather in the corner of the staff room and murmur, had fallen silent. It appeared that they, too, were now cautious around me. During this time, the school felt more like a Communist Party training camp than an educational institution.

One day, Principal Jeon Ui-won called for me. Although he was a member of the communist party, he liked me. He informed me that it was an order from the Jeongju education department for me to transfer to Jeongju Middle School. It was located near the communist party's local military unit, and it seemed clear that they wanted to keep me close for surveillance. Principal Jeon said, "You could have stayed at Osan School, but it seems things have changed." However, I later learned that Shin Sang-cho, too, had received an order to work at Jeongju Middle School. Both Shin Sang-cho and I saw this as an opportunity. We were in a situation where we would likely have to head south, and while leaving from our hometown school might bring trouble to our relatives, it seemed that departing from Jeongju would leave fewer complications behind.

Despite this, my mother was saddened when she learned that my wife and I were moving to Jeongju, which was approximately 15 kilometers away. After all, a parent's heart finds comfort in having their children close by. I, too, had never truly fulfilled my filial duty and had only caused my parents worry and concern. And now, under orders from the communist party, I was once again leaving my hometown. Somehow, it felt as though this departure was a final farewell — as if I were turning my back on my hometown forever, and that made me feel deeply sorrowful. I left for Jeongju with a heavy heart, unable even to properly say goodbye to the teachers and students at Osan School, as if I were fleeing.

Chapter 14
Road to South Korea

Transfer to Jeongju Middle School

When I was appointed to Osan Middle School, it was located in a narrow alley called Osan in Jeongju (定州) county. In the local area, it was considered an educational institution with a longstanding tradition of educating Korean people, despite its remote location. On the other hand, Jeongju county, which was a transportation hub during the Japanese colonial era in north Pyongan Province and a major industrial area, lacked secondary and high schools. Therefore, the people of Jeongju had long advocated for the relocation of Osan Middle School to Jeongju for its development.

In 1942, Park Moon-gyu (朴文圭), the head of the hometown and a well-known businessman, with the support of Lee Jeong-geun (李貞根), who was the governor of north Pyongan Province at the time, established

Jeongju Technical School. After liberation, this institution was transformed into a liberal arts middle school and elevated to the status of Jeongju Middle School.

Jeongju had historical significance as it was the site of the Northern Jangdae (北將臺), built by Hong Gyeong-rae (洪景來) to fight against the government forces, and it was also a key area later during the Korean War. With the opening of the Jeong-Sak train line (定朔線), the region developed rapidly, and with the development of land reclamation projects on the western coast, it became rich in agricultural products. Moreover, as it was the last major city connecting to Sinuiju, it had been notorious during the Japanese occupation for the sharp-eyed surveillance of the special higher police. Therefore, Jeongju Middle School could be seen as the epicenter of education in this region.

When I first arrived at this school, the principal was Lee Seok-yoon (李錫潤), who was originally from this area. He had graduated from Rikkyō University (立敎大學) in Japan with a degree in English literature and had expertise in Shakespearean studies. During my study abroad in Tokyo, I had lived in the same boarding house as him, which gave us a special bond. At that time, he was clearly a fervent communist, and he openly praised communism without hesitation, seemingly to satisfy the ideological demands of the authorities.

The head of the academic affairs department was Kim Yong-ha (金龍河), my maternal uncle. As previously mentioned, he had studied art during his early years in Tokyo and was one of the founders of the communist party in Jeongju county. I had come to believe that the reason he had been active as a radical communist at the time was because he saw becoming a communist as the most effective way to enjoy freedom. Since we had once lived together in the same room in Tokyo, I can say we knew each other very well.

Almost all the intellectuals in the Jeongju county area gathered at Jeongju Middle School at that time, making it truly a place of intellectual activity. The teachers there were brilliant. The discipline teacher, Choi Sung-min (崔成珉), was a graduate of Osan School and was highly respected for his outstanding mathematical skills. Choi Yong-rin (崔龍麟), another Osan School alumnus, had studied at the Musashino (武藏野) Music School in Japan and passionately advocated communism. He should be highly commended for recognizing the exceptional vocal talent of one of his students, Ahn Hyung-il (安炳一), and for providing him with free personal instruction, ultimately guiding him to great success as a professor at the college of music, Seoul National University.

Kim Gong-sik (金公植), a fellow classmate from Osan School, had graduated from the philosophy department of Sophia University in Japan. Despite his academic background, he was at the forefront as a vanguard of communism, which didn't seem to match his field of study. There were also the writer Seok In-hae (石仁海) and Tak Si-yeon (卓時淵), another classmate of mine from Osan School. Tak supported himself through school for five years and graduated from the Bunka Gakuin (文化学院) in Japan. Although he came from a background that would typically lead one to become a communist, he never lost his composure or discipline. Seeing him made it clear that becoming a communist wasn't determined solely by one's background.

On the other hand, seeing people like Choi Yong-rin and Kim Gong-sik—who everyone believed would walk a right-wing path—become fervent communists and recklessly charge ahead, I couldn't help but lament their petty heroism. Choi Yong-rin, my classmate and peer whom I knew better than anyone else, was selected by the Communist Party to travel to the Soviet Union. Upon his return, he went around exclaiming, 'The air in Moscow has flavor! That's because it's the air of a pure communist country, free from exploitation.' I couldn't help but feel a sense of void as I thought, 'Air may be clean, but how can it possibly have flavor?

Figure 94: Professor Ahn Hyung-il.

I want to share a story about Ahn Hyeong-il, who was a student of Choi Yong-rin. During the Korean War, Choi Yong-rin, as part of the cultural propaganda unit, came to Seoul and sent a letter requesting to meet Ahn Hyeong-il. At the time, Ahn deeply longed to see his former

328

teacher, but in the end, he didn't meet him out of fear that Mr. Choi might pressure him—perhaps even forcibly—to go north. Once again, I was reminded that the wall of ideology stands taller than the wall of friendship, and that it can overshadow even the bond between teacher and student. Ahn Hyeong-il has now reached retirement age at Seoul National University.

During my time at Jeongju Middle School, there were many beautiful moments of camaraderie among the teachers. My wife and I lived in a small room provided by the school, and, on one occasion, a student came to our house and saw that we had no firewood. He went back to his own home, brought a log, and even chopped it into firewood for us. Jeon Gye-hyeon, our math teacher, was originally from Hamgyeong Province. I still can't forget the times when the teachers would sit together drinking *soju*, using the salted pollock roe his family had sent from back home as a side dish.

There was also a student named Seung Gye-ho (承啓浩), who showed remarkable intelligence. Though his family was poor, I still can't forget the bright, smiling face he always wore. He went on to graduate from Seoul High School after leaving for South Korea during the Korean War. He received a scholarship and went to the United States, where he earned a Ph.D. in philosophy from Yale University. Currently, he leads an honorable life as a philosophy professor at the University of Houston in Texas. When I visited the United States a few years ago, we had a heartfelt reunion. I was delighted to see him living a happy life with his wife, a musician, and his talented children.

Figure 95: Professor Seung Gye-ho.

The day Seung Gye-ho left for the United States is the one I can never forget, as it was the very day President Syngman Rhee unilaterally released approximately 25,000 anti-communist North Korean POWs detained on Geoje Island, South Korea. The night before his departure, Seung Gye-ho came to my house, and I could see that he was trembling from hunger and cold. All I could do to bless his hopeful journey was to give him a pair of socks and enough money for a modest meal. At the time, I was teaching at Seoul Middle School, but I had so little to give. Looking back now, I realize just how painfully poor I was then—it makes me shudder.

The students I taught at Jeongju Middle School back then are now all past their 60s. Whenever they gather, they fondly reminisce about how I was once regarded as a stylish teacher, how I made history an engaging and lively subject, and how, though never a leftist, I never seemed rigidly right leaning either. Their conversations often blossom into cheerful laughter with these memories. I spent that winter at Jeongju

330

Middle School, and looking back now, I believe 'the path of a teacher was a truly rewarding one.'

Resolution to Cross to South Korea

The town of Jeongju was relatively small, and it seemed like there were no watchful eyes around me. I regained peace of mind and dedicated myself to my work at school. At home, I became a loving father. My son, born during this time, is now around 50 years old. Whether at school or at home, I couldn't shake off the constant pressure that I had to flee to the South as soon as possible. With the 38th parallel expected to become even more firmly sealed once the winter of 1946 passed and spring arrived, I resolved to go south before the new school term began.

I was already planning to go to South Korea with Shin Sang-cho. However, our colleagues, Choe Sung-min and Hyon Pong-chan (玄鳳讚), who were also teachers, noticed our intentions and suggested that we all escape to South Korea together. We thought that four teachers from the same school escaping together would raise suspicions. Moreover, Shin Sang-cho and I had already been labeled as reactionary elements and had been detained for two months in the People's Security Agency, so we were certain that if we were caught on the way to South Korea, we would never see the sunlight again. Therefore, we discouraged Choe and Hyon from joining us and advised them to find their own way to South Korea.

By that time of 1947, there had already been elections for local representatives in North Korea. I also cast my vote in the so-called "black-and-white election" where they asked about our preferences. North Korea was organizing its system in its own way. We were becoming anxious. We knew that every day we delayed our escape to South Korea, the journey would become even more challenging. However, leaving my wife and parents behind, abandoning my bright-eyed students, and departing from my growing son was an unbearable pain. Leaving meant parting, and there was no guarantee of reuniting. Moreover, if we were captured by the authorities, I couldn't predict what fate awaited me.

Nevertheless, there was an undeniable force pushing me to hurry and escape to South Korea. But would a successful escape solve all my problems? In reality, I had no base or connections in Seoul. Seoul was just a place I had passed through a few times during my college days in Tokyo. However, the vague belief that Seoul held the freedom I yearned for was the driving force behind my determination to risk this adventure.

I sought my wife's approval. It seemed impractical for the three of us to carry our belongings and board a train bound for South Korea from Jeongju Station, so I suggested that I go ahead alone, and my wife and son could follow later. My thoughtful wife, to my gratitude, immediately agreed and urged me to go south without worry or delay.

Since there was a locomotive depot within the Jeongju Station yard, all southbound trains passing through would stop for about 30 minutes to take on water. I made a firm promise with Shin Sang-cho to board the southbound train passing through Jeongju station at noon the next day, and we parted ways. I didn't tell anyone—not even my parents—that I was defecting to the South, because although I might fail in my duty of filial piety, I didn't want to cause them worry.

In truth, my journey to the South was a bold undertaking that put my life at risk, and the chances of success were not high. When I escaped from the Japanese army, my actions were seen as just, and all my relatives and neighbors supported me. But this time, escaping from the communist society was viewed as 'a reactionary act against an already established order,' and while some relatives might understand, receiving support from neighbors was unthinkable.

Because of this, I considered my defection entirely a personal act for which I alone would bear the responsibility. At that time, my father was serving as the Democratic Party's chairman for Galsan-myeon, so it was unlikely he would disapprove of my decision to defect. Also, my older brother, a graduate of Osan School, was running a business in Goeup (古邑). He had once followed Ham Seok-heon (咸錫憲) and was involved in Bible Chosun (聖書朝鮮), for which he served over six months in prison. He had always regretted that I, his younger brother, was not walking the true path of a Christian. But now, seeing me escape from the den of communists, he would have no reason to oppose it.

Uncle Kim Yong Ha

As I thought about leaving my beloved hometown tomorrow, my heart felt heavy. Although I had kept it a secret from everyone, I wanted to inform my uncle Kim Yong-ha (金龍河), who had taken such good care of me. It wasn't about seeking his understanding for my decision to go to South Korea, but rather, it was a gesture of gratitude for all the kindness he had shown me. In other words, I didn't want to quietly leave for South Korea, as I thought it might make him feel betrayed. I disliked the idea of betraying anyone, even if it meant facing death.

In the evening, I went to visit him and suggested having a drink together at a Chinese restaurant. I spoke directly to him, saying, "I've decided to leave for South Korea tomorrow. I've been feeling an overwhelming urge to go to South Korea due to the anxiety that has been haunting me without my realizing it."

He closed his eyes for a while, lost in thought, and then said the following, "I, too, have been feeling the attraction of the South. However, I can't go. In Seoul, Sunwoo Gi-seong (鮮宇基成 , Kim Yong-ha's fellow student at Osan School and the leader of the Northwestern Youth Association, which opposed the communist party) is making his move." I listened to his honest confession, and my heart ached.

He was a radical member of the communist party, but, as I had thought, he was essentially a libertarian. Libertarians are drawn to the bait of freedom, and it was clear that he, too, was caught up in the bait of liberty. In the case of an intellectual, once caught, they would struggle not to fall, becoming even more fervent. As mentioned earlier, he was one of the founding members of the communist party in Jeongju, but his deep interest in the arts couldn't be denied. How could he deny his desire to engage freely in artistic activities on the land of the free South? Kim Yong-ha had gone on to achieve prominence, even rising to the position of the director of culture for the provincial party committee in North Pyongan Province.

People who had been close to him during his time in eastern Manchuria all lamented that if he had defected to South Korea, he would have blossomed his talents and left a remarkable mark in the South Korean art scene. I can't remember who it was, but I heard a story that his profile was featured as the first person in an article titled "Unforgettable people" in the monthly *Shin dong-a* (新東亞) magazine.

Road to South Korea

On the morning of the day Shin Sang-cho and I had promised to defect to South Korea; I went to work at the school as usual. After finishing the first class, I returned to the office, but I couldn't see the face of the promised defector, Shin. He had gone to his hometown in Deogeon-myeon (德彦面) the previous evening. When he came to the office around 11 a.m., he appeared calm and emotionless. I saw him and felt relieved, so I proceeded with my third-period class.

Around noon, at 12 p.m., the sound of the northbound train's whistle could be heard. I opened the classroom window and looked towards Jeongju Station, where the train was approaching the station. I told the students that today's lesson would end here, set down the chalk, and hurriedly left the classroom. Passing through the school gate, I ran straight toward the station.

At Jeongju station, all passing trains stopped for about 30 minutes to refill water and coal for the locomotives. The distance from the school to Jeongju station was roughly a 10-minute walk, so we had enough time to catch the train. When I arrived at the station waiting room, my wife was there with our son on her back, holding the ticket for the Pyongyang-bound train I was to take. I took the ticket from her and, without even properly saying goodbye, hurried through the gate and found a seat in a corner of the train car. Since I didn't run into anyone I knew, I tried to calm my trembling heart and quietly prayed that I could at least reach Pyongyang safely.

I wondered how my wife felt about seeing me off on this journey to South Korea. I was still dressed in the same suit as when I went to school, with chalk dust on my hands and carrying no luggage. I had only a few red bills with me. If there were any security checks, I hoped to appear as if I were in a hurry to visit Pyeongyang. Finally, the train started moving, and the train car filled with people. I looked around, and in a distant seat, I saw Shin Sang-cho. Seeing him eased my mind.

But Shin Sang-cho was wearing a shabby pair of loose pants and a cap, making him look like a peddler. Beside him was a sack filled with rice — he was apparently disguised as a rice merchant. I couldn't help but smile inwardly. Looking at his intellectual face, refined speech, and manner, I wondered whether any security agent would truly be fooled. Fortunately, we made it to Pyongyang station without being inspected on the train. The station's gate area was extremely crowded, which allowed us to slip through safely. It was at that moment that I once again felt, deep in my skin, how painfully difficult life is when you're constantly on the run.

The atmosphere at Pyeongyang's streets felt cold, matching the chill in my heart. The streets seemed desolate because of my despondent mood. Only the numerous banners painted in red paint fluttered in the wind, catching my eye. We had relatives near Pyeongyang, but we were worried that if something went wrong, they would face repercussions, so we decided to spend the night at an inn. We decided against going outside, fearing we might encounter someone who recognized us as defectors from North Korea. Now that we had reached Pyeongyang, crossing the 38th parallel would require taking another train to Namcheon (南川).

However, Pyeongyang station seemed like a risky place to board the train due to the possibility of security checks. The station staff constantly monitored passengers next to the gate. It seemed dangerous for us to voluntarily present our tickets for Namcheon to the inspectors and pass by. Therefore, we decided to walk to Jungwha (Chunghwa, 中和) station and take the train from there to Namcheon. Jungwha station was a rural stop, so we thought the surveillance would be less stringent. We walked, asking for directions, and reached Jungwha station. As we had expected, we could board the southbound train safely. Even though it was midnight, there were many passengers, and the crowded train was advantageous for us. Thankfully, we did not undergo any security checks, and the train arrived at Namcheon station.

At that time, Namcheon station was the final stop for southbound trains. We got off the train, and it was past midnight, but Namcheon station was quite crowded, perhaps due to ongoing construction. We couldn't determine the direction in the pitch-dark night. We had to spend the night safely somewhere, and since inns near the 38th parallel were likely to have strict security checks, we decided to avoid them. In the dark, we could faintly see a range of hills to the south. So, we decided to go to those hills and spend the night hidden, hoping to avoid any trouble. We walked down an untraveled path towards the dimly lit hillside.

Security Officers

As we continued on our way, suddenly two young men emerged from a house by the road and challenged us, asking who we were. We stopped in our tracks. The two young men had their guns pointed at us, and there were several security officers inside the house. Ah, it turned out that this house was a security office! We had inadvertently passed by it while wandering through the streets without knowing the direction.

One of the security officers asked me, "Who are you and what are you doing here?" I recalled the saying that even in a tiger's den, one can survive as long as they keep their wits about them. So, I calmed my nerves and replied, "I received a message from the communist party leader in Namcheon county that I was hired as a teacher at this middle school. I just arrived at Namcheon station, and I'm looking for his house." He seemed to accept my response and then turned his attention to Shin Sang-cho, asking him the same question. Shin Sang-cho replied, "I'm a farmer and a trader. I got off at Namcheon station to buy rice." He even showed them the bags of rice he had.

The security officer looked back and forth between the two of us, then turned to me and said, "You can go. If you keep going down this road, there's a bridge. Turn left there, and you'll see a big tree. The house after that tree is the home of the district party official in charge." He even gave me directions to the house. But to Shin Sang-cho, he said, "You need to be investigated, so come inside."

I quickly withdrew from the spot as if fleeing. But I was worried about Shin Sang-cho. I had a bad feeling he wouldn't be released easily. Left alone, I had nowhere to go. I started walking toward the mountain I had vaguely seen earlier. When I reached the foot of the mountain, there were several farmhouses, and a bit away from them, I saw a straw hut.

As I approached the straw hut and peeked inside, I saw that no one was there. I pushed open the wattle gate and entered. Inside, there was a kiln for firing pottery—it was clearly a pottery site. The night air in May felt cold, so I felt incredibly fortunate to have found a place to spend the night.

At dawn the next morning, as soon as the sky began to lighten, I left the place. I was afraid I might run into villagers. Bathed in the dazzling morning sunlight of May, I walked along the rice field path back into the town of Namcheon, my mind still troubled over what might have happened to my friend.

The person I now had to find was Kim Yong-hyun (金龍鉉). He was another one of my maternal uncles and the younger brother of Kim Yong-ha, to whom I had confessed my plan to cross to the South the day before leaving Jeongju. He used to run a business in his hometown of Osan, but after liberation, he moved to Namcheon and managed an orchard. He would sometimes introduce local guides to fellow villagers who were on their way to the South.

Uncle was startled to see me enter, looking so gaunt and disheveled, and asked if I had come down to go South. When I said yes, he suggested we first go see the party committee chairman of Namcheon county, a certain Mr. so-and-so. I had wanted to meet him from the beginning as well. He had originally lived in Osan and had embraced communist ideology early on. During the Japanese occupation, he had lived in hiding in his hometown. He had been a close and inseparable friend of my father, often coming to our house to sit in the guest room in our house and talk with him about the state of the world.

When he saw that I, a university graduate, was being dragged off as a student soldier before I even had the chance to start a new life, he was deeply pained—almost as if it were his own misfortune—and showed me heartfelt sympathy.

Even though he had since become the county party committee chairman of Namcheon after liberation, I believed that his feelings—once like a father's toward me—would not have changed. That's why I wanted to meet him. I also thought that, depending on the situation, I might be able to ask for his help regarding Shin Sang-cho.

I went to his house with my uncle leading the way. He happened to be in the middle of breakfast, but when he saw me, he welcomed me with the joy of someone receiving back a long-lost prodigal son.

I sat and shared breakfast with him, telling him everything I had been through: how I had escaped from the Japanese military camp, how I had no choice but to flee from the Korean Independence Alliance, how I had been imprisoned for two months by the north Pyongan provincial security office, and how I had now come all the way to Namcheon in order to go south.

I then pleaded with him, telling him that the night before, while wandering after getting off the train, my dear friend Shin Sang-cho had been taken by the security office—and that he must, by any means, help rescue him.

After hearing my story, he seemed to grasp the urgency of the situation. He told me to stay quietly at his house and hurried out, saying he would go to the security office to find out more.

When he returned, he looked dejected and told me that Shin Sang-cho had already been handed over to the Soviet army at dawn, and that there was nothing he could do beyond that point. He said Shin would have to stand trial.

Then, he urged me to stay, saying that since he was the party secretary in charge of the county, he could arrange for me to work here if I wanted. He encouraged me not to go south, but to stay and live together, working for the cause.

Though I was deeply grateful for his offer, I firmly declined. I didn't know exactly how he had become connected with the communist party or risen to his current position, but I was certain that once the system solidified, he would inevitably be demoted. That was because, before being a communist, he was above all a warm-hearted human being— someone whose nature overflowed with compassion and humanity.

Later, I heard that our departure from Jeongju Middle School caused quite an uproar once it was discovered that we had set out on the road to the South. The right-wing teachers remained silent, but my classmate and a leftist agitator, Kim Gong-sik, reportedly shouted that "those reactionary bastards finally fled to the South."

The communist party's Jeongju county committee even held a meeting of devoted members, during which the county party secretary is said to have declared with great fervor, "At Jeongju Middle School, four reactionary elements among the teachers have betrayed the revolution and gone South. Of them, the ringleader, Shin Sang-cho, has been caught by us and is now in our hands."

Later, Shin Sang-cho was charged with the crime of attempting to defect to the South, brought to trial, and sentenced to two years of hard labor. He was assigned to work as a coal miner at Anju (安州) coal mine, extracting coal deep in the mine face. He was likely the first person in North Korea to receive a heavy sentence specifically for the "crime" of attempting to go South.

During his work in the mine, his lungs deteriorated, and he was transferred to a medical ward due to illness. While undergoing treatment, he bravely escaped and finally made his way to Seoul in May of the following year.

Shin Sang-cho experienced the outbreak of the Korean War in Gunsan (群山), where he was working at a maritime college, and fled to Busan. Afterwards, he had a brilliant career in journalism and politics, eventually becoming a member of the Korean National Assembly. As chairman of the Anti-Communist League, he played a prominent role on the front lines of the anti-communist movement in South Korea.

He had left two sons behind in North Korea, and, grieving that they did not know their father, he lamented that they must deeply resent him, a man who served as chairman of the anti-communist league. Tormented by the pain of national division, he closed his eyes for the last time on this land—and now, several years have quietly passed since his death.

Crossing the 38th Parallel

After returning to my uncle's house, I had to spend several days there. We needed to gather information about guides to lead us to South Korea, gather the people who were planning to defect to the South, and, most importantly, choose a moonless night for our escape. Finally, the day we had been waiting for had arrived. I had to leave my childhood friend, Shin Sang-cho, behind at Namcheon prison and cross the 38th Parallel alone. The thought of leaving him and imagining the hardships he would face weighed heavily on my heart.

As the sun set and darkness blanketed the land, about ten people gathered in a humble house deep in the mountains. They exchanged hushed conversations and sighed heavily. It was clear they were negotiating. They needed to pay the guide who would lead them across the border, and they also had to give a gratuity to the middleman who arranged the guide. The guide had to traverse the treacherous mountains through the night, and if detected by Soviet soldiers or border guards, they would face extreme hardships and potentially risk their lives. Therefore, demanding a substantial sum of money appeared to be only reasonable.

Negotiating was not going smoothly, and it seemed that getting the guide's assistance wouldn't come cheap. The increased security had made the journey even riskier, so they argued that they needed more money. Since this was a clandestine operation, there was no fair market price. I handed over all the red banknotes I had with me. Once I reached South Korea, these red banknotes would be useless anyway, and I didn't want to be bound by money when my life was at stake.

As the night deepened, our group set out from that place. We walked along mountain paths and climbed over hills. When we came upon a rock, we hid beneath it and observed our surroundings. We were strictly told not to smoke. If any children cried, we were to cover their mouths to keep them from making noise anymore.

When the guide ran, we ran after him; when he walked slowly, we slowed our pace as well, staying alert to avoid losing sight of the person ahead. After midnight, everything around us was silent, with only the faint sound of flowing water in the background. Suddenly, the guide told us to run quickly. He crossed a stream and dashed up a mountain path. Then he said we had just crossed the 38th parallel. It was around 1 a.m.

Following the guide's instructions, we gathered beneath a large tree, where we were finally allowed to smoke freely. As I lit a cigarette, I was deeply moved once again by how precious this freedom was. They said that if we continued down the open road, we would reach Kaesong (開城) by morning. At last, I truly felt that I had come to the land of freedom. Urging myself to forget everything that had happened in the past, I began walking toward Kaesong.

Chapter 15

Did I find freedom?

Nam-o Inn

When I arrived in Seoul by train from Kaesong, the evening sun was setting in the west. The Seoul train station square was bustling with many people. After buying a pack of Lucky Strike cigarettes, which had just recently hit the market, I was left with not a single penny in my pocket. The cigarette pack had a white background with a red circle drawn on it, giving it a distinct appearance. But as I lit a cigarette and gazed at *Namdaemun* (南大門, South Great Gate), I could feel a sense of relief. In truth, I had no personal connections in Seoul. During my time studying abroad in Tokyo, I would occasionally transfer trains in Seoul on my way to Busan, but that was the extent of my experience in the city.

In Seoul, there were two inns run by people from my hometown. One was the Asia Guesthouse managed by a senior from Osan High School, located at 10 Da-dong (茶洞). The other was Nam-o Inn (南五旅館) in Namdaemun 5-ga. Since the owners of these two inns had personal connections with my father, I thought that even if I had no money, they would let me stay for a few days on credit.

Figure 96: Lucky Strike Cigarettes.

Nam-o Inn was particularly crowded because it was where Kim Gi-hong (金基鴻), a member of the board of directors of the Osan Foundation, had settled after coming from North Korea. The former principal of Osan High School, Mr. Joo Ki-yong, had also sought refuge here, making it a gathering place for individuals related to Osan High School. It was always bustling with people from my hometown, and I could get updates on the situation in North Korea from them. Not only were there people related to Osan High School, but it was also a hub for

346

those who wanted to know about the North Korean situation because of the school's long history in Pyongan Province.

My friend Ahn Guk-ju

That's where I learned about the whereabouts of Ahn Guk-ju (安國柱). As I mentioned earlier, his hometown was Sinuiju, and he was my comrade from my days as a student soldier in Choyangcheon (朝陽川), Kangdo. When he arrived in his hometown, Sinuiju was already completely under the control of the Korean People's Army, and the communist party was in power. Therefore, he immediately decided to escape to South Korea the next day.

His family was a distinguished and well-known household in Sinuiju, owning a business called Ahn-guk Trading Company (安國商會). His father was an elder at the First Church of Sinuiju, and during the time when Reverend Han Kyung-jik (韓景職)—now an emeritus pastor of Youngnak Church (永樂教會)—was serving at the Second Church, his father was the one who took good care of Reverend Han.

Ahn Guk-ju had rented a single room in a dilapidated Japanese house in Hangangno 2-ga and was living a very modest life on his own. Quietly, he was continuing his studies—interrupted by his forced conscription as a student soldier—hoping to fulfill his parents' wish for him to become a scholar. I decided to rely on his hospitality and began living with him.

At that time, my daily routine consisted mostly of cooking and eating breakfast, then walking out to the Nam-O Inn, where I would gather with acquaintances and hear news from my hometown.

Around this period, many teachers and students from Osan School and Jeongju Middle School had also come down to the South. Most of the young men among them joined the Northwest Youth League, taking the lead in cracking down on communists. Occasionally, some managed to find jobs and moved to other regions.

Two other friends

I had two friends I wanted to meet in Seoul. One was my middle school classmate, Kim Deok-yu (金德裕), and the other was a college friend who had graduated with a degree in English literature. Kim Deok-yu had been living in Seoul after graduating and was also a former student soldier like me. I made inquiries and found his residence in Changsin-dong, Jongno (Seoul), in the eastern part of Seoul. However, to my surprise, he didn't seem very pleased to see me. He immediately questioned why I had come to Seoul, given that South Korea had become an American colony after liberation, and leftists were suffering severe persecution. He asked if I had heard that I was rumored to be working as a middle school teacher in the North and scolded why I had chosen to escape to this chaotic situation. He even mentioned that he was planning to defect to the North because he couldn't stand how things were going in the South.

His ability to say such things stemmed from his ignorance of the path I had walked since becoming a student soldier. I had risked my life in search of freedom, and it was bewildering to hear such words from an old friend. He seemed to have an extreme leftist view without truly understanding what the communist party was like. I didn't even want to consider him a classmate anymore.

As I left his house and walked along the streets of Jongno, I couldn't shake off a feeling of solitude. Kim Deok-yu had been a short-distance track and field athlete in school, agile and quick-witted. I had thought he would be astute in assessing the political situation, but he had changed a lot. It saddened me to see how much he had changed, and I felt sorry for him. I never had the chance to meet him again, and I heard he eventually defected to the North.

One day, I set out to meet another friend from my college days who had graduated from Waseda University with a degree in English literature. He was also a former student soldier and was working as an English teacher at Yongsan High School at the time. I wanted to meet him not only because I missed him but also because I hoped to find a job at his school. However, much to my surprise, when he saw me, he didn't welcome me at all. Instead, he pointed to a newspaper and angrily showed me an article about American soldiers assaulting Korean women. He questioned why I had come to South Korea and proclaimed his intention to defect to North Korea, where he believed true democracy was being upheld. I simply thought to myself that he was unbelievably ignorant.

Who would refuse the independent and truly equal society where everyone can enjoy freedom, and no one exploits or is exploited? But the equality and freedom claimed by the North Korean Communist Party were freedoms only for the Party, not for the people as a whole. Their so-called alliance of various parties and factions was limited only to those who supported the communist party's leadership and agenda. Unless someone had seen and experienced it firsthand, they could never truly understand—let alone imagine—what it was really like.

I once participated in a black-and-white election in North Korea. It was not a genuine free election, but merely a vote to approve or reject the candidate designated by the communist party.

Though intellectuals tend to long for freedom and harbor discontent with the political situation, I felt that many people in the South viewed the North with an unrealistic and overwhelming sense of illusion. Could he truly enjoy the genuine freedom he desired if he crossed over to the North? After that, I never saw him again.

Unjust assault

April (1947) had passed, and May had arrived. On a sunny morning, I left my house on Han River Road and walked to Nam-o Inn. There was no news from my hometown. However, I waited without any slightest doubt that 'my wife and son would soon escape to the South.'

But on May 1st, it was May Day. Namdaemun Street was bustling with the activities of communist party members, who were wearing red ribbons on their heads. On that day, there were May Day events organized by the communist party on Namsan Mount and also a commemorative ceremony organized by the right-wing at Dongdaemun Stadium, Seoul.

I had heard that leftist forces were strong even in the South, and out of idle curiosity, I wanted to see what their May Day rally would be like. Having witnessed so many mass gatherings in China and North Korea, I only wished to watch this one from a distance for a short while.

The crowd wasn't very large, but the leftist agitators were shouting fierce slogans in a loud standoff with the police. Caught in the chaos of the crowd—pushed this way and that—I suddenly felt myself ridiculous and embarrassed to be there just watching. I quickly changed my mind and left the scene.

My motive was nothing more than scholarly curiosity, as a student of history, about how such rallies were organized in the South. Of course, I didn't meet anyone I knew.

However, the next day, I was unexpectedly attacked by fellow hometown youths due to this curiosity. They mistook me for a communist sympathizer, both in North Korea and now in South Korea, and subjected me to a beating. They accused me of attending the leftist rally without any remorse for my actions and claimed that if I sympathized with the leftists, I should have stayed in North Korea. I tried to explain that I was merely observing out of curiosity, but I was met with hostility and had to struggle to get away.

After this unexpected attack, I lay in bed, staring at the ceiling, feeling utterly desolate. I was not a leftist, and I had no reason to be beaten like this. I had no money left in my wallet, and I was dependent on the hospitality of friends. In this situation, having been physically attacked and also receiving ideological scorn, I felt that my future was bleak and uncertain. I did not expect a warm welcome in Seoul, but the rejection and hostility I encountered left me bewildered. There seemed to be no escape now, as I had no place to go. My pockets were empty, and I was staying at a friend's place, yet amid the ideological struggles I even managed to incur the hatred of some. It was a dark and trying time.

The ever-kind Ahn Guk-ju comforted me, saying, "Looking back on everything we've been through, when have we not run into obstacles? But at least now, we have the freedom to push through if we set our minds to it. As far as I know, the assault you experienced came purely from a misunderstanding by the anti-communist youth, so there's no need to worry."

I, too, believed that if people truly tried to understand our past, no one could rightfully denounce us as communists.

In 1947, the political situation in our country was chaotic. By that time, North Korea had already established the North Korean People's Committee with Kim Il-sung as its chairman, initiating socialist economic policies. It began with the land reform in March 1946, turning peasants into their support base. In August 1946, they formed the North Korean Labor Party, involving the intellectual class, and in the following year, 1947, they established the North Korean People's Committee. They also created the People's Army, focusing all their national power on the goal of invading South Korea.

This became more certain when I recalled what Jang Ji-min, the head of the provincial security office, had said to me on the day I was released from the North Pyongan Province Security Bureau. He said emphatically, "Comrade, don't run away to the South. We will surely take over the South, and then where will you go?" I could tell that his words were neither a lie nor a mere threat.

Teaching jobs

In North Korea, the communist party was systematically preparing and organizing itself towards its established goals without any gaps. In contrast, the political landscape in South Korea, where I sought freedom, was chaotic and uncertain. The struggle between left and right forces in South Korea was intense, with the left appearing to dominate. Large-scale communist party protests were happening in various places, and it seemed like people were embracing the idea of a new socialist order. Except for those who had come from North Korea like me, everyone I met in South Korea criticized the U.S. military administration and seemed to sympathize with socialism. At the time, I felt a deep sense of despair, and my freedom was severely limited.

I needed to find employment in this society where I had to settle down. While I was earnestly searching for a job, a friend from my hometown approached me with the decision to enlist in the South Korean military. He told me about a special recruitment program for officers and suggested that I join him. However, becoming a military officer was something I had never dreamed or considered suitable for my personality, so I politely declined his offer. My only wish at that time was to move to a rural area and become a teacher to lead a quiet life.

I took a résumé and went to see my former teacher, Mr. Hong Jeong-sik (洪貞植), who was then the director of planning at the Ministry of Education. A man of gentle character who never hesitated to help others, he looked over my résumé, drew a line under the part that said I had graduated from the department of history at Waseda University, and confidently said he would make arrangements right away.

He wrote me a letter of introduction and told me to meet with Mr. Lee Deok-bong (李德鳳), the principal of Kyungsung Teacher's School. This school, the predecessor of today's College of Education, Seoul National University, was an institution for training elementary school teachers. When I visited, the principal immediately decided to hire me!

They even fixed up a room in the school's affiliated warehouse and provided it as official housing. There, I began my first life in Seoul with my wife, who had fled south.

At that time, Kyungsung Teacher's School did not have its own school building, so it shared facilities with Yongsan Middle and High School. Even though the school had no buildings of its own, the professors were distinguished, including Yu Kyung-chae (柳景採, art teacher), Hong Woong-seon (洪雄善, director of education), and Jung Hae-jin (director of student affairs), who would later achieve great success in the field of education in South Korea.

I had only been at the school for three days when I heard students singing the communist party anthem (赤旗歌, Jeog Gi Ga) in the classroom. I couldn't believe what I was hearing! How could this be happening? I realized that the atmosphere in the early days of liberation was very different from what I had expected. Kyungsung Teacher's School, like other national schools, had many economically disadvantaged students because graduates were usually appointed as teachers. As a result, left-wing forces were particularly strong among the

354

student body. I was shocked to hear students singing the communist party anthem so openly.

I suspected that the music teacher, Jung Jong-gil (鄭鐘吉), had encouraged the students to sing the communist party anthem. However, what surprised me even more was that no one tried to stop them, and the situation seemed as though they were simply listening to a song. This was the atmosphere in the early days of liberation when schools had just opened their doors.

Because the profession was limited, there was no atmosphere for building a solid foundation of knowledge at the school. Nevertheless, I wholeheartedly engaged with my students. As summer vacation approached, the Seoul city government organized a nationwide training program for teachers, held at Baejae (培材) High School. I was assigned to teach history. I enthusiastically delivered my lecture, thinking that the audience was enjoying my teaching. However, everyone in the audience was laughing, and I had no idea what was so funny.

Later, the teachers told me that my Pyongan Province dialect was so strong that they couldn't quite understand what I was saying—they just smiled in response. It was then that I keenly realized that if I was going to work as a teacher, the first thing I had to do was quickly learn to speak standard Korean.

I began giving lectures at school and having meals prepared at home, gradually building a household, I slowly started to feel the sense of freedom in the atmosphere of Seoul.

After three months of teaching at Kyungsung Teacher's School, I transferred to Seoul High School. Principal Lee Deok-bong had kindly asked me to stay at the school, but due to the presence of many teachers from North Korea and its left-leaning faculty, I decided to move on. The principal also recommended me to Seoul High School, where Kim Won-kyu was the principal.

At that time, Seoul High School had a significant number of teachers from North Korea. Principal Kim Won-kyu (金元圭) had been actively promoting education, and my teacher at Osan School, Kim Ki-seok (金基錫), had highly recommended me. This was how my connection with President Choue Young-Seek (趙英植), who later founded Kyung Hee University, began. I was committed to my teaching profession.

During this time, I also participated in the first parliamentary elections of the Republic of Korea. Thinking back to the days when I participated in one-sided black-and-white elections in North Korea, I was deeply moved to be able to cast my precious vote among many candidates. This experience further reinforced my sense of gratitude for the freedom and opportunities that South Korea offered, despite being far from my hometown and relatives. The elected representative from Jongno district was Lee Yun-young (李允榮), who had come from North Korea.

With the establishment of the Korean National Assembly and the election of the president, the Republic of Korea was officially founded. The U.S. military, having completed its tasks, withdrew from South Korea in June 1949. However, I couldn't help but feel uneasy about the U.S. military's withdrawal, as I believed it would provide an opportunity for the North Korean military to invade South Korea.

Figure 97: Professor Uhm Young-sik

Figure 98: Professor Uhm Young-sik (嚴永植, Author, during his tenure as a professor at Kyung Hee University).

End of Manuscript (The author ceased writing beyond this point).

Appendix

List of Figures and Maps

Figure1: The entry of the Japanese Kwantung Army into Fengtian (present-day Shenyang) on September 18, 1931. http://www.atlasnews.co.kr

Map 2: The Expansion of the Japanese Empire in China, 1940. https://ko.wikipedia.org/wiki/중일_전쟁

Figure 3: Osami Nagano, Chief of the Naval General Staff.

https://ko.wikipedia.org/wiki/나가노 오사미

Figure 4: Hajime Sugiyama, Chief of General Staff of the Army https://namu.wiki/w/스기야마 하지메

Figure 5: Emperor Shōwa (Reign: 1926–1989).

Figure 6: The surprise attack on Pearl Harbor by the Imperial Japanese Combined Fleet, December 1941.

Figure 7: Prime Minister Fumimaro Konoe. https://namu.wiki/w/ 고노에 후미마로

Figure 8: General Tojo Hideki https://ko.wikipedia.org/wiki/도조 히데키

Figure 9: A scene from the movie *Midway*.

Figure 10: U.S. Marines at the shores of Guadalcanal, 1942. https://ko.wikipedia.org/wiki/과달카날_전역

Figure 11: Admiral Yamamoto Isoroku (山本五十六). https://ko.wikipedia.org/wiki/ 야마모토_이소로쿠

Figure 12: Government-General Building in Seoul, Korea. 출처: ko.wikipedia.org/wiki/ 조선총독부_청사와_관사

Figure 13: General Jirō Minami. https://namu.wiki/w/ 미나미 지로

Figure 14: Uhm Jin-seung (right), my father, with a friend.

Figure 15: The image of a Korean youth who was forcibly conscripted into the Japanese military in 1944. 한국사회문화연구원 [source] 파란만장 심영순씨의 인생

Figure 16: Teacher Ham Seok-heon with the First-Year Class A students of the 1936 school year at Osan School, Jeongju. https://www.ingn.net/news/articleView.html?idxno=23861

359

Figure 17: Cho Man-sik (曺晩植). Source: 오산학교 그리고 평북 정주 작성자 SonKJ,
　　　https://blog.naver.com/sonwj823/221257813471

Figure 18: Shin Chae-ho (申采浩). Source: 오산학교 그리고 평북 정주 작성자 SonKJ,
　　　https://blog.naver.com/sonwj823/221257813471

Figure 19: Lee Kwang-soo (李光洙). Source: 오산학교 그리고 평북 정주 작성자 SonKJ,
　　　https://blog.naver.com/sonwj823/221257813471

Figure 20: A Shinto shrine enshrining Amaterasu Ōmikami, the sun goddess in Japanese mythology
　　　ko.wikipedia.org/wiki/ 아마테라스_오호미까미

Figure 21: Governor-General Kuniaki Koiso. Source:
　　　namu.wiki/w/고이소 구니아키

Figure 22: Han Un-sa (韓雲史)　https://ko.wikipedia.org/wiki/한운사

Figure 23: Thousand-stitch belt (千人針: Seninbari)
　　　https://blog.naver.com/korngold/50135577693

Figure 24: Railroad route through the Japanese-occupied territories, connecting Fengtian (present-day Shenyang, 奉天), Tianjin (天津), and Xuzhou (徐州).

Map　25: Henan Operation, 1944.　https://namu.wiki/w/ 대륙타통작전

Map　26: Guilin in Kwangsi (Guangxi, 桂林) Province, China.

Map　27: Anhui Province (安徽省), China.

Figure 28: Jungyangkwan Pass (正陽關) in Anhui Province.
　　　https://kr.people.com.cn/n3/2017/0816/c207555-9255905.html

Figure 29: Jang Do-yeong (張道暎)
　　　https://ko.wikipedia.org/wiki/장도영

Map　30: Longhai Line and Jinpu Line at Xuzhou.

Map　31: Locations of Xuzhou and Chongqing

Figure 32: Kamidana used for enshrining kami (spirits or deities).

　　　Source: ko.wikipedia.org/wiki/가미다나

Figure 33: Boseong Girls' School in Seoncheon, Korea.
　　　https://namu.wiki/w/선천 보성여자고등학교

Figure 34: Seung Yeong-ho. https://namu.wiki/w/ 승영호

Map　35: The arrow indicates our intended direction after escape.

Figure 36: Eighth Route Army's Anti-Japanese Campaign.
https://ko.wikipedia.org/wiki/ 팔로군

Figure 37: Huangjiu, one of the two traditional Chinese liquors.
https://ybea12.tistory.com/2908

Figure 38: Foot binding, a traditional Chinese custom. Google

Figure 39: Crispy fried pig ears.

Map 40: Location of Jiangsu Province (江蘇省)

Figure 41: Commanders of the New Fourth Army.
https://ko.wikipedia.org/wiki/ 신사군

Figure 42: Shin Sang-cho (申相楚） https://namu.wiki/w/ 신상초

Figure 43: Shim Young-soon, at Tapgol Park, Seoul. 출처: photo
유창우 조선영상미디어 기자, 파란만장 심영순씨의 인생,
https://blog.naver.com/cfa20/150026134186

Figure 44: General Mu Jeong.
http://korean.people.com.cn/73554/309003/15321764.html

Figure 45: Prominent leaders of the Korean Volunteer Army. From
left: General Mu Jeong (on horseback), Unit Commander Park
Hyo-sam, Political Commissar Kim Hak-mu, Lee Cheol-jung,
Yi Ik-sung, and Lee Chun-am. http://www.tongilnews.com

Figure 46: Prominent leaders of the Eighth Route Army. From left:
Peng Dehuai, Zhu De, and Deng Xiaoping (on the far right).
http://kr.chinajilin.com.cn/qihua/content/2012-
12/03/content_99367.htm

Figure 47: Peng Dehuai (彭德懷). https://ko.wikipedia.org/wiki/

Figure 48: Zhu De (朱德). https://ko.wikipedia.org/wiki/주더

Figure 49: Choi Chang-ik (崔昌益). https://ko.wikipedia.org/wiki/
최창익

Figure 50: Kim Du-bong (金枓奉) https://ko.wikipedia.org/wiki/
김두봉

Figure 51: Han Bin. https://encykorea.aks.ac.kr/Article/E0061658

Figure 52: Anti-Japanese Military and Political University.
https://ko.wikipedia.org/wiki/ 중화인민항일군사정치대학교

Figure 53: Officers and Soldiers of the New Fourth Army with
Identification Tags and Insignia
https://blog.naver.com/pkschina505/220672171798

Figure 54: Five Four Movement (五四運動), 1919.
https://ko.wikipedia.org/wiki/5·4_운동

Acknowledgements

I am deeply grateful to my son, Joseph, whose skill and dedication made it possible to translate this book from Korean into English.

I also extend my sincere thanks to my wife, Sunyoung, for her careful proofreading of the English manuscript.

Young-il Cho

Editor, Professor